Days of the Lord

THE LITURGICAL YEAR

Volume 2.

Lent

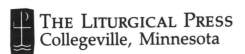

THE LITURGICAL PRESS
Collegeville, Minnesota

The English translation of Volume 2 of this series is by Madeleine Beaumont, with assistance from Thomas J. Hallsten, O.S.B. The original French text of *Days of the Lord* (*Jours du Seigneur*, Brepols: Publications de Saint-André, 1988) was written by the authors of the *Missel dominical de l'assemblée* and *Missel de l'assemblée pour la semaine* under the direction of Robert Gantoy and Romain Swaeles, Benedictines of Saint-André de Clerlande.

ACKNOWLEDGMENTS
Excerpts from the English translation of *The Roman Missal* © 1973, International Committee on English in the Liturgy, Inc. (ICEL); excerpts from the English translation of *The Liturgy of the Hours* © 1974, ICEL; excerpts from the English translation of *Eucharistic Prayers for Masses of Reconciliation* © 1975, ICEL; excerpts from the English translation of *Documents on the Liturgy, 1963–1979: Conciliar, Papal, and Curial Texts* © 1982, ICEL. All rights reserved.

Scripture selections are taken from the New American Bible *Lectionary for Mass,* © 1970 by the Confraternity of Christian Doctrine, Washington, D.C., and are used by license of said copyright owner. All rights reserved. No part of the New American Bible *Lectionary for Mass* may be reproduced in any form without written permission from the copyright owner.

Scripture quotations are from the *New American Bible with Revised New Testament,* © 1986 Confraternity of Christian Doctrine. The text of the Old Testament in *The New American Bible with Revised New Testament* was published in *The New American Bible,* © 1970 Confraternity of Christian Doctrine. Other quotations, as indicated, are from *The Jerusalem Bible,* © 1966 by Darton, Longman & Todd, Ltd. and Doubleday & Company, Inc.

Cover design by Monica Bokinskie.

LIBRARY OF CONGRESS CATALOGING-IN-PUBLICATION DATA

(Revised for vol. 2)

Days of the Lord.

Translation of: Jours du Seigneur.
Includes bibliographical references.
Contents: v. 1. Season of Advent. Season of Christmas/Epiphany — v. 2. Lent —   — v. 6 Ordinary time, Year C.
1. Church year. 2. Catholic Church—Liturgy.
BX1970.J67313 1990   263'.9   90-22253
ISBN 0-8146-1899-5 (v. 1)
ISBN 0-8146-1900-2 (v. 2)
ISBN 0-8146-1901-0 (v. 3)
ISBN 0-8146-1902-9 (v. 4)
ISBN 0-8146-1904-5 (v. 6)

Contents

Forty Holy Days

Despite all that can blur our perception of it—secularization, neopagan carnival celebrations, less rigorous penitential observances, etc.—for today's Christians, Lent remains the unparalleled time of the liturgical year. Throughout history, Lent has maintained its powerful orientation and strong emphases received through various channels from centuries-old ecclesial traditions.

The history of Lent in the Roman Church can be divided into three main periods. The first extended from the end of the third century, or the beginning of the fourth, to the eighth—or even to the twelfth century.[1] The second period is that of stabilization, which lasted until the Second Vatican Council.[2] The third began in 1969 with Paul VI's promulgation of the Missal, Lectionary, and Roman Calendar.

Space does not allow us to review Lent's long and tortuous history.[3] However, when beginning a study of Lent as expressed by today's liturgy, we must briefly recall its most important historical lines and principal components.

A Joyful Walk Toward Holy Easter

The weekly celebration of Christ's passover, "the first day of the week,"[4] is the primitive kernel of what will become the Christian liturgical year; it also constitutes its framework and basic unity.[5] The annual Easter celebration towers above these Sundays.[6] Together with the date of the First Sunday of Advent, the date of Easter determines each year's liturgical calendar.[7] But beyond these questions of computation, the paschal celebration is the summit of the entire liturgical year.[8] Since its beginning, the structure and development of Lent has been designed as preparation for Easter.

All through Lent we have constant reminders of this basic function. This is a guide for our reading and, at the same time, a help for us to grasp the spirit in which the Church invites us to live it. "The wonderful works of God among the people of the Old Testament were but a prelude to the work of Christ our Lord in redeeming mankind and giving perfect glory to God. He achieved his task principally by the paschal mystery of his blessed passion, resurrection from the dead, and glorious ascension."[9] This is why the first reading of each Sunday of Lent recalls one

1

of these great steps that have moved us toward the passover of Christ, summit of all salvation history. And at the Easter Vigil, we will evoke them again, starting with creation, the beginning of all things and the first decisive mighty work of God and of his universal plan of salvation.

The celebration of the ancient Passover commemorates the journey of the Israelites, from their exodus from Egypt to their entrance into the Promised Land. The Passover is the memorial of this founding exodus, of the covenant, and of all the great deeds of God who saves his people.[10] Jesus, assuming and accomplishing what the covenant signified, made it into the sacrament of the new covenant sealed by his blood when he passed from this world to his Father; thus he opened the path of the last exodus on which he draws us. Lent, then, is strongly marked by the spirituality and dynamic of the Exodus.

Easter is also the liturgical and sacramental celebration of renewal, of the passage from death to life, of new birth by participation in the death and resurrection of Christ. Consequently, Lent, the preparation for the celebration of Easter, fosters a particularly characterized baptismal, penitential, and Eucharistic spirituality.

From the fourth century on, the preparation of the newly converted for baptism—the catechumenate—has been integrated into the setting of Lent. This preparation concerns first of all those who are going to receive the sacrament of baptism at the Easter Vigil. But it is the whole community that walks with them toward this celebration and welcomes them into its bosom, including the sharing of the Body and Blood of the Lord. This baptismal and catechumenal dimension more particularly characterizes Year A, with the readings from Matthew and the "great Gospels" of the Samaritan woman (John 4:5-42), the man born blind (John 9:1-41), and the raising of Lazarus (John 11:1-45).[11] We are not concerned here with a vestige from Lenten times of long ago or of a characteristic that is pertinent only to communities that accompany catechumens.

In a certain sense, believers remain catechumens all their lives: they are always on the road of the never completed Christian initiation.[12] During the Easter Vigil, those who have already been baptized are called to return to their baptism, to renew their profession of faith and their commitment, whether neophytes are present among them or not.

Moreover, Lent is for everyone a preparation for the paschal Eucharist of Holy Thursday, memorial of what the Lord did and what he directed us to do until his return. To this paschal Eucharist are related all those Eucharists the Church celebrates during the year.[13]

Finally, Lent is a penitential preparation for the solemnity of Easter. This does not mean, first and foremost, works of ascetical penance, but rather interior conversion and acts done in view of sacramental reconciliation as a preliminary to participation in paschal celebrations. In the early Church, reconciliation took place—at least in Rome—on Holy Thursday. That day remains a particularly fitting time for the sacramental reconciliation of Easter, which gives Lent its penitential dimension. The forty days of Lent are also a period of preparation for personal reconciliation and the public celebration of the sacrament of penance. The celebration of Ash Wednesday is the first step on a penitential journey, during which we hear calls for conversion and oracles on the mercy of God, always ready to forgive. We respond by repeating in different ways, "Return to us and we shall be saved!"; "Make us return and we shall return!" Becoming conscious of their sin by looking at the one who saves, Christians, individually and in community, take advantage of the weeks of Lent to break away from sin by the grace of God. This often requires rectifying thoughts, judgments, habits, and individual and collective behavior. To bring about these changes by the light of the Word, to reconcile ourselves with others, to atone for wrongs and injustices, we need time: the weeks of Lent offer this year after year.[14]

Thus, Lent is not a period of voluntaristic, tense concentration on ourselves, but a joyful walk toward Holy Easter, a progression in the Church toward the summit of the liturgical year.

A Journey to Reform Ourselves—Individually and as Church

"The life of a monk ought to be a continuous Lent. Since few, however, have the strength for this, we urge the entire community during these days of Lent to keep its manner of life most pure and to wash away in this holy season the negligences of other times." What St. Benedict says about monks[15] has value for individual Christians, whatever their status, and for the entire Church. At the same time, this way of speaking about Lent expresses a great deal about its very dynamic.

If Lent is a preparation for Easter, it is important to correctly understand in what way and in what spirit this preparation should take place. A Lenten journey at the end of which we would return to our previous state would have only a very relative interest. Of course, it would be worth something by reason of the effort put forth during this period. But we might derive from it more self-satisfaction—even some pride for the feats accomplished—than real progress. In any case, we might forget that asceticism is not an end in itself. As a preparation for the paschal celebration, Lent is a path of personal and communal renewal. "Let us celebrate the feast, not with the old yeast, the yeast of malice and wickedness, but with the unleavened bread of sincerity and truth" (1 Cor 5:8—Mass of Easter Sunday). In concrete terms, Lent is about rejecting everything that tarnishes or warps Christ's image, whether in the individual or the community. Lent is concerned with making repeated amends, rectifying what can and must be corrected so that Christians—individually and collectively—may present themselves in a fashion that is more direct, purer, and livelier. We are invited and given the opportunity to drink from a "Fountain of Youth." In a certain way, nothing after Lent should be as it was before, since having rid ourselves of the "old yeast," we are renewed in "sincerity and truth."

This Christian reform may bear upon things seemingly small but of considerable importance for ourselves, others, the community: ways of thinking and judging, attitudes, modes of behavior, personal and collective habits—all of these, on the religious, ecclesial, familial, social, and political levels. However, the point is not to seek a cure aiming solely at giving us new moral health or enabling us to accept the future with the assurance and the dignity of persons getting back on our feet. The "sincerity and truth" are measured by our love for God and its criterion, our love for others. The word of the Lord, which the prophet proclaims at the top of his voice, leaves no doubt about this. The sort of Lent that is pleasing to God is

> . . . releasing those bound unjustly,
>   untying the thongs of the yoke;
> Setting free the oppressed,
>   breaking every yoke;
> Sharing your bread with the hungry,
>   Sheltering the oppressed and the homeless;
> Clothing the naked when you see them,
>   and not turning your back on your own.
> (Isa 58:6-7)[16]

We reform ourselves in order to practice love, or rather *by* practicing love. For the Lord concludes:

> Then your light shall break forth like the dawn,
>   and your wound shall quickly be healed;
> Your vindication shall go before you,
>   and the glory of the LORD shall be your rear guard.
> Then you shall call, and the LORD will answer,

you shall cry for help, and he will say: Here I am!
If you remove from your midst oppression,
  false accusation and malicious speech.
(Isa 58:8-9)

A More Attentive Listening to the Word of God

In order to observe the sort of Lent that is pleasing to God, we must, before all else, apply ourselves to a more attentive listening to the word of God, especially to the Scriptures designated by the Church for this period of the liturgical year. We would derive great profit from the integral reading, conducted in a meditative and prayerful atmosphere—the sort of reading called *lectio divina*[17]—of one or the other biblical book, for instance, Exodus or Jeremiah.[18] But, we must begin with the more attentive reading of the scriptural passages selected for the time of Lent in the Lectionaries of Sundays and weekdays[19] and in the Liturgy of the Hours.

Reading and meditating on the liturgical texts primarily—be it in the secrecy and silence of one's room or in one's "prayer corner"—immediately places this *lectio divina* in a communal and ecclesial setting by the very fact that the same scripture readings are proclaimed in all Christian communities gathered for the Eucharist or the Liturgy of the Hours.[20] For the same reason, one should choose to read the books of the Bible from which the Church borrows more abundantly during this time of the year.[21] Because of the union with all other Christian communities, personal *lectio divina* is not simply an exercise of private devotion.[22]

Finally, this reading will gain by being done in common, in a family, a group, a community whose members agree to read the same book, with allowances for each one's pace and according to each one's possibilities of time, place, etc. Union in listening to the Word will naturally lead to union in prayer.

A More Constant Attention to Prayer and Liturgy

All forms of prayer are born from listening to the word: praise and thanksgiving for God's wonders and mercy; entreaty for forgiveness of the sin that God unveils and denounces in order to bring us back to him; intercession for God's grace and aid so that he will provide for the needs of his children, especially the poor, the powerless, the outcast, those who suffer injustice and find in God their only defender. The time of a more attentive listening to the word of God can only be that of a more constant attention to prayer and liturgy.

By the time of Pope Leo the Great (440-61), Mondays, Wednesdays, and Fridays of Lent were days when the assembly was successively convened in different Roman Churches.[23] At the beginning of the sixth century, the other days of the week also became assembly days and, as was not the case previously, days of Eucharistic celebration.[24]

We do not intend to return to the past and contest the soundness of subsequent evolution and resulting development. But we must not forget too quickly that, in the centuries in which Lent took shape (the fourth and fifth), Lenten practices on weekdays consisted of Liturgies of the Word, homilies, and prayer. Beyond the successive developments, the liturgical reforms, and the fortunate renewal of participation in the Eucharist by the faithful, it is important for us to attend to the primitive tradition: Lent is a time characterized by a more assiduous observance of prayer and liturgy. We would miss the grace of this time if we ignored the urgent call of the Church. Anyway, this would be tantamount to remaining deaf to God's word.

To repeat, what we are all about when we observe this liturgical time, is the correction of our habits in order to learn or relearn normative Christian behavior. By applying ourselves more assiduously to prayer and liturgy during Lent, we prepare to find or rediscover the paths of personal and communal prayer, the full, conscious, and active participation in the liturgy, all things that hold a central and irreplaceable position in the lives of believers and the Church.

The help of the Holy Spirit is indispensable to all who want to reach this goal, taking into consideration their personal possibilities, vocations, and ways of life. But we should not dismiss the help that brothers and sisters in the faith can bring one another by encouraging one another to run the risk of prayer.

Fasting is so much a part of Lent that it has come to be identified with it. In any case, for many people the main, if not the only, characteristic of this liturgical period is privation.[25]

Fasting did not originate with Christians; they received this practice from Judaism,[26] and it is also a part of numerous non-Christian religions. The practice of fasting was observed in the Church from its beginning, therefore long before the establishment and development of Lent, as the *Didache* or *Teaching of the Twelve Apostles*, which dates from the first century, attests: "Here is the way of life: in the first place you will love God, who created you, then your neighbor as yourself. All that you do not want done to you, do not do to anyone else. Here is the teaching contained in these words: Bless those who curse you, pray for your enemies, and fast for those who persecute you."[27] This fasting was observed on Wednesdays and Fridays all year long, except during Eastertide. When Lent was officially organized, fasting was extended to every day of the week except Sunday, and thus became an element of the preparation for the Easter celebration.[28]

Christian fasting is nothing like an ascetical performance that would have absolute value in itself.[29] A Christian fast, whether in or out of Lent, is not a self-imposed penitential punishment.[30] Neither does it imply any contempt for the body or food, as is shown by table prayers, thanksgivings and blessings to God for the good things he gives to his children.[31] But moderation in food and drink is a virtue, so is frugality. To fast at certain times is a way of checking on those virtues in ourselves and probably a necessity if we want to avoid times when our hearts "become drowsy from carousing and drunkenness" (Luke 21:34)[32] and to keep, or find again, mastery over our instincts. But all spiritual masters recommend discretion and discernment,[33] knowing that the goal is to keep "the heart" light and not to exhaust the body, that lack of moderation can entail consequences opposed to those one expects.

Christian fasting, therefore, is a spiritual practice in the strictest sense;[34] and this is why it is never considered in isolation.

Fasting, Prayer, Sharing

Christian fasting is always associated with prayer and the sharing of goods. The New Testament maintains the connection, already found in the Old, between fasting and prayer.[35] It is said of the prophetess Anna that "she never left the temple, but worshiped night and day with fasting and prayer" (Luke 2:37). Paul and Barnabas prayed and fasted with the disciples before installing presbyters in the Churches at Lystra, Iconium, and Antioch (Acts 14:23). While fasting expresses the strongest form of prayer, this is not all. From earliest times, it was also associated with almsgiving.

Today we do not like the term "almsgiving," because it brands gift-giving to the poor as condescension, and gift-receiving as humiliation. So a more acceptable term is "sharing," which is precisely the meaning of almsgiving as traditionally understood from the beginning. This is why tradition joins almsgiving to fasting in the phrase, "One fasts to be able to share."[36]

Around A.D. 130 an apologist writes, "When there are poor persons among them needing assistance, Christians fast for two or three days and customarily send them the food that they had prepared for themselves."[37] Similarly, we read in the *Didascalia Apostolorum* ("Teaching of the Apostles"), "Christians having nothing to spare will fast and bring to their brothers and sisters what they would have spent for food on that day."[38] For this reason the Church Fathers point out time and again in their preaching on the importance of fasting, that it is more a work of mercy than of mortification,[39] a work that has value only in relation to prayer and compassion.

> There are three things, my brethren, by which faith stands firm, devotion remains constant, and virtue endures. They are prayer, fasting and mercy. Prayer knocks at the door, fasting obtains, mercy receives. Prayer, mercy and fasting: these three are one, and they give life to each other.
>
> Fasting is the soul of prayer, mercy is the lifeblood of fasting. Let no one try to separate them; they cannot be separated. If you have only one of them or not all together, you have nothing. So if you pray, fast; if you fast, show mercy; if you want your petition to be heard, hear the petition of others. If you do not close your ear to others, you open God's ear to yourself.
>
> When you fast, see the fasting of others. If you want God to know that you are hungry, know that another is hungry. If you hope for mercy, show mercy. If you look for kindness, show kindness. If you want to receive, give. If you ask for yourself what you deny to others, your asking is a mockery. . . .
>
> . . . Fasting bears no fruit unless it is watered by mercy. Fasting dries up when mercy dries up. Mercy is to fasting as rain is to the earth. However much you may cultivate your heart, clear the soil of your nature, root out vices, show virtues, if you do not release the springs of mercy, your fasting will bear no fruit.
>
> When you fast, if your mercy is thin your harvest will be thin; when you fast, what you pour out in mercy overflows into your barn. Therefore, do not lose by saving, but gather in by scattering. Give to the poor, and you give to yourself. You will not be allowed to keep what you have refused to give to others.[40]

Today

The discipline of fasting has evolved in the course of time to the point where, today, it is obligatory only on Ash Wednesday and Good Friday. On the other hand, Lent today is the occasion for extensive sharing programs in the form of collections for the poorest of the poor, particularly those in the Third World. The generosity with which these appeals are met bears witness to our growing consciousness of the duty of rich countries to share its riches with poor countries; we can only rejoice over this generosity. Still, the link between sharing and fasting is in danger of disappearing. We give, but we do not fast. Our generous donations are not—at least directly—the fruit of fasting, even in the broad sense of the word. Even if we deprive ourselves of something by making a financial sacrifice, can we say that we give of our substance? In the Gospel, the poor widow who put two small coins into the temple treasury gave all that she had to live on (Mark 12:41-44; Luke 21:2-4), the fruit of fasting.

As meritorious and meaningful as it is to give or to reserve for the Lenten sharing the money we would normally spend for two days' food, this would not enable us to participate as generously as we usually do in a Lenten campaign or drive. Neither would this allow the organizers of such campaigns and drives to contribute, as they do, to the causes they have chosen to fund. In financial terms, and in terms of effectiveness, the traditional fast is not and cannot be, today, the immediate source of almsgiving and sharing. The shocking and intolerable inequalities, between people, classes, rich and poor countries, have social, economic, and political dimensions; and they cannot be set right by the collection of individual alms. But should not Lent be a call to us, an occasion for us to ask ourselves what part we can have in bringing about more justice, a beginning of sharing at least with the poor who are among us, and a greater solidarity among children of the same Father? This is an immense problem, whose magnitude and complexity are discouraging: "What can we do? What can I do?" This is a problem that the Church Fathers knew of, even if they did not see it on the global scale as we do now. It remains that their preaching, often vehement, is relevant to the contemporary scene and gives us food for thought.

> The rich declare themselves the masters of the common goods they usurped because they are the first to claim them. If people kept only what is required for their daily needs and if the surplus were given to the poor, both riches and poverty would be abolished.[41]
>
> Are you not a thief? The goods entrusted to your stewardship, you have hoarded. The bread you reserve belongs to the hungry. The coat hidden in your chest belongs to the naked. The shoes rotting in your house belong to those who walk barefoot. Thus you oppress as many people as you fail to help.[42]
>
> The Lord our God wanted this earth to be the common possession of all human beings and its fruits to be for the use of all, but greed has produced the division of the land. Consequently, if you claim as your own part of what has been given for the use of all humankind and even of all the animals, it is fair for you to distribute at least part of it to the poor. They have the same rights as you; therefore, do not deny food to them.[43]

> How could it not be evil to alone possess the Lord's goods, to alone en-
> joy what belongs to everyone? Therefore, if we can call our own the goods
> that belong to the Lord of all, they also belong to everybody else, just as
> do we his servants. For the Lord's things belong to all.[44]

These authoritative and powerful words are not isolated in patristic literature.[45] It is hard to believe that they were written so long ago, such is
their pertinence today to any reflection on sharing. Is not Lent the best
time to change our lifestyle in a consumer society to whose laws Christians too often submit through some complicity, even though a passive
one? Should not the fasting/sharing of Lent in the Church-at-large and
in Christian households be made manifest by actions, concrete plans, firm
positions resulting from the fundamental duty of Christians to love? Certainly, injustice would not suddenly disappear from the earth in a universal rush of sharing. But death-dealing egoism would at least be denounced
in the name of faith and of the Lord's command, rather than in mere
words and resounding statements.

In spite of today's mitigations of the Lenten observance, fasting/shar-
ing is as binding on Christians today as yesterday, even more. Fasting
and almsgiving (sharing) are "the two wings of prayer," as St. Augustine
says.[46]

> Here comes God:
> *Let God pass by.*
> Open my eyes, Jesus:
> Make me see.
> *Let God pass by.*
>
> Here comes God:
> *Let God pass by.*
> Come, call me, Jesus:
> I am deaf.
> *Let God pass by.*
>
> Here comes God:
> *Let God pass by.*
> Lift me up, Jesus:
> Lead me.
> *Let God pass by.*
>
> Here comes God:
> *Let God pass by.*
> Walk with me, Jesus:
> I am alone.
> *Let God pass by.*

Here comes God:
Let God pass by.
Give me light, Jesus:
It is dark.
Let God pass by.

Here comes God:
Let God pass by.
Come, speak with me Jesus:
Be my voice.
Let God pass by.[47]

Contemporary Structure and Discipline of Lent

When Lent took shape in Rome during the second half of the fourth century, it lasted six weeks, beginning on the first of the Sundays in Lent. This added up to exactly forty days before the Easter Triduum, but only to thirty-six days of fast, because Sundays were not counted as fast days. Therefore, at the beginning of the sixth century, the Wednesday, Thursday, Friday, and Saturday before the first Sunday of Lent were added so as to have forty days of fast.[48] The preceding Sunday became Quinquagesima Sunday (from "fifty"), itself preceded by Sexagesima, then Septuagesima Sunday; these added up to three weeks before Lent. This is the structure that endured until Vatican II.

The Council returned to the initial, simpler structure. Lent now extends from Ash Wednesday to the Mass of Holy Thursday, which opens the Easter Triduum. Therefore, we have five Sundays of Lent, followed by Passion Sunday, also called Palm Sunday. Depending on the year, Lent begins between February 10 and March 10; it ends between March 19 and April 22. During Lent we celebrate few feasts and solemnities.[49]

Looking Forward to Holy Easter and the Joy of Spiritual Desire

Lent is certainly a period marked by seriousness, and even gravity; but, contrary to certain stereotypes, it is also a time of joy. Lent is serious and grave because it causes us—individuals and Church—to confront the image of God in Christ, which we have blurred and tarnished by individual and collective sin. But we gain this awareness by contemplating the Holy Trinity, the love of the Father revealed by the Son in the Spirit, rather than by remaining fixated on ourselves. The word of God no doubt denounces sin, but at the same time proclaims the divine mercy always ready to forgive. The call to conversion, which insistently echoes throughout Lent, is an invitation to stand up once more, and not a pronouncement that overwhelms us and keeps us prostrate with our faces to the ground.

Lenten penance, an effort freely accepted "with the joy of the Holy Spirit,"[50] is the opposite of a self-imposed punishment that would have its own intrinsic justification and value. Nothing shows us this better than the practice of fasting in order to share with others one's goods or one's wants with a feeling of love toward others and God.

Finally, Lent is looking "forward to holy Easter with joy and spiritual longing," a hope that cannot be disappointed. If the Church refrains from singing Alleluia[51] during this whole time, it is not to have us robed in sadness, but to deepen our joy and to cause the Resurrection Alleluia to burst out more vibrantly and endlessly reverberate from one assembly to another to the four corners of the world on the night when Christ appears bathed in light.

Light of humankind, we walk toward you.
Son of God, you will save us!

Those who seek you, Lord, you lead toward the light,
You, the Road of those who lost their way.

To those who find you, Lord, you promise eternal life,
You, the Easter of those who are baptized.

Those who follow you, Lord, you feed with your Word,
You, the Bread of those you invite to your table.[52]

The Porch of Lent

Lent is the only liturgical time that begins on a weekday, with a solemn celebration marked by particular practices: fasting and ashes.

The liturgies of the three following days—Thursday, Friday, and Saturday—prolong the liturgy of Ash Wednesday. The biblical texts read at the Masses stress the spirit in which we must begin Lent and practice its "works," the meaning and goals of this liturgical time, the call to follow Christ, who revealed by his actions the mercy of God to which we must turn in a movement of genuine conversion.

The threshold of Lent is crossed on Ash Wednesday. But the following days constitute a "porch" leading to the great door that will be opened on the following Sunday. This is a threshold that we must take time to cross step by step, in prayer, reflection, and assessment of our strengths. This is the moment to throw aside what could uselessly weigh us down as we walk, and to check whether we are properly equipped for the Lenten exodus.

This is a porch on which the whole Christian community is called to gather because it is important to start together, at a brisk pace, toward the Lord's pasch and its celebration.

Ash Wednesday

The beginning of Lent—the Wednesday before the First Sunday—is marked by the giving of ashes. To cover oneself with ashes to signify mourning or contrition is a gesture often mentioned in the Bible.[1] It was natural that this practice be used by Christians and it was, for sinners, a public sign of penitence. For several centuries, however, this remained a private observance without liturgical expression. The use of ashes became a rite in Rhenish regions in the tenth century; it spread to Italy and finally to Rome in the twelfth century. It was only in the thirteenth century that the papal liturgy used ashes with the pope himself submitting to the rite. From that time until 1970, the liturgical imposition of ashes took place before Mass.[2] Since then, it has taken place after the Gospel reading and the homily. The Missal provides that if ashes are distributed outside of Mass, this rite is to be integrated into a celebration of the Word, utilizing the texts assigned to this day's Eucharist. The opening celebration of Lent, Ash Wednesday, normally comprises the Liturgy of the Word according to a Mass formulary, a penitential rite with the giving of ashes, and the Liturgy of the Eucharist.

The opening antiphon sets the tone.

> Lord, you are merciful to all, and hate nothing you have created. You overlook the sins of men to bring them to repentance. You are the Lord our God.

This is a sort of profession of faith. It is taken directly from the Book of Wisdom.

> But you have mercy on all, because you can do all things;
>   and you overlook the sins of men that they may repent.
> For you love all things that are
>   and loathe nothing that you have made;
>   for what you hated, you would not have fashioned.
> And how could a thing remain, unless you willed it;
>   or be preserved, had it not been called forth by you?
> But you spare all things, because they
>   are yours, O LORD and lover of souls,
> for your imperishable spirit is in all things.
> (Wis 11:23–12:1)

This profession of faith is found in similar terms in many passages of the Bible and in a considerable number of prayers. Every confession of sin, every movement of repentance, goes hand in hand with a profession of faith in the love, kindness, and mercy of God. We address ourselves to God with confidence because he is God, and for no other reason. He could not reject our prayer without denying himself, without ceasing to be God. Therefore, the act of repentance, of conversion, is before all else and at bottom, an act of faith, an action of our faith: "I believe in God . . . , in Jesus Christ the only son . . . , in the Holy Spirit . . . , in the forgiveness of sins." We must always put acts of penance in this dynamic movement, in this place, particularly when we deal with the sacrament of penance and reconciliation.

Return to the Lord

The Lord himself calls his people to enter into Lent, as proclaimed by the Church, which has chosen a text from the Book of Joel to express this call. It is an oracle of the most solemn kind: "Word of the Lord." This is much more than a vibrant and urgent exhortation; it is a word of revelation (Joel 2:12-18).

It is God himself who is at the center of this oracle, God who speaks and addresses his people. He defines himself in startling terms, "[tender] and merciful . . . , slow to anger, rich in kindness, and relenting in punishment." This is not how we imagine the "Almighty." This is not how we conceive of a strong person capable of dominating others and exercising sovereign authority over them. We are not accustomed to imploring the mercy of a powerful person of this world by saying,

> Spare, O LORD, your people,
>   and make not your heritage a reproach,
>   with the nations ruling over them!
> Why should they say among the peoples,
>   "Where is their God?"
> (Joel 2:17)

"Tender and merciful." The first of these terms evokes a feeling we know; the admirable thing is that it characterizes God. The second term has taken on a peculiar sense, with a strong connotation of pity, especially with regard to the wretched and guilty. This is not truly what the Bible means; there, mercy stems from a love that grips us to our innermost depths, our guts.[3] Tenderness and mercy are concrete attitudes rather than feelings or, in other words, feelings that are expressed in concrete attitudes. Tenderness and mercy define God, in whom doing and being are one and the same thing; God, who reveals himself and who is known not in himself—no one can see God—but by what he does, by his way of acting.

This is why we trustfully ask God to "return," to "forgo punishment," to "fill his own with blessings" so that we may "offer a sacrifice." This last request makes it clear that God is not appeased by what we offer him and that offerings do not force him to change. On the contrary, the opportunity to offer a sacrifice to God comes from the tenderness-mercy that is in him and which he manifests.

Therefore, we must "rend" our own closed hearts in order to open them to God and no longer "rend our garments" in a gesture of mourning or despair. In his "tenderness," God cannot help but show himself "moved" and having pity—mercy—on his people.

This is why a fast is announced at the sound of the trumpet and people are called into a solemn assembly from which no one is excluded, not even "the children and the infants at the breast." All business comes to a standstill, everyone hastens to join in the prayer that "the priests, the ministers of the Lord," address to God "between the porch and the altar," where the veil is about to be lifted.

> *Be merciful, O Lord, for we have sinned.*
> Have mercy on me, O God, in your goodness;
>   in the greatness of your compassion wipe out my offense.
> Thoroughly wash me from my guilt
>   and of my sin cleanse me.
> For I acknowledge my offense,
>   and my sin is before me always:
> "Against you only have I sinned,
>   and done what is evil in your sight."
> A clean heart create for me, O God,
>   and a steadfast spirit renew within me.
> Cast me not out from your presence,
>   and your holy spirit take not from me.
> Give me back the joy of your salvation,
>   and a willing spirit sustain in me.
> O Lord, open my lips,
>   and my mouth shall proclaim your praise.
> (Ps 51:3-6b, 12-14, 17)

Not Receiving the Grace of God in Vain

What Paul writes to the Corinthians echoes Joel's oracle (2 Cor 5:20–6:2).

At the moment of Christ's death, the veil of the sanctuary is torn from top to bottom, rendering free access to God. Now, God's justice can directly touch humankind and communicate with it. Christ, "who did not know sin," was made "to be sin, so that we might become the righteousness of God in him."

Such is the unimaginable effect of grace: "we . . . become the righteousness of God."[4] Jesus' identification with the sin of humanity assures our identification with God's justice. How could we receive such grace in vain?

Those who have known the good news cannot keep it for themselves. Like the apostles, ambassadors of Christ and spokespersons of God, they have the duty to call others to consent to be reconciled also to God.

For everyone, "now is a very acceptable time . . . now is the day of salvation." Christians must proclaim this message in their words and acts, in their way of living during Lent, this time of grace.

Prayer, Fasting, Almsgiving According to God

On this opening day of Lent, we must reread and meditate on Jesus' words as recorded by Matthew, on the works that characterize this time (6:1-6, 16-18).

What Jesus says to his disciples, gathered around him on the mountain, is particularly important for two reasons. First of all, because his words are part of what we call the Evangelical Discourse or the Sermon on the Mount. They are even placed in the last part of this "evangelical charter," and by this very fact, have a general impact, even beyond what is said of prayer, almsgiving, and fasting.

In fact, what is meant is that we must live as the just live, that is, by observing the Law (Matt 5:17-19) according to the new justice Jesus has proclaimed, "You have heard that it was said. . . . But I say to you. . . ." (Matt 5:21-48) before concluding, "So be perfect, just as your heavenly Father is perfect." What is in question, therefore, is our identification with God's justice, the righteousness of which Paul speaks (2 Cor 5:21).

Second, by speaking as he did, Jesus wanted not only to hold his listeners' attention but, the better to do it, to stir their imaginations. People do not have a trumpet blown before them when giving alms. But a certain ostentation in religious practices—more or less subtle and also more or less ridiculous—is not all that rare. Usually, we claim that we do not want to make a show of ourselves, but rather that we want to avoid yielding to human respect and to set a good example.

Jesus is aware of this necessity, since he has just said "Your light must shine before others, that they may see your good deeds and glorify your heavenly Father" (Matt 5:16). There is no contradiction between this teaching and that of almsgiving, prayer, and fasting done "in secret" and remaining unknown to other people. On the contrary, in both cases, what is enjoined is that we must please God and not people, to act in such a way that they will turn to God.

Likewise, there is no condemnation here of "public" prayer, of liturgical celebrations. Jesus himself participated in temple liturgies, and he was faithful to synagogue meetings on the sabbath. After Pentecost, the apostles regularly frequented the Temple, to which they went especially for the evening sacrifice (Acts 2:46; 3:1). From the beginning, the Christian community held regular gatherings. "They devoted themselves to the teaching of the apostles and to the communal life, to the breaking of the bread and to the prayers" (Acts 2:42). The assembly of the first day of the week goes back to the very beginnings of the Church. It is what most clearly characterizes Christians and most immediately manifests the presence of an ecclesial group in a given place.[5]

But no more than personal religious acts must the liturgy, the assembly, public worship, and prayer become spectacles "in order that people may see them." Otherwise, worship "in Spirit and truth" (John 4:23-24) has vanished. In sum, it is the truth of the heart that must be expressed; it is the heart that must be strengthened and converted by the liturgical acts, as well as by prayer, fasting, and almsgiving, which are the "works" of Lent. Lacking this attitude of heart, there is only vainglory, which neither deceives God nor fools humans, who denounce the practices as hypocritical and are scandalized.

On the other hand, what is done only for God's glory "in secret" and in the truth of the "heart" is not only "seen by the Father" but will soon shine clearly, unambiguously before people and lead them also to "glorify [the] heavenly Father" (Matt 5:16).

See How They Know That God Loves Them

The mark of Christians is love, manifested without ostentation, because it flows from their hearts, good as the heart of God revealed by Jesus. The Lord's disciples are recognized by their charity: "See how they love one another." The way they live Lent should lead observers to say, "See how they know that God loves them!" Lenten observances, the effort at personal and communal conversion, have their raison d'être in the tenderness and mercy of God. This is to say that there is no sadness or distress in the seriousness and gravity of this liturgical period. Dejected countenances are not acceptable. The hardships of our exodus are mixed with joy because we know that the Easter light will brightly shine at the end of the journey. It dawns already; it guides the steps of the Church on the path of freedom, renewal, and resurrection.

The Sign of Ashes

Now placed after the Liturgy of the Word, the giving of ashes has clearly become an entrance rite into Lent and into the penitential process it inaugurates.

Not long ago, the blessing of ashes was quite lengthy: an entrance hymn followed by four prayers noticeably longer than those of the Mass. The giving of ashes was done with the formula, "Remember, man, you are dust and to dust you will return" (see Gen 3:19). The rite ended with a final prayer.

Everything is much simpler today, since the blessing and giving of ashes follow the Liturgy of the Word. There is one single prayer before the giving of the ashes.[6] To the former phrase, "Remember, man, you are dust. . . ." another formula is offered as an alternative, "Turn away from sin and be faithful to the gospel" (see Mark 1:15). Finally, the rite concludes with the general intercessions. The Eucharistic liturgy follows.

The two prayers to choose from for the beginning of the rite[7] directly place Lent and the rite of ashes in the perspective of preparation for Easter.

> Lord,
> bless the sinner who asks for your forgiveness
> and bless ✛ all those who receive these ashes.
> May they keep this lenten season
> in preparation for the joy of Easter.
> We ask this through Christ our Lord.[8]

> Lord,
> bless these ashes ✛
> by which we show that we are dust.
> Pardon our sins
> and keep us faithful to the discipline of Lent,
> for you do not want sinners to die
> but to live with the risen Christ,
> who reigns with you for ever and ever.[9]

Finally, ashes are not blessed as something one can eventually take away or use outside the celebration—like the water blessed on Holy Saturday, for instance—and they are intended for a communal rite.[10]

The encouragement of others certainly spurs us to undertake and pursue the effort at renewal of Christian life to which Lent calls us. But Lent's communal dimension has a deeper foundation: We are going to God, we meet him, he comes to us, we are converted in the midst of—and even by—the believers' community. Lent is, therefore, also an opportunity to recapture—sometimes at the price of a genuine conversion—the ecclesial character of the search for God and an opportunity to free ourselves from an ever-threatening individualism.

Fasting Deepens the Longing Fulfilled by the Eucharist

Whether under its individual or ecclesial aspect, Christian life is moved by the tension between the waiting for the Lord's coming and the manifestations of his presence. Jesus said, "The days will come when the bridegroom is taken away from [the wedding guests], and then they will fast'' (Matt 9:15; Mark 2:20; Luke 5:35). But at the moment of his being taken away, he solemnly declared, "And behold, I am with you always, until the end of the age" (Matt 28:20). From that time on, the Church has been living under the regime of the absence-presence of her Lord. While fasting is inspired by this absence, the Eucharist is the sacrament of this presence. But it is not a question of two successive steps: alternating times of absence and times of presence. Christ is present at the core of the absence. The manifestation of his presence, particularly in the Eucharist—in memory of him, until he comes again—remains a remembrance and an experience of his absence:

> We proclaim your death, Lord Jesus,
> until you come in glory.[11]
> Come, Lord Jesus!

Fasting deepens the longing that is fulfilled by the Eucharist; the Eucharist sharpens the hunger that will be completely satisfied by the return of the Bridegroom, who has been "taken away" from his own. On that day, "he will gird himself, have them recline at table, and proceed to wait on them" (Luke 12:37). There will no longer be any fast, Lent, or Eucharist because, the world as we know it having disappeared (1 Cor 7:31), the signs will yield to the reality already germinating today.

> If you loose the chains of bondage,
> if you free your fettered brothers and sisters,
> the night of your road will be noontime light.
>
> Then from your hands,
> a spring will well up,
> the spring that invigorates tomorrow's earth,
> the spring that invigorates God's earth.
>
> If you share your God-given bread
> with those who are your very flesh,
> the night of your love will be noontime light.
>
> Then from your hearts,
> living water will spring up,
> the living water that irrigates tomorrow's earth,
> the living water that irrigates God's earth.
>
> If you destroy what oppresses humankind,
> if you raise your humiliated brothers and sisters,
> the night of your struggle will be noontime light.
>
> Then from your steps,
> a dance will be born,

the dance that invents tomorrow's earth,
the dance that invents God's earth.

If you denounce the evil that breaks humankind,
if you uphold your abandoned brothers and sisters,
the night of your call will be noontime light.

Then from your eyes,
a star will shine,
the star that announces tomorrow's earth,
the star that announces God's earth.

If you break down the walls between humans,
if you forgive your enemy brothers and sisters,
the night of your passion will be noontime light.

Then from your bread,
a church will live,
the Church which gathers tomorrow's earth,
the Church which gathers God's earth.[12]

Thursday after Ash Wednesday

Lord, may everything we do
begin with your inspiration,
continue with your help,
and reach perfection under your guidance.[1]

We have here the prayer of a caravan about to set out, the day after Ash Wednesday. We know from the experience of previous years that we are embarking on an uncommon journey. This year, we find ourselves in new spiritual conditions. At every moment, a call will be made to everyone's freedom and initiative. God's grace is absolutely necessary to inspire our actions and sustain them to the end. We run the risk of getting discouraged, of being overcome by weariness. As we travel, we also run the risk of drawing sustenance from sources other than God's will, of choosing our activities according to criteria insidiously inspired by mixed motives, including the desire "to perform righteous deeds in order that people may see them" (Gospel of Ash Wednesday).

The Hour of Choice
Conversion consists in turning—or turning again—toward the one we have chosen. A time of conversion, Lent is therefore the time of the choice proposed by God (Deut 30:15-20).

God does not force anyone to follow him; he does not chain anyone to himself; he offers a choice by clearly enunciating what the options are, "life and prosperity, death and doom." Given this choice, we cannot hesitate. Why then such insistence, as if it were possible to be tempted to prefer death and doom? Would it be because we suspect such an advantageous deal to hide exorbitant conditions? "Too good to be true."

In fact, this is not a question of a deal, but of a covenant that is binding on both parties. There are no hidden clauses, only "loving [the Lord, your God], and walking in his ways, and keeping his commandments, statutes and decrees": this is the code of the covenant (Deut 30:10).

There is nothing here that resembles arbitrary regulations and prohibitions. Rather, the commandments, statutes, and decrees are beacons that stake out the right road, guideposts that indicate dead ends or ways that lead nowhere and on which we might get lost for lack of clear signs.

But it is true that a covenant of love is not concluded lightly: it implies the total gift of self; there is no room for haggling; it is unlike a contract whose clauses are determined once and for all and can be verified one by one to see whether they have been observed to the letter. "The measure of the love for God is to love him without measure."[2] It is all or nothing. To bind ourselves by this bond can be frightening. We do not doubt the happiness brought by such a covenant. But how can we be sure of ourselves and others? When this other is God, there can be no hesitation: nothing can prevail against his faithfulness.

Happy are they who hope in the Lord.

Happy the man who follows not
    the counsel of the wicked
Nor walks in the way of sinners,
    nor sits in the company of the insolent,
But delights in the law of the LORD
    and meditates on his law day and night.
He is like a tree
    planted near running water,
That yields its fruit in due season,
    and whose leaves never fade.
    [Whatever he does, prospers.]
Not so the wicked, not so;
    they are like chaff which the wind drives away.
For the LORD watches over the way of the just,
    but the way of the wicked vanishes.
(Ps 1:1-4, 6)

Life and Happiness, the Way of the Cross

The law of the Lord is not only a "code of the covenant" that the just repeat day and night and whose observance insures life and happiness. To cling to the Lord God is, for us Christians, to follow Christ, to do the Father's will as he did, to take the same the path he took—the path that leads to the life he received to keep or give away. At the moment of going from this world to his Father, he said to his disciples: "Whoever loves me will keep my word, and my Father will love him, and we will come to him and make our dwelling with him. Whoever does not love me does not keep my words; yet the word you hear is not mine but that of the Father who sent me. I have told you this while I am with you. The Advocate, the holy Spirit that the Father will send in my name—he will teach you everything and remind you of all that [I] told you" (John 14:23-26).

Moses reported God's words and transmitted the commandments dictated to him, whose observance would insure the Lord's blessing and life. Jesus, for his part, says that to love him is to love the Father, that to remain faithful to his word is to welcome the word of the Father. Jesus is, in person, "the way and the truth and the life" (John 14:6)[3] because he can say, "The Father and I are one" (John 10:30). "To walk in God's ways" (first reading) is, therefore, to follow Christ—the Way; to love him is to love the Father; to cling to him is to be attached to the Truth and the Life.

Now, Jesus says: "The Son of Man must suffer greatly and be rejected by the elders, the chief priests, and the scribes, and be killed and on the third day be raised" (Luke 9:22). "This command I have received from my Father" (John 10:18). And, "This is why the Father loves me, because I lay down my life in order to take it up again" (John 10:17). As a consequence, it is impossible to follow the Way without renewing oneself and taking up one's cross "each day." It is impossible to save one's life without losing it for the Truth. It is impossible to be a Christian without being conformed to Christ, following him only.

Every life meets its share of trials, of "crosses." All beings must pass through death at the end of their earthly journey. Faith gives a new meaning to these crosses and to this death: it teaches us to live them in a Christian way with God's grace. But what Jesus says goes well beyond the trials of human life and beyond death itself. "If anyone wishes to come after me, he must deny himself and take up his cross daily and follow me" (Luke 9:23).

What is in question here is the condition of discipleship, and not a requirement of self-imposed penitential practices. "We know that our old self was crucified with him, so that our sinful body might be done away with, that we might no longer be in slavery to sin" (Rom 6:6). "I have been crucified with Christ; yet I live, no longer I, but Christ lives in me" (Gal 2:19). "Now those who belong to Christ [Jesus] have crucified their flesh with its passions and desires" (Gal 5:24). "But may I never boast except in the cross of our Lord Jesus Christ, through which the world has been crucified to me, and I to the world" (Gal 6:14). We are taught by these texts why and how we must take up our cross each day. Christian life springs up and rises again—daily—from the putting to death, in Christ, of sinful humanity. It is the mystery of death-resurrection, the paschal mystery, through Christ, with him, and in him. "Christ is our life in every way, his divinity is life, his eternity is life, his flesh is life, his passion is life. Thus Jeremiah speaks of him: "In whose shadow . . . we . . . live. . ." (Lam 4:20). The shadow of his wings is the shadow of his cross, the shadow of his passion. His death is life, his blood is life, his burial is life, his resurrection is life for all."[4] Such is the choice that God urges us to make after we have been instructed, the option of faith in Jesus, the Son of Man, who entered glory through his way of the cross.

"What is this new mystery in me? I am small and great, low and exalted, mortal and immortal. I am the one with the world, the other with God; the one with the flesh, the other with the Spirit. I must be buried with Christ, rise with him, inherit heaven with him, become the child of God, become God!"[5]

Friday after Ash Wednesday

Lord,
with your loving care
guide the penance we have begun.
Help us to persevere with love and sincerity.[1]

Marked by prayers and readings, the time spent on the "porch of Lent" on the Thursday, Friday, and Saturday after Ash Wednesday is more than an idle waiting period in front of the doors that will open on the following Sunday. Conscious of beginning a particularly important phase of the liturgical year, which is the sacrament of salvation, the Christian community recollects itself and fervently prays. It needs the "loving care" of the Lord—of his grace—in order to make the discipline proper to this time into a work of love.

The Manner of Fasting, the Test of Religion

"Show me your religious practices and I shall see what your religion is." The Letter of James applies this principle to faith:[2] without works it is useless; it is actually "dead."[3] A famous passage from the third part of the Book of Isaiah had already made of behavior the criterion of the fast that is pleasing or, on the contrary, offensive to God (Isa 58:1-9a).

Who would not applaud this categorical denunciation of a practice that has value neither in itself, nor in human eyes, nor in God's judgment when it is vitiated by formalism and hypocrisy? Perhaps we applaud the louder, since we are dealing with fasting, a practice that today appears to have little to do with religion. "Releasing those bound unjustly, untying the thongs of the yoke; setting free the oppressed, breaking every yoke; sharing one's bread with the hungry, sheltering the oppressed and the homeless; clothing the naked when one sees them, and not turning one's back on one's own (see Isa 58:6-7). Yes, by all means. To devote oneself to the service of the most deprived? Admirable! To participate in Lenten sharing? Certainly. But, to fast! . . ." To reason thus is to consider fasting an isolated practice. We undoubtedly recognize that the practice of fasting symbolizes sharing, especially if it is meant as a gesture of communion with the poor, as for instance the bowl of rice that is our only food for one day while we think of all those who daily suffer from hunger. This is not the sort of fasting the prophet is talking about; he speaks of that which expresses concern for sharing and justice and leads us to work at bringing them about.

> Then your light shall break forth like the dawn,
>   and your wound shall quickly be healed;
> Your vindication shall go before you,
>   and the glory of the LORD shall be your rear guard.
> Then you shall call, and the LORD will answer,
>   you shall cry for help, and he will say: Here I am!
> (Isa 58:8-9b)

The fast that is pleasing to God must be a serious matter if it has such consequences as justice, efficacious prayer, and even a share in the Lord's glory. Truly, this is a particularly significant test of religion.

> Prayer, almsgiving, and fasting are the three fundamental works of personal religious life. Those who do not pray to God, do not assist others,

and do not curb their nature by abstinence, are strangers to any sort of religion, even though they have spent their lives meditating on religious sub-
jects and speaking or writing of them. These three fundamental activities
of religion are so closely linked that the one has no efficacy without the
others. . . . Only when prayer, charity, and abstinence are united does
the one divine grace operate. Not only does this grace attach us to God
(in prayer), it assimilates us to the all-clement divinity (in charity) and to
divinity exempt from all need (in abstinence).[4]

We cannot approach God by any other way than fasting, prayers, and almsgiving. For God himself is at once merciful, without greed, and perfectly
holy. This is why those who want to be close to God must imitate what
God himself is.[5]

Voluntary Almsgiving and Social Justice

When we read the oracle from the Book of Isaiah (58:1-9), we usually skim
over the first part, which denounces the sorts of fast God cannot accept.
This is, on the one hand, because to ''bow [one's] head like a reed and
lie in sackcloth and ashes'' do not appear to us today as reprehensible
actions. On the other hand, the picture is so exaggerated that we feel
it has nothing to do with us.

Lo, on your fast day you carry out your own pursuits,
and drive all your laborers.
Yes, your fast ends in quarreling and fighting
striking with wicked claws.

But if transposed into another context, this denunciation is still pertinent.
In sum, it tells us that almsgiving in conjunction with fasting is a demand
of justice, not a manifestation of good will, an act of generosity left to
the free decision of the rich. This demand flows from the principle that
no matter what our financial situation is, we all have power over our
goods, whatever might be the radical injustice of inequalities that go
against God's will. ''There should be no one of you in need'' (Deut 15:14).
The early Christian community took this command literally: ''There was
no needy person among them, for those who owned property or houses
would sell them, bring the proceeds of the sale, and put them at the feet
of the apostles, and they were distributed to each according to need''
(Acts 4:34-35). However much this picture has been idealized, it exactly
describes a world and society that would reflect God's views. For he gave
the earth and all that it contains for all human beings to share. ''The land
is mine, and you are but aliens who have become my tenants,'' says God
(Lev 25:23). We are far from this ideal.[6]

Since its origin, the Church has urged Christians to voluntary poverty in connection with almsgiving-sharing. Modern nations, for their part, have promulgated laws in an attempt to establish some social justice, to regulate the uncontrolled accumulation of wealth by some at the expense of others mercilessly exploited. Would we be doing violence to Isaiah's text by rereading it in this context? "You fast, you willingly agree to give alms, and sometimes even very generously. But you evade the obligations of social justice. On your fast day, you know how to look out for your own interests and harshly treat those who serve you. You look for ways to save money at their expense by not providing the social benefits to which they are entitled. It is not with almsgiving of this sort that you will be heard on high."

Whatever the value of these paraphrases, we must rigorously test the whole of our conduct and practices, as well as the three traditional Lenten works, by the standard of God's word.

God's holiness is involved and, through the witness we give of it, God's credibility with humans. It is not holocausts that God wants from his people, but effective justice and charity that give him glory.

A broken, humbled heart, O God, you will not scorn.

Have mercy on me, O God, in your goodness;
    in the greatness of your compassion wipe out my offense.
Thoroughly wash me from my guilt
    and of my sin cleanse me.
For I acknowledge my offense,
    and my sin is before me always:
"Against you only have I sinned,
    and done what is evil in your sight"—
For you are not pleased with sacrifices;
    should I offer a holocaust, you would not accept it.
My sacrifice, O God, is a contrite spirit;
    a heart contrite and humbled, O God, you will not spurn.
(Ps 51:3-6b, 18-19)

Fresh Meaning of the Christian Fast

In the tradition of the prophets, Jesus preached the true spirit of fasting by denouncing the risks of formalism, pride, and ostentation that threaten to corrupt this practice (Gospel for Ash Wednesday). These censures imply the proclamation of the high value of fasting when it is observed with a sincere heart, with humility, with the desire to open oneself to the justice coming from God. As a new Moses and a new Elijah, Jesus inaugurated his mission by a fast of forty days. As a faithful observer of the Law, he surely took part in the "great fast" of Yom Kippur (Day of Atonement), which was the condition for belonging to God's people (Lev 23:29). Finally, he knew the fasts practiced by Jews out of personal devotion (Luke 2:37), by the disciples of John the Baptist, and by the Pharisees (Mark 2:18), a certain number of whom fasted twice a week (Luke 18:12).[7]

However, Jesus did not enjoin this sort of fast on his disciples who, in fact, accepted the tradition concerning fasting and integrated it, in their own way, into the practice of the Church.[8] On the other hand, he insisted on detachment from riches (Matt 19:21), on voluntary continence (Matt 19:12), and above all on self-denial (Matt 10:38-39). One day, however, Jesus had to express his opinion on fasting (Matt 9:14-15).

The opportunity arose for Jesus in a question framed as an objection put to him by disciples of John the Baptist: " 'Why do we and the Pharisees fast [much] but your disciples do not fast?' Jesus answers them, 'Can the wedding guests mourn as long as the bridegroom is with them? The days will come when the bridegroom is taken away, and then they will fast.' "

The way this answer is worded is unexpected. Jesus could have simply said, "Penance is not for my disciples as long as I am with them. They will fast later after I have left them." Instead, Jesus speaks of the "bridegroom" and "wedding guests." The use of these biblical images gives to his answer a meaning and amplitude beyond those of a mere response to an objection. At the same time, the newness of the fasting of Jesus' disciples is revealed.

This fast must be understood and practiced from the perspective of messianic times evoked by the image of the wedding. These times have come since Jesus is here, he who designates himself as the bridegroom. Consequently, his answer is a question asked of those who interrogate him, "Why do you do penance? In order to prepare yourselves to welcome him who has already come? This is out of the question, but what matters now is to recognize him present among you and to join him at the wedding banquet to which you are invited." Fundamentally, fasting is the sign of the faith professed in the heart. Therefore, the first part of Jesus' response does not concern only the disciples of John the Baptist who questioned him. It remains a word for us, today.

What follows completes this first teaching for Jesus' disciples who, since his being "taken away" to the right hand of the Father, live in the "meantime" that separates us from the Lord's return. It is still the time of invitation to the wedding, which the sacraments, and especially the Eucharist, prefigure and anticipate. "Happy are those invited to the table of the Lord, the wedding feast of the Lamb." But on that day, after the doors of the banquet hall have been closed (Matt 25:10), this long-awaited wedding, for which the guests have prepared themselves while waiting for the bridegroom's coming (Matt 25:1-13), will at last take place.[9]

During this meantime, which is that of today's Church, fasting expresses in its own way what we, in fact, proclaim at each Eucharist, "Lord Jesus, we await your coming in glory. Come, Lord Jesus!"

When the groom is again among his own, they will no longer fast; moreover, the sacraments of his presence in absence will lose their raison d'être. Joy, still held back for now, will burst forth untrammeled when the immense crowd will proclaim with one voice:

"Alleluia!
The Lord has established his reign,
[our] God, the almighty.
Let us rejoice and be glad
and give him glory.
For the wedding day of the Lamb has come,
his bride has made herself ready.
She was allowed to wear
a bright, clean linen garment."
(The linen represents the righteous deeds of the holy ones.)
Then the angel said to me, "Write this: Blessed are those who have been called to the wedding feast of the Lamb."
(Rev 19:6-9)

Saturday after Ash Wednesday

Father,
look upon our weakness
and reach out to help us with your loving power.[1]

Tomorrow, the assembled Christian community will leave the porch of Lent. Those who have been detained will arrive and the procession will begin to advance. At the beginning of the last celebration of the four days of preparation, a prayer is raised to God. May he consider the weakness of which his faithful have become more clearly aware. They bow before him while he stretches over them his "all-powerful hand"—a solemn liturgical gesture. Once more they listen to what God says through the prophet's voice.

The New Charter of the Covenant
The text of today's first reading is the conclusion of the great proclamation begun yesterday (Isa 58:9b-14).

This ending concisely and vigorously rephrases the exhortation that just precedes it:

> If you remove from your midst oppression,
>   false accusation and malicious speech;
> If you bestow your bread on the hungry
>   and satisfy the afflicted,
> Then light shall rise for you in the darkness,
>   and the gloom shall become for you like midday.

After so much insistence, there is no possible hesitation on the meaning of Lent and its works to which the Church calls the faithful. We must commit ourselves to the service of the poor in order to establish a more just world. Asceticism, fasting, self-renunciation, all animated by prayer, have for their motive and aim the exercise of charity.

The promises that follow evoke the paradise regained after the "Holy City" has been rebuilt, "prepared as a bride adorned for her husband" and in which "there shall be no more death or mourning, wailing or pain" (Rev 21:1-4).

> Then the LORD will guide you always
>   and give you plenty even on the parched land.
> He will renew your strength,
>   and you shall be like a watered garden,
>   like a spring whose water never fails.
> The ancient ruins shall be rebuilt for your sake,
>   and the foundations from ages past you shall raise up;
> "Repairer of the breach," they shall call you,
> "Restorer of ruined homesteads."
> (Isa 58:11-12)

Mortification and penitential practices are contrary to a destructive undertaking. They aim at rebuilding the world on the foundation of the spiritual values God has given his people, into which, through Christ, the whole of humankind is incorporated.

> Jonah began his journey through the city, and had gone but a single day's walk announcing, "Forty days more and Nineveh shall be destroyed," when the people of Nineveh believed God; they proclaimed a fast and all of them,

great and small, put on sackcloth. When the news reached the king of
Nineveh, he rose from his throne, laid aside his robe, covered himself with
sackcloth, and sat in the ashes. Then he had this proclaimed throughout
Nineveh, by decree of the king and his nobles: "Neither man nor beast,
neither cattle nor sheep, shall taste anything; they shall not eat, nor shall
they drink water. Man and beast shall be covered with sackcloth and call
loudly to God; every man shall turn from his evil way and from the violence he has in hand. Who knows, God may relent and forgive, and with-
hold his blazing wrath, so that we shall not perish." When God saw by
their actions how they turned from their evil way, he repented of the evil
that he had threatened to do to them; he did not carry it out.
(Jonah 3:4-10)

This narrative reminds us of the missionary dimension of Lent, during
which the Church, with a fresh burst of energy, commits itself to announce the good news to all nations, to all human beings for whom Jesus
died and rose from the dead, Jesus whom we all must follow carrying
our own crosses each day (Luke 9:23—Gospel for Friday).

The Day of the Lord

The oracle concludes with a few lines on the sanctification of the Lord's
Day.

We would expect a reminder of our obligation to worship. But apparently, the prophet thought it was unnecessary, since the persons he spoke
to were faithful to that duty. In any case, again the emphasis is placed
on actions.

If you hold back your foot on the sabbath
    from following your own pursuits on my holy day;
If you call the sabbath a delight,
    and the LORD's holy day honorable;
If you honor it by not following your ways,
    seeking your own interests, or speaking with malice—
Then you shall delight in the LORD,
    and I will make you ride on the heights of the earth;
I will nourish you with the heritage of Jacob, your father,
    for the mouth of the LORD has spoken.
(Isa 58:13-14)

Jesus gave us the example of the sanctification of the Lord's day by works
of mercy. The Gospels record several cures accomplished on the sabbath
in the synagogue.[2] To those who reproached him, Jesus one day went
so far as to say, "The sabbath was made for man, not man for the sabbath" (Mark 2:27).

Teach me your way, O Lord, that I may be faithful in your sight.

Incline your ear, O Lord; answer me,
for I am afflicted and poor.
Keep my life, for I am devoted to you;
save your servant who trusts in you.
You are my God; have pity on me, O Lord,
for to you I call all the day.
Gladden the soul of your servant,
for to you, O Lord, I lift up my soul;
For you, O Lord, are good and forgiving,
abounding in kindness to all who call upon you.
Hearken, O LORD, to my prayer
and attend to the sound of my pleading.
(Ps 86:1-6)

Jesus the Physician

At the beginning of this celebration, we turned to God, asking him to look upon our weakness (Opening Prayer). The call of Levi, a publican, recounted with great economy by Luke, confirms this prayer and gives to those who say it with a humble and sincere heart the assurance of being heard. For Jesus says: "Those who are healthy do not need a physician, but the sick do. I have not come to call the righteous to repentance but sinners" (Luke 5:27-32).

The initiative comes from Jesus, who notices a publican seated at his table, therefore busy at his work. He simply says to him, "Follow me." And Levi, "leaving everything behind, . . . got up and followed him." Moreover, to celebrate this insane behavior and to make sure no one will miss it, Levi organizes a great banquet to which, along with Jesus and his disciples, he invites "a large crowd of tax collectors and others" from their circle. We wonder at what this fashionable company must have thought and said of the abrupt decision of their colleague and friend. The evangelist is satisfied with recording the recrimination of "the pure ones," the "Pharisees and their scribes," probably because he reckons that the readers of his Gospel have nothing in common with the publicans and the sinners of their ilk.

Jesus' statement is a word of revelation regarding his person and mission, and on God, who sent him. But, on the eve of the First Sunday of Lent and after the reading from Isaiah, it also describes the mission of the Church and the disciples.

Conscious of their weakness at the onset of their effort at conversion, healed by the Lord, they must go to their brothers and sisters who are still ill, even if they are engaged in business as usual. Was Levi perhaps expecting the call of Jesus without daring to believe in such a grace? Was he surprised by it? What does it matter? It was still necessary that Jesus should notice him and say, "Come."

> There is more joy in heaven
> over a little useless song
> than over those great speeches supposed to change
> the world.
>
> More joy
> over one repaired wall
> than over a whole city,
>
> over one ray of sunshine in the shadow
> than over a flawless day,
>
> over a thin trickle of water
> than over a wide river.
>
> More joy
> over an adventure attempted
> than over a deal successfully concluded,
>
> over a crazy action
> than over reasonable proceedings.
>
> More than over all the immobile scribes:
> joy over a person who stands up![3]

Starting Off on the Right Foot

In truth, the days spent under the porch of Lent are not wasted days. It would be a shame to withdraw after Ash Wednesday to come back only on the following Sunday. After Advent and the feasts of Christmas/Epiphany, plus a few weeks in Ordinary Time, we are now entering a six-week period unlike any other period in the Church's year. The change in climate is too sudden to be approached without a brief but intense preparation. It is time to assess our strength, to take a deep breath, to attach ourselves to others with a rope in order to start off on the right foot and to courageously undertake the ascent toward Easter. Let not our weakness or the watchful eyes of those who judge our undertaking as being strange, presumptuous—even useless—dishearten us.

> People of God, do not be ashamed,
> show your sign to our times!
> While crossing the ages of the world,
> seek your breath in the Spirit;
> raise your hymn to his power,

turn your natural bent to his glance:
So that he may dwell in your praises
and be visible to his children.

Hold onto his love, hold onto his trial;
it is in joy that he has entrusted to you
the whole burden of his work
so that it may sing through your voice:
Do not withdraw within yourselves
as if God acted like this!
It is when you love that God loves you,
open your heart, imitate him.

Go, draw from your inheritance
and, without counting, share it;
win the test of our times,
carry the name of God everywhere!
Let him shake you, let him wake you:
You are his Body, in his Spirit!
People of a God who works marvels,
be his marvel of today.[4]

The Three Paths of Lent

The entrance into the Lenten season is always made through the same porch where we gather from Ash Wednesday through the following Saturday. Depending on the liturgical year, Sunday opens one of the huge doors marked A, B, C. Each one gives access to a Lenten itinerary that has its own characteristics but is fundamentally the same as the other two.

The Sunday Lectionary

The First Sunday is always focused on Jesus' fast and temptation in the desert, and the Second Sunday on the transfiguration, according to Matthew, Mark, or Luke. From the Third to the Fifth Sunday, however, the paths are different.

In Year A, we read three important passages from John's Gospel: the Samaritan woman (John 4:5-42—Third Sunday), the cure of the man born blind (John 9:1-41—Fourth Sunday), and the raising of Lazarus (John 11:1-45—Fifth Sunday).

These Gospel texts were the framework of the preparation for Easter when Lent lasted only three weeks and was geared to the celebration of baptism. For we have here three baptismal catecheses on water and spirit, the light of faith, death and life.[1] They constitute what has been called the "Johannine Lent," directed primarily to catechumens and also rousing the baptismal faith of those around them.[2]

In Year B, the Gospels for the Third, Fourth, and Fifth Sundays, also taken from John, are more explicitly oriented to the passover of the Lord: the prediction of the destruction of the Temple and its rebuilding in three days (John 2:13-25—Third Sunday), words concerning the Son of Man, who must be raised up so that all who believe in him may have eternal life (John 3:14-21—Fourth Sunday), and the teaching on the grain that dies and bears much fruit (John 12:20-33—Fifth Sunday).

Finally, in Year C, the Gospels for these three Sundays have a more penitential theme: the necessity of conversion (Luke 13:1-9—Third Sunday), the parable of the prodigal son (Luke 15:1-3, 11-32—Fourth Sunday), the woman taken in adultery (John 8:1-11—Fifth Sunday).

As usual outside of Ordinary Time, the second reading—sometimes the first—of each Sunday has been chosen to complement the Gospel.

During Lent, however, the first reading stands by itself. Each selection is an Old Testament text relating an important and significant stage in salvation history.

In Year A: the creation of man and woman and the first sin (Gen 2:7-9; 3:1-7—First Sunday), the call of Abraham (Gen 12:1-4a—Second Sunday), the gift of water from the rock Moses struck with his staff (Exod 17:3-7—Third Sunday), the anointing of David by Samuel (1 Sam 16:1b, 6-7, 10-13a—Fourth Sunday), God's promise to raise up his people (Ezek 37:12-14—Fifth Sunday).

In Year B: the first promise of the covenant made to Noah after the Flood (Gen 9:8-15—First Sunday), Abraham's sacrifice of Isaac (Gen 22:1-2, 9a, 10-13, 15-18—Second Sunday), the giving of the law on Mount Sinai (Exod 20:1-17—Third Sunday), the exile of the people at the time of Nebuchadnezzar and its liberation by Cyrus (2 Chr 36:14-16, 19-23—Fourth Sunday), the promise of a new covenant (Jer 31:31-34).

Finally, in Year C: the ancient creed of Israel (Deut 26:4-10—First Sunday), the covenant between God and Abraham and his posterity (Gen 15:5-12, 17-18—Second Sunday), the burning bush (Exod 3:1-8a, 13-15—Third Sunday), the Passover at the time of the entrance into the Promised Land (Josh 5:10-12—Fourth Sunday), the promise of a new, triumphant exodus (Isa 43:16-21—Fifth Sunday).

At Sunday Masses in Lent, the first reading is independent from the other two. Each of the three series constitutes a catechetical unit, as do the seven Old Testament readings at the Easter Vigil. Hence, their importance during the five Sundays of Lent.

On Passion (Palm) Sunday, the first two readings are the same every year (Isa 50:4-7; Phil 2:6-11). They are followed by the Gospel narrative of the Passion According to Matthew (Year A), Mark (Year B), or Luke (Year C).

The Weekday Lectionary

The biblical readings for the Lenten Masses remain the same every year. Lent is the only time, on weekdays, when the first reading (from the Old Testament) is related to the Gospel. Its perspective is that of Lenten catechesis and spirituality.

From Monday of the fourth week on, we read, in order,[3] large excerpts from chapters 4, 5, 7, 8, 10, and 11 of John, which are especially appropriate for this liturgical time.

On the days preceding the Easter Triduum, we read the account of the anointing at Bethany (John 12:1-11—Monday), the prediction of Judas' betrayal and Peter's denial (John 13:21-33, 36-38—Tuesday), the pact between Judas and the chief priests, the preparation of the paschal meal, and the last warning to the traitor (Matt 26:1-25—Wednesday).

The Road to Easter According to Scripture

The Lenten liturgies do not contain a more abundant reading of scriptural texts than those of the rest of the year, although some excerpts are longer than average.[4] Their arrangement conforms to the principle followed outside of Ordinary Time.[5] However, the Liturgy of the Word during Lent turns out to be of a remarkable spiritual and doctrinal richness. This is due to the fact that the biblical texts have been admirably selected so that the meaning of Lent and the actions it entails might be really brought to light by God's word.

The recalling of the important steps of revelation and salvation history— first reading of Sunday, in the three years—helps us to better perceive the paschal mystery in the unity and dynamic of God's plan that leads to this summit.

> The wonderful works of God among the people of the Old Testament were but a prelude to the work of Christ Our Lord in redeeming mankind and giving perfect glory to God. He achieved his task principally by the paschal mystery of his blessed passion, resurrection from the dead, and glorious ascension, whereby "dying, he destroyed our death, and rising, restored our life." For it was from the side of Christ as he slept the sleep of death upon the cross that there came forth "the wondrous sacrament of the whole Church."[6]

The Gospels of the temptation of Jesus in the desert—First Sunday of Lent, every year—immediately place before our eyes Christ victorious over Satan, whose dominion of humankind he destroys, calling all of us to fight, with him, in a similar combat against the enemy of humanity.

The transfiguration of the Lord—Second Sunday of every year—imparts a certain character to Lent by offering for our contemplation the icon of Christ raised up into glory after suffering his passion.

He gives us living water and cures blindness; he raises up those "who were indeed buried with him in baptism into death; so that . . . we too might live in newness of life" (Rom 6:4; Col 2:12). For the whole Christian community, as well as for the catechumens, Lent is a baptismal itinerary (from the Third to the Fifth Sunday—Year A).

Lent is also a catechumenal itinerary for all; it prepares everyone of us and the entire ecclesial community to renew, at the Easter Vigil, our profession of faith in Christ, who is the grain of wheat fallen into the earth to rise on the third day, in the Son of Man lifted up on a cross to draw all to himself so that through faith we may obtain eternal life (from the Third to the Fifth Sunday—Year B).

Finally, Lent is a privileged time for the conversion of sinners whose return the Father awaits in order to establish them in their dignity as his children, forgiving them through Christ (from the Third to the Fifth Sunday—Year C).

It is in this profoundly theological—even mystical—context that we must place personal and communal efforts proper to Lent and to its works: prayer, fasting, and almsgiving-sharing. God's word ousts all sorts of illusions that threaten to more or less seriously vitiate Lenten practices. Prophets and Jesus never cease to vigorously denounce them: ostentation, vainglory, feigned justice.[7] The Scriptures read during Lent proclaim the sorts of fasting and Lent that are pleasing to God and make us holy because they are inspired by the love of God and neighbor.

Such is the Christian Lent, and beyond it, every Christian life of which Lent is in some way the model,[8] according to Scripture, source of truth and authenticity and criterion of options, practice, personal, and communal mortifications.

The First Two Weeks

At the time of St. Leo, pope from 440 to 461, the first two Sundays of Lent were respectively characterized by the Gospels of the temptation of Jesus in the desert and of his transfiguration, both according to Matthew (4:1-12; 19:1-9).[1]

The Sunday Lectionary, published in 1969 in the wake of the liturgical reform of Vatican II, kept these two Gospels for Year A. But since there is now a three-year cycle for the Sunday biblical readings, the parallel narratives in Mark (1:12-15; 9:2-10) were chosen for Year B and those in Luke (4:1-13; 9:28b-36) for Year C.

The Gospels of the first two Sundays in Lent, in Years A, B, and C, are parallel. But this is not the case for the other readings.

Thus, these Sundays of Jesus' temptation and transfiguration have, each year, their originality, not only because of this difference between the first two readings, but also because, next to Mark's brief mention, we find two detailed stories by Matthew and Luke. Moreover, we observe notable differences between these last two. We must attentively read each of the Gospels of Jesus' temptation rather than rely on our own memory, a composite remembrance that blends several elements: the desert, Jesus' fasting, and three temptations that he foils. There is also good reason to read these texts with our minds free from memories of various interpretations aimed at making Jesus' temptations immediately relevant to us. This is not to say—far from it—that these interpretations are suspect (a priori) of illegitimate stretching of the texts. But it is important to apply ourselves first to what each evangelist says, trying to understand what he himself suggests.[2]

With Jesus in the Desert

The liturgies of the first two Sundays of Year A are the oldest of Lent; in fact, they go back to the fourth century.[3] From that time until the middle of the sixth century, the months were counted starting with March. Lent was the beginning of the liturgical year and apparently also the beginning of the continuous reading of the Bible. In this case, the account of the first sin in Genesis would have suggested the reading of Jesus' temptation and his victory over Satan.[4] Whatever the case, these two texts, to which the passage from the Letter to the Romans on the justification of all humans through the obedience of the new Adam has been more recently associated, form a particularly homogeneous group.[5]

The Origins of Sin and Death

The first pages of the Bible are devoted to the origins of the universe, humankind, and sin. In common parlance, we speak of the "stories" of the creation and fall. This term does not accurately describe the genre of these texts and their true value, which goes beyond those of a narration. What is in question here is a reflection, sapiential in character, a reflection born of wisdom into which the author—a sage—draws his reader. Therefore, it is a test of one's own wisdom to understand the sage's teaching. The more so as the question asked is a difficult one: What was the beginning of humanity and what were the origins of sin? We do not have in the first pages of Genesis a "naive" story of origins that the subsequent progress in knowledge would allow us to relegate to the category of so-called "primitive" legends. Such a judgment would betray a lack of discernment. We must, therefore, listen with great attention and perspicacity to the first reading for this Sunday (Gen 2:7-9; 3:1-7a).[6]

It is composed of two brief excerpts from a rather large unit.[7] The beginning briefly recounts that after having created heaven and earth, God "form[s] man out of the clay of the ground and [blows] into his nostrils the breath of life," then places him in the Garden of Eden. All this is told with an extreme and effective economy. The original condition of humankind is a gift from God, and a fragile gift. Humans are not the owners of this garden in which God places them. They are not destined for death, but they can die if they disobey the command they have received. How is it that death, from being only a threat, has become the unavoidable fate of humankind? Even more precisely: How were human beings led to a disobedience they knew would be punished by death? The inspired sage ponders these questions, this enigma.

He does not give the solution in the manner of a teacher magisterially stating the correct answer. Instead, he imagines the dialogue between the "cunning" serpent and the woman, leaving it to the discerning reader to grasp the meaning of this story. Sin is disobedience, but a disobedience rooted in the heart. The tempter insidiously leads Adam and Eve to doubt God, to see in him a jealous rival whose law prevents them from living a full life.

Sin is not born of the attraction of the forbidden fruit, but of a perversion within oneself of God's image, of the nature and intent of the divine law. Only then does the forbidden fruit appear "good for food, pleasing to the eyes, and desirable" since it allows us to seize something that a tyrant God would like to keep out of our reach.

Is God he who loves and gives, or he who obstructs and jealously keeps things for himself? Is the law a yoke which holds us in subjection and which we must cast off, or a guide offering us a responsible choice free from worldly interpretation? Finally, is God an object of lust or a partner in a relationship of love and trust?

> Here then, I have today set before you life and prosperity, death and doom. If you obey the commandments of the LORD, your God, which I enjoin on you today, loving him, and walking in his ways, and keeping his commandments, statutes and decrees, you will live and grow numerous. . . . If, however, you turn away your hearts and will not listen, but are led astray and adore and serve other gods, I tell you now that you will certainly perish. . . . I have set before you life and death, the blessing and the curse. Choose life, then, that you and your descendants may live, by loving the LORD your God, heeding his voice, and holding fast to him.
> (Deut 30:15-20)

Here is where sin and death come from: rather than listening to God and trusting him, we allow ourselves to be seduced and tricked by the suggestions of the evil one. Everything else follows, in particular the perturbation of the relationship between man and woman. The body, the first gift of God, who fashioned it and blew life into it, ceases to be a sign and becomes an object of lust and of power-hungry seduction, attracting all eyes to itself. It arouses shame.[8]

The tone of this reflection on the entrance of sin and death into the world is undeniably serious. Could it be otherwise? However, we do not have here a passage that dramatizes the present situation of humankind, causes fright or even despair. On the contrary.

The woman was the victim of the serpent's wile and was foolish enough to fall into the trap into which the man allowed himself to follow. In the beginning, therefore, there was a wrong move, heavy with consequences to be sure. But this mistake is evoked with a gravity tempered with the gentleness of a sage who has knowledge of the subsequent history of humankind. We, too, know what happened afterward, as we join the author in this meditation. Man and woman—humanity—will be able to backtrack from this disastrous move; choose anew, with fuller knowledge, good and life; recognize the truth of God, who loves them, and the intent and proper domain of the law. This is why the meditation over the origin of sin and its entrance into the world is followed not by a song of lament and mourning, but by a psalm of repentance, that is, a confession of the Lord's merciful love, a song of humble trust and hope.

> *Be merciful, O Lord, for we have sinned.*
>
> Have mercy on me, O God, in your goodness;
>   in the greatness of your compassion wipe out my offense.
> Thoroughly wash me from my guilt
>   and of my sin cleanse me.
> For I acknowledge my offense,
>   and my sin is before me always:
> "Against you only have I sinned,
>   and done what is evil in your sight"—
> A clean heart create for me, O God,
>   and a steadfast spirit renew within me.
> Cast me not out from your presence,
>   and your holy spirit take not from me.
> Give me back the joy of your salvation,
>   and a willing spirit sustain in me.
> O Lord, open my lips,
>   and my mouth shall proclaim your praise.
> (Ps 51:3-6b, 12-14, 17)

In Jesus, the New Adam, Justice and Life

By entering the world, sin and death have plunged humankind into a peculiarly gloomy state, although not a desperate one. Humans cannot reach God through their own strength. Some, withdrawing into themselves, have fallen into numberless perversions (Rom 1:18-32). Others have not succeeded in remaining faithful to the Law and the Covenant symbolized by circumcision (Rom 2:1-3:8). All, Jews and Gentiles, have sinned, following Adam, and by the same token, are deprived of the glory of God (Rom 3:1-19).

The situation is reversed and another era begins with the coming of Christ. For whoever relies on faith in Jesus Christ, life is radically transformed. This is salvation, for in his Son, God himself comes to restore to humanity its former orientation and fulfill its expectation. Humans recover the possibility of entering again into communion with God, a state willed by the Creator "in the beginning" (Rom 3:21-5:11).

The first five chapters of Paul's Letter to the Romans paint a vast fresco of this human condition before and after Christ's coming. The second reading for this Sunday condenses this description in a strong synthesis that, following the reading from the Book of Genesis, has an especially compelling unity in itself.

What strikes us at the outset is the contrasted parallels: a world of darkness and death, a universe of light and life; the unity of humanity vitiated in Adam, renewed in Jesus Christ. In a word, on one side sin and death dominate; on the other, life and grace reign.

Furthermore, what disproportion between Adam's fault and Christ's work!

> But the gift is not like the transgression. For if by that one person's transgression the many died, how much more did the grace of God and the gracious gift of the one person Jesus Christ overflow for the many. And the gift is not like the result of the one person's sinning. For after one sin, there was the judgment that brought condemnation; but the gift, after many transgressions, brought acquittal. For if by the transgression of one person death came to reign through that one, how much more will those who receive the abundance of grace and the gift of justification come to reign in life through the one person Jesus Christ. In conclusion, just as through one transgression condemnation came upon all, so through one righteous act, acquittal and life came to all. For just as through the disobedience of one person the many were made sinners, so through the obedience of one, the many will be made righteous.
> (Rom 5:15-19)

Many topics for endless meditation are proposed in this final picture of the drama of humanity:[9] human solidarity beyond all imagination, the realism of the incarnation without which Christ would not have really reached the whole of humankind, the unity of sacred history from its origins "when God created the heavens and the earth" (First Reading) up to its completion, the destiny of the world and humankind, the problem of sin and grace, the certainty that Christ is the sole savior, victorious once and for all over death and evil. The answer is full of hope: grace will have the last word in the new world, liberated by Christ from sin and death.

Jesus and the Devil in the Desert

In the three Synoptic Gospels—Matthew, Mark, and Luke—the story of Jesus' temptation immediately follows that of the theophany at the time of his baptism.[10] The three note that Jesus was led into the desert by the Spirit. But Matthew's Gospel, read in Year A, says that Jesus went there "to be tempted by the devil."

The evangelist immediately adds, however, that it is after having "fasted for forty days and forty nights" that Jesus' hunger is the occasion of the devil's first assault. And he concludes that after failing three times, the devil leaves Jesus, and angels come and serve him.

We must guard against understanding this passage as the simple account of what Jesus does in the desert and of what happens to him.[11] We must take the time to hear the harmonics of this story resonating in us. The forty days and forty nights that Jesus spends in the desert remind us of the forty years the people of God spent on their way to the Promised Land. The desert is the place of trials[12] as well as of revelations. Matthew emphasizes the first aspect, without forgetting that a stay in solitude can be peaceful: angels are near Jesus and serve him. There is no contradiction here. Solitude places us humans in the presence of God and ourselves without any possible escape; it forces us to make radical choices. We must decide to answer "yes" or "no" to God; the "yes, but," used routinely in ordinary life, proves impossible. The choice cannot be made without a violent struggle against the self and against the enticing solicitations of the devil. But when we succeed in answering "yes" to God's call, the devil departs and peace takes possession of our whole being.[13]

Because he was truly human, the beloved Son of the Father could not bypass the test of the desert and of temptation; temptation was the more violent as his mission was loftier and more exacting than that of any other person. But his initial victory over the devil was definitive; nothing could cause him, who had received the fullness of the Spirit, to take back the "yes" said to the Father.

"If You Are the Son of God"

We need to withdraw into solitude in order to discern God's calls and to test the authenticity of the calls we have perceived. On the banks of the Jordan, Jesus heard the Father's voice and saw the Spirit descend and rest on him. The tempter would love to lead him to doubt God's proclamation, just as he had succeeded to make the woman doubt the truth of God's words: "God told you that you would die if you should eat the fruit of the tree. Nothing of the sort! You certainly will not die! God is deceiving you. To prove it, eat of the fruit of the tree."

With Jesus, Satan uses the hunger resulting from a prolonged fast. Had not the search for food in the desert led the people to doubt God and Moses, his spokesperson, by questioning whether God had really chosen them? "You had to lead us into this desert to make the whole community die of famine" (Exod 16:3). To silence their grumblings and to have them recognize him who led them, God sent a covey of quail and bestowed the manna (Exod 16:11-15). The devil suggests to Jesus that he ascertain the authenticity of his being the Son of God by changing stones into loaves that will appease his hunger. "One does not doubt God's word," Jesus answers. "It and it alone gives us life."

The second temptation is to talk Jesus into making sure that God really loves him and watches over him. Jesus is to jump into empty space from the parapet of the Temple. Jesus answers, "You shall not put the Lord, your God, to the test." Jesus will not challenge the Lord as the people did at Massah and Meribah, in order to see whether, yes or no, God was with them (Exod 17:7).[14]

"Prostrate Yourself Before Me"

At first sight, the third temptation appears completely unlikely. Prostrating oneself before the devil to adore him in the belief that dominion over all the kingdoms of the world will be granted by him! How could Jesus ever have toyed with such a transaction? Are we not into irrationality?

On second thought, we see that this last insinuation of the devil logically follows the first two. Jesus has just evoked the Lord God. The devil counters, "Precisely, let's talk about it. Who is he for you? Look at all the kingdoms of the world. You can see that I am their master. Therefore, if you want them, you must come to an understanding with me; prostrate yourself and worship me. Then they will be yours."

Was this temptation too crass for Jesus to have fallen for it? We must resist the urge of going into psychological explanations, for we cannot speak with any certainty about the human psychology and spirituality of Jesus. But at least two remarks are in order. How could the Son of Man be the new Adam, the head of the new humanity, if he had not had to choose to adore God and him alone, explicitly, with full knowledge and freedom? Where would his victory over Satan be if he had not unmasked[15] and dismissed him by resolutely turning to God?

Superficially read, this Gospel seems to record a kind of exegetical joust between a fundamentalist[16] tempter and Jesus, who opposes the devil's scriptural quotations with other texts that shed light on the meaning of the passages used by the devil. In fact, this Gospel narrative projects a decisive light on the person of Jesus. We foresee that his teaching will bear upon concrete priorities of life, upon the meaning of the Law, upon God. At the same time, everyone is called to unmask Satan behind whatever contests the authority of the Son fully obedient to his Father, confident that he, and he alone, will provide for his needs, his prestige, his glory. Temptation may take on multiple forms. One can—one must—give examples of it. But however well founded these applications, they remain mere examples of interpretation that do not exhaust the meaning of this Gospel.

Christ's Victory and Christian Combat
"I have today set before you life and prosperity, death and doom" (Deut 30:15). This word of God, transmitted through Moses in his last discourse to the people of the covenant, has not ceased to be heard since the creation of humankind. The devil's deceit subjected humanity to the power of death and sin. Afterward, God gave the Law to his people in order that they might choose again life and prosperity, but the human condition was not changed. With the incarnation of the beloved Son, the new Adam, perfect Image of God, humanity was radically reoriented. Before undertaking his ministry of teaching and revelation in words and actions, Jesus confronted Satan in a decisive single combat. Jesus defeated him by foiling his trickery through his unshakable attachment to God's word, stable and unique foundation of life and happiness. In him and through him, the whole of humankind was again and definitively turned toward its creator.

When Jesus began to teach, his victory over Satan was behind him; it is also behind us. No longer do Christians fight against the tempter and his snares in an unequal combat. They enter the fight with the solid support of the initial victory of the Head of the new humanity, with the weapons of faith in Christ. They have learned to unmask Satan, whatever his disguise. Finally, Christians have been instructed by Christ to use the sword of the Word, the true meaning of which Jesus authoritatively revealed.

Solidarity of Humanity in Adam and in Jesus Christ

"Just as through one person sin entered the world, and through sin, death . . . so through one righteous act acquittal and life came to all" (Rom 5:12, 18—Second Reading). What Paul says rests on the principle of the solidarity of humankind, which is becoming today more and more influential in many domains. Could Paul have had the intuitive genius to perceive what we see better and better today? Indubitably not. We must not stretch his thought. But his teaching on the reign of sin and death through the fault of one man, on justification through the obedience of one man, gives us cause for reflection.

> If such a solidarity exists, is it unthinkable that a fundamental change reaching into the very heart of humankind (its ordination to God) have immediate effects on the whole of humanity in the manner of a chain reaction? Then perhaps we would better understand the unique place of Adam's sin, and its transmission. Humankind was made for God. The first explosion produced the disintegration of the whole. From that point on, successive explosions have no common measure with the first. This lasts until the day when someone has the power to oppose this endless disintegration, thanks to an element of cohesion. It is Jesus Christ's work that triggers, in the opposite direction, a chain reaction, now irreversible, for all those who receive the gift of justification.[17]

Such solidarity gives to Christ's followers unsuspected powers. Every movement of conversion, every victory over evil mysteriously but efficaciously contributes to direct or maintain the orientation of humankind toward life and toward God, in whose image it has been created. Likewise, sin appears for what it is: a leaven of decay with tragically grave consequences. Only God's intervention can regenerate the diseased tissue by eradicating what impedes the diffusion of life in the entire body or one of its members.

> Lord Jesus, sent by the Father,
> you came to fight in an immense combat
> to deliver Adam's children.
> Grant that we may be so close to you
> in battle and toil,
> that we may also share in your victory.[18]

First Sunday of Lent—Year B

The Future Saved
by the Just One

The first important step of salvation history recalled on the First Sunday of Lent, Year B, is the new covenant concluded between God and the universe in the days of Noah (Gen 9:8-15).

The initial eruption of sin provoked a series of chain reactions that spread and increased more and more. "The LORD saw how great was man's wickedness on earth, and how no desire that his heart conceived was ever anything but evil." To describe the depth of the disaster, the author says that God himself was so sickened that he regretted having created and placed humans on the earth (Gen 6:8-11). He attributes to God the feelings and thoughts of parents in despair over their children's reprehensible behavior, reproaching themselves for having given them birth. This is an admirable anthropomorphism of the Bible, which has an acute sense of the visceral love the Creator has for his creatures. The love of God allows him to be appeased by the justice of one single child. The Creator is not going to destroy his work; rather he will save it by making Noah, the just one, descendant of Adam, the father of a renewed humanity (Gen 6:11–8:22). Therefore, the Flood is followed by a new covenant—more explicit than the original one—not only with humankind, but with the whole cosmos.

When Noah and his family leave the ark, God pronounces the same blessings over them as he had over Adam and Eve, "Be fertile and multiply and fill the earth." He renews their power "over the fish of the sea, the birds of the air, and all the living things that move on the earth" (Gen 9:1-3, repeating 1:28-30). These words again found humanity upon one father on the first day of history—Adam; "on its first morrow"[19]—Noah. But already we perceive the figure of the new Adam, who will be the head of a new humanity and, as the Noah of the end of time, will save the believers gathered in the ark of the Church through the waters of baptism.

As on the first day, God's blessing is paired with an interdict, "Every creature that is alive shall be yours to eat. . . . Only flesh with its lifeblood still in it you shall not eat. For your own lifeblood, too, I will demand an accounting: from every animal I will demand it, and from man in regard to his fellow man I will demand an accounting for human life" (Gen 9:3-5; see 2:16-17). In reality, this interdict commands respect for others' lives.[20]

Therefore, after Adam, Noah is the father of the whole of humankind, prior to distinctions of race and religion; he is the new leader of the universe that survived the Flood.

The Cosmic Covenant in the Days of Noah

When Noah and his family and the animals leave the ark to take possession of the land, God concludes a covenant with them. This covenant comes after a period when sin had become universal; therefore, it is a covenant of mercy and forgiveness that sets in relief God's goodness, undiminished by numberless human sins. It is a cosmic covenant that reaches "every living creature that was with you: all the birds, and the various tame and wild animals that were with you and came out of the ark." It is a covenant by which God himself guarantees the permanence of life on earth, no matter what may happen through human fault.

Noah himself is not personally a sinner; therefore, he has no need of forgiveness. In spite of this, he is not presented as the man whose justice saves others.[21] Rather, he is the just man thanks to whom everything can be rebuilt more soundly than before, like those foundations on which, after a disaster, one can build a new, more spacious and better-planned house.

This first explicit covenant will undergo developments throughout salvation history. With Abraham, it will become the election of a people chosen to keep and transmit divine blessings and promises constantly repeated in wider and wider perspectives. Finally, Christ will come, in whom and through whom the covenant will embrace all humans of all races and peoples.[22]

The Sign of the Rainbow in the Sky

After a storm, the rainbow announces the imminent return of a clear sky and the end of atmospheric disturbances. We modern people are more sensitive to the beauty of its colors; people of old were more struck by its shape. They saw it as the bow with which God "sent forth his arrows . . . with frequent lightnings" that spread terror (Ps 28:15).[23]

Is this a primitive, prescientific conception of a natural phenomenon whose mechanisms we now understand? Without a doubt. But it is also a poetic and religious vision which scientific explanations do not invalidate and which we cannot do without.[24] The rainbow, the weapon hanging in the clouds and unused by God, is thus the sign of the covenant: in some way, God holds himself back from destroying his work and he will not cease to affirm it.

> For a brief moment I abandoned you,
>> but with great tenderness I will take you back.
> In an outburst of wrath, for a moment
>> I hid my face from you;
> But with enduring love I take pity on you,
>> says the LORD, your redeemer.
> This is for me like the days of Noah,
>> when I swore that the waters of Noah
>> should never again deluge the earth;
> So I have sworn not to be angry with you,
>> or to rebuke you.
> Though the mountains leave their place
>> and the hills be shaken,
> My love shall never leave you
>> nor my covenant of peace be shaken,
>> says the LORD, who has mercy on you.
> (Isa 54:7-10)

A Sage Ponders the Story of the Flood

The story of the Flood has not been recorded in the Bible so that we may keep the memory of a cataclysm that occurred thousands of years ago or even, for that matter, that we may learn about a certain Noah.[25] What we have here is a sage's meditation on the future of humankind now guaranteed by God's promise and the universal covenant that God has initiated. The sage sees in the sky a sign of this cosmic covenant. Along with this covenant we find a a prohibition concerning food, which must be understood not as a legal pronouncement but as an absolute command to respect life—signified by blood—given by God when he created humans in his image.

> *Your ways, O Lord, are love and truth,*
>> *to those who keep your covenant.*
>
> Your ways, O LORD, make known to me;
>> teach me your paths,
> Guide me in your truth and teach me,
>> for you are God my savior. . . .

Remember that your compassion, O LORD,
and your kindness are from of old . . .
in your kindness remember me,
because of your goodness, O LORD.
Good and upright is the LORD;
thus he shows sinners the way.
He guides the humble to justice,
he teaches the humble his way.
(Ps 25:4-5b, 6, 7b-9)

The Prisoners of Death Liberated by Christ

In the early Church, the First Letter of Peter was proportionately the most often quoted New Testament writing.[26] The reason for this is that it has transmitted very important expressions of faith to us, particularly, three Christological formulas, one of which is contained in the second reading of this Sunday (1 Pet 3:18-22).[27]

> For Christ also suffered for sins once, the righteous for the sake of the unrighteous, that he might lead you to God. Put to death in the flesh, he was brought to life in the spirit. . . . [He] has gone into heaven and is at the right hand of God, with angels, authorities, and powers subject to him.

This is a remarkable profession of faith. As early as that time—about A.D. 64—the Church already had fixed formulas at its disposal, as in a creed. Our Apostles' Creed deserves its name.[28]

On the other hand, the mission of Christ, who goes to proclaim his message "to the spirits in prison," poses a problem. We would dodge it if we identified his preaching with the liberation of the just of the Old Testament, to which the New alludes (Matt 27:51), or to the descent of Christ into hell, which is an article of our creed. We cannot really call these just ones "spirits in prison."[29]

The First Book of Enoch, an apocryphal writing composed between the second century B.C. and the middle of the first century A.D.,[30] calls the fallen angels, mentioned in the Book of Genesis (6:1-6) "imprisoned spirits." We are told that Enoch was sent to them to tell them that they will not receive their pardon. They beg Enoch to intercede with God, but God remains inflexible. Enoch then returns to tell them of the final answer. This book was well known in early Christianity; some New Testament texts make reference to it.[31] If the First Letter of Peter does allude to these mythological stories, it sets in relief the dazzling success of Christ, who at the time of his descent into hell succeeded in doing what Enoch had been unable to do.[32]

In any case, the letter clearly says that the risen Christ has announced his message to those who were regarded as the worst of sinners: those who, formerly, had revolted when the patience of God continued unflagging "during the building of the ark, in which a few persons, eight in all, were saved through water."

The Flood as an Image of Baptism
At the time of the Flood, a small number of persons were "saved through water," thanks to the ark, made of "frailest wood," says the Book of Wisdom (10:4), which adds, "For blest is the wood through which justice comes about" (14:7). For Christians, the wood of salvation is that of the cross (1 Pet 2:24), since it is "through the waters" that they pass, with Christ, from death to life. This is how the Flood "prefigure[s] baptism, which saves [us] now" by purifying us of a defilement that is not material, i.e., "carnal."[33]

This passage through the waters of baptism introduces us into the new covenant, sealed by Christ on the wood of the cross. It implies a personal commitment to God that, traditionally, the catechumens express before being immersed into the baptismal bath that makes them Christians, i.e., sharers in the resurrection of Jesus Christ, who conquered sin and death.

From the Temptation in the Desert to the Announcement of the Gospel
Unlike the other evangelists, who give a rather well-developed account of the temptation, Mark makes only a brief mention of it. Besides, this initial test is placed in immediate relation to the beginning of the Lord's preaching (Mark 1:12-15).

It is "at once" after his baptism that Jesus is "driven" into the desert by the Spirit, with a certain violence and haste. This urgency is in keeping with Mark's style. All through his Gospel, he shows Jesus hurrying from one place to another, always on the move.

Without going into detail, Mark notes that during his forty days in the desert, Jesus is tempted by Satan. He adds, "He was among wild beasts, and the angels ministered to him." All of this is said so rapidly that we wonder what we are to understand by it. In our imaginations, the presence of "wild beasts" evokes the insecurity of inhospitable places, and the fact that it is mentioned, increases the terrifying character of the stay in the desert. But then what is meant by the ministry of angels? Is there not a contradiction between angelic assistance and hostile environment?

In response to the prayer of the just one who takes refuge in God, the psalm says,

> No evil shall befall you,
> nor shall affliction come near your tent,
> For to his angels he has given command about you,
> that they guard you in all your ways.
> Upon their hands they shall bear you up,
> lest you dash your foot against a stone.
> You shall tread upon the asp and the viper;
> you shall trample down the lion and the dragon.
> (Ps 91:10-13)

In Luke's Gospel, the victory over Satan is associated with protection from dangerous animals. Addressing the seventy-two disciples returning from their mission, Jesus says, "I have observed Satan fall like lightning from the sky. Behold, I have given you the power 'to tread upon serpents' and scorpions and upon the full force of the enemy and nothing will harm you" (Luke 10:18-19). Jesus can give this power to his disciples because he has received it from the Father and because, in the desert, he has personally defeated the devil. Finally, we are reminded of the oracle of Isaiah:

> Then the wolf shall be a guest of the lamb,
> and the leopard shall lie down with the kid;
> The calf and the young lion shall browse together,
> with a little child to guide them.
> The cow and the bear shall be neighbors,
> together their young shall rest;
> the lion shall eat hay like the ox.
> The baby shall play by the cobra's den,
> and the child lay his hand on the adder's lair.
> (Isa 11:6-8)

Mark's brief notice on Jesus' stay in the desert turns out to be quite meaningful. "At once" after his baptism and before the beginning of his public mission, the Lord wins a decisive victory over Satan. By the same token, he has lived the return to Paradise, in the peace of a world in which humans are given back their power over the forces unleashed by sin. Therefore, he can proclaim: "This is the time of fulfillment. The kingdom of God is at hand. Repent, and believe in the gospel."

A Future for Humanity and the Universe

In the liturgy, the biblical narratives are chosen and arranged according to a viewpoint, and with a coherence that is original. The task at hand is not to build a structured development, as in a discourse or a catechesis, but to illuminate the sacramental action by the light of the Word. This, in turn, is qualified by the context of the liturgical time, the mystery being celebrated. Certainly, we must begin by listening to the biblical passages that are proclaimed, so that we may welcome their message without prejudice—a message that is often disconcerting—or at least be surprised.

It is also important for us to be attentive to the lighting that the texts project, one upon the other; these beams of light intersect one another, varied in their intensity and color. These plays of light illuminate now one, now another theme of these texts. Perspectives take shape, opening on vast horizons; this Sunday, those of the future.

Noah is, in effect, "the just one who saves the future"[34] because he does not allow himself to be taken in by the perversity and sin that surround him. God takes him and sets him apart to make of him the father of a new humanity and the new Adam of a universe never again to be submerged by a flood. It is not Noah's righteousness or astuteness that obliges God to change his mind or foil his plan of destruction, but the faithfulness of the Creator to his work that saves it and recreates it. God wants life for humankind and other living things. Nothing will be able to make him deviate from his first intention. On the contrary, he will tirelessly pursue his design for a world and a humanity intent on fulfilling their potential.

When the time came, he sent his Son, the just one. Although subjected to death for a while, he was not overcome by it. Restored to life, the risen Christ has freed "the prisoners of death" who in the past had rebelled against God. He empowers those who follow him to walk, through baptism, on the way that leads to God, that they may arrive at eternal life and at the glory of his resurrection.

This paschal itinerary crosses the desert where, after his baptism, Jesus was "driven" by the Spirit. There he confronted Satan and his temptations. Having passed through the ordeal, strengthened by the power of God, who has subjected everything to him in heaven—the angels—and on earth—the wild beasts—he proclaimed the good news with authority and preached conversion because "the kingdom of God is at hand."

Saved for us by Christ, the future is in our hands. Each liturgy unveils it anew and opens its doors wider and wider.

> Into what land of solitude,
> forty days and forty nights,
> will you go, driven by the Spirit?

May it test you and strip you!
See, the times are fulfilled,
and God invites you to forget
your ancient servitudes.[35]

Salvation and Glory Near God

The Presence of the Past in the Act of Worship

The first reading for this Sunday is an old creed that accompanies the liturgical offering of earthly goods and explains its meaning by recalling the long periods during which God has been forming his people (Deut 26:4-10).[36]

Here, then, is the basic outline of the main phases of salvation history: the time of the patriarchs, vagrant Arameans, a period ending with Jacob's going into Egypt; that of the long years of slavery under Pharaoh's rod until God's liberation of his people through Moses; finally, the period extending from the Exodus to the people's entrance into the Promised Land under Joshua.

The recalling (anamnesis) of this history is a profession of faith in God, who gathers and leads his people. But this recollection does not turn us backward to a past not to be forgotten; it makes us contemporaries with the events that are recounted; that history is our history today; it encompasses and assumes the future. The threefold dimension of the liturgy is yesterday, today, and tomorrow, the offering of what "earth has given and human hands have made"—all a gift from God who was, who is, who is to come.[37]

But it is not sufficient to know and to repeat from celebration to celebration, "My father was a wandering Aramean. . . . [T]he God of our fathers . . . heard our cry. . . . Therefore, I have now brought you the first fruits of the products of the soil which you, O LORD, have given me." This profession of faith and the ritual offering that accompanies it would be vain without a personal commitment.

> Lord God, we ask you to receive us
> and be pleased with the sacrifice we offer you
> with humble and contrite hearts.[38]

We may be assured then that God, seeing our poverty, will hear our voices and not abandon us.

Be with me, Lord, when I am in trouble.

You who dwell in the shelter of the Most High,
  who abide in the shadow of the Almighty,
Say to the LORD, "My refuge and my fortress,
  my God, in whom I trust."
No evil shall befall you,
  nor shall affliction come near your tent,
For to his angels he has given command about you,
  that they guard you in all your ways.
Upon their hands they shall bear you up,
  lest you dash your foot against a stone.
You shall tread upon the asp and the viper;
  you shall trample down the lion and the dragon.
Because he clings to me, I will deliver him;
  I will set him on high because he acknowledges my name.
He shall call upon me, and I will answer him;
  I will be with him in distress;
I will deliver him and glorify him. . . .
(Ps 91:1-2, 10-15)

Salvation for All by the Invocation of the Name

The first reading recalls the place of the "memorial" (anamnesis) in worship. The text of Paul's Letter to the Romans, chosen for the second reading, stresses the importance of the invocation (epiclesis) of the Lord's name, through which we obtain salvation (Rom 10:8-13).

Paul takes off from what Moses said in his last discourse to the people:

"The word is near you,
  in your mouth and in your heart."

Moses was speaking of the Law: "For this command which I enjoin on you today is not too mysterious and remote for you. It is not up in the sky, that you should say, 'Who will go up in the sky to get it for us and tell us of it, that we may carry it out?' Nor is it across the sea, that you should say, 'Who will cross the sea to get it for us and tell us of it, that we may carry it out?' " (Deut 30:11-13). Paul is speaking of the "word of faith," the object of apostolic preaching that announces Jesus dead and risen. To profess on the lips and from the heart that God has raised Jesus from the dead brings righteousness and gives access to salvation: none of those who have this faith will regret it at the time of judgment.[39] Calling on the name of the Lord is having the assurance of being saved. But where does the power of this invocation come from?

To say the name of someone is to recognize, in his or her profound identity, the person it designates. To call on the name of Jesus is, therefore, a total act of faith in the risen Lord who saves. It is an unconditional welcome to his power of resurrection, his strength for salvation. Nothing comes between the one who calls upon the name and the Lord. At the time of judgment, we shall not regret having put our entire trust in him; we shall not know the disappointing experience of counting our merits or appraising our faithfulness to the law.[40]

Such a path to salvation is open to all. Again, Paul quotes a scriptural text, "Everyone who calls on the name of the Lord will be saved." He takes this from the Book of Joel (3:5) but gives it a universal meaning that it did not have in Joel.[41] What Paul says is that it is no longer a matter of observing a great number of precepts, but only of believing in the "word of faith" preached by the apostles. Moreover, Jesus having been made "both Lord and Messiah" (Acts 2:36), Peter says that "God shows no partiality" (Acts 10:34), observing, not without surprise, the faith of the centurion Cornelius in Caesarea (Acts 10:34), and the faith Paul repeatedly noticed in his ministry to the Gentiles. To all, indeed, the Spirit is given freely and abundantly (Acts 10:44-48; 11:15-18).

Jesus Led by the Spirit Through the Desert

Before Luke tells us, Matthew and Mark say that Jesus, after his baptism, was led into the desert by the Spirit. But Luke's Gospel introduces the story of the temptation in a more original way; we also recognize in this introduction other traits proper to Luke (4:1-13).

"Filled with the holy Spirit," Jesus leaves the banks of the Jordan, in which he has been baptized. Under the guidance of the Spirit, he goes into the desert "for forty days, to be tempted by the devil." An impression of peaceful docility to the Spirit emanates from this introduction, written in a flowing literary style. Jesus obeys spontaneously. He will do so again at the beginning of his ministry when, after his test in the desert, "Jesus return[s] to Galilee in the power of the Spirit" and begins to teach. The evangelist tells us that Jesus' first sermon takes place in the synagogue at Nazareth. Having read the passage from Isaiah where it is written

> The Spirit of the Lord God is upon me,
>   because he has anointed me" (Isa 61:1),

he proclaims, "Today, this scripture passage is fulfilled in your hearing" (Luke 4:14-22). In his Gospel and in Acts, Luke reserves an important place for the Holy Spirit.[42]

Finally, Luke suggests in his introduction that Jesus walked through the desert, unceasingly harassed by the devil. It is a discreet way of introducing us to the three confrontations later mentioned, three temptations presented in the wilderness to Jesus, who had to repel many others as well.

The Three Temptations According to Luke

At the end of forty days of absolute fast, Jesus is hungry. If Jesus is the Son of God, let him "command this stone to become bread." The devil speaks to Jesus in the same manner as the soldiers at the crucifixion, "If you are King of the Jews, save yourself" (Luke 23:37; see also 23:35). In the desert, as later on, Jesus refuses to use the power of his word solely to save himself. He will use this power in order to save others, as when, with a single word, he will free the demoniac (Luke 4:35), cure the sick (6:10; 18:42), call his disciples (5:27), raise the dead (7:14; 8:54), forgive sins (7:50).

Then, Luke records another kind of temptation that in a certain way is an extension of the first; for again it is a question of power, this time Jesus' power. Power characterizes his ministry and teaching (Luke 5:17). But it is from the Father that Jesus gets his power, because only the Father has the initiative to give it to whomever and whenever he wills. Jesus will communicate it to his disciples with the gift of the Spirit, so that they may be his witnesses to the ends of the earth (Acts 1:8). This power has nothing in common with that of "the ruler of the world" already "condemned" (John 14:30; 16:10). However, this illusory "power" and "glory" are nonetheless tempting, as was proved in the case of Adam, whose son Jesus is (Luke 3:38). In any event, the power and the glory that God gives to his Christ, and through him to the disciples, are fully revealed only at the end of their paschal journey. Then "the Son of Man will be seated at the right hand of the power of God" (Luke 22:69); the disciples will eat and drink at the Lord's table in his kingdom and "will sit on thrones judging the twelve tribes of Israel" (Luke 22:30). Then all will be "recapitulated."

This is why Luke presents a genealogy tracing our Lord to Adam and containing seventy-two generations. Thus he joins the end to the beginning and gives us to understand that the Lord is the one who has recapitulated in himself all nations scattered since Adam, all tongues and generations of humans, including Adam himself. This is also why Paul calls Adam, himself, "the type of the one who was to come," because the Word, Maker of the universe, had begun beforehand to plan in Adam the new "economy" of the human nature that the Son of Man was to take upon himself. God indeed had first created the "natural" man in order that, obviously, he might be saved by the "spiritual" Man. For, since the One who would save him was already in existence, it was necessary that what was to be saved also come into existence so that this Savior might not be without a raison d'être.

Therefore, it was indispensable that, coming to seek the lost sheep, recapitulating such a vast "economy," and looking for his own handiwork, the Lord should save that man who had been made in his image and likeness, that is, Adam, when Adam would have fulfilled the time of his condemnation caused by disobedience (the Father had fixed that time by his power since the whole "economy" of human salvation was unfolding according to his will) in order that God might not be vanquished and that his art might not be held in check.[43]

Jesus knew all this, since he taught it to his own. But he does not discuss it with the demon. He merely murmurs in his heart the daily Jewish prayer, the *Shema Israel,*

"You shall worship the Lord, your God,
   and him alone shall you serve" (see Deut 6:13),

as he will do at the time of the ultimate trial in Gethsemane, "Father, . . . not my will but yours be done" (Luke 22:42).

The third temptation that Luke records takes place in Jerusalem, on the parapet of the Temple. This precise locale comes as no surprise in Luke's Gospel. Everything began in the Temple with the announcement of John the Baptist's birth (Luke 1:5-25). In the Temple, the infant Jesus was recognized by Simeon and Anna as the light of the nations that had been foretold (Luke 2:22-38). It is in the Temple that he first manifested his extraordinary wisdom (Luke 2:41-50). These references to the Temple found in the Third Gospel from its prologue on, are landmarks on the road that leads Jesus to Jerusalem, where he must die (Luke 13:33-34) and rise from the dead, where the Christian community will be born on the day of Pentecost (Acts 2:1-47).

The temptation in Jerusalem, "on the parapet of the Temple," is a prelude to the ultimate confrontation that will take place in the city "at the appointed time." On that day, Jesus will not yield to the voices of those who challenge him to come down from the cross (Luke 23:35-36, 39). In an act of supreme trust, he will commend his spirit into the hands of the Father (Luke 23:46).

The Last Assault of the Demon at the Appointed Time

"Having exhausted all these ways of tempting him, the devil left him, to return at the appointed time."[44] The conclusion of the battle between Jesus and the devil will take place later on. In fact, he reappears at the beginning of the passion narrative when "Satan entered into Judas, the one surnamed Iscariot, who was counted among the Twelve" (Luke 22:3). "Satan has demanded to sift all of you like wheat" (Luke 22:31). But Jesus prays for Peter that his own faith may not fail and, having turned back, that he may strengthen his brothers (see Luke 22:32).

Jesus does not falter either when, hung on the wood of the cross, he hears railing voices challenging him again, "Let him save himself if he is the chosen one, the Messiah of God" (Luke 23:35; see also 23:35-39). At the culminating point of the drama, Jesus addresses not the tempter but his Father, to express, one last time, his unfailing attachment and confidence. In Gethsemane, in the throes of his unspeakable agony and anguish, he had said, "Not my will but yours be done" (Luke 22:42). Now he turns to his Father to implore forgiveness for his executioners (Luke 23:34); then, before breathing his last, to say "in a loud voice, 'Father, into your hands I commend my spirit' " (Luke 23:46).

What happened after the Lord's baptism finds its epilogue here. The devil's first attack against Jesus helps us to understand the drama played out in the passion. At this time, as at the temptation, the true question concerns the person of Jesus, Son of God. The answer lies in his obedience to the Father unto death itself, in death itself. In this obedience, the Lord's sovereign power is manifested. To one of his companions in suffering he says, "Amen, I say to you, today you will be with me in Paradise" (Luke 23:43). And "the centurion who witnessed what had happened glorified God and said, 'This man was innocent beyond doubt.' When all the people who had gathered for this spectacle saw what had happened, they returned home beating their breasts" (Luke 23:47-48).

The Scandal of the Cross

All the trials overcome by Jesus, including the temptations in the desert that act as prologue, apply only to the Son of God, if we want to speak with exactness. They cannot really be transposed into the lives and conditions of Christians. But the cross of Christ remains for all a scandal, the scandal that could sink even the faith of believers if the Lord did not intercede for them as he did for Peter. Even so, they are unconsciously tempted to echo the devil, not to be on his side by defying the Son of

God, but to reject the cross, to pull it away from their Lord, so to speak. When, for the first time, Jesus taught his disciples "that the Son of Man must suffer greatly, be rejected by the elders, the chief priests, and the scribes, and be killed, and rise after three days. . . . Peter took him aside and began to rebuke him. At this, [Jesus] turned around and, looking at his disciples, rebuked Peter and said, 'Get behind me, Satan. You are thinking not as God does, but as human beings do' " (Mark 8:31-33).

Christians and the Church as a whole do not find themselves confronted by the same temptations as the Lord, because they do not know and will not know the sort of test that only he had to endure. But their faith stumbles against the scandal of the cross. They must surmount it by following their Master, whom the devil never succeeded in persuading to deviate from his path.

> If hope has made you walk
> farther than fear,
> you will raise your eyes.
> Then you will be able to hold firm
> until you reach the sun of God.
>
> If sadness has made you doubt
> on one evening you felt abandoned,
> you will know how to carry your cross.
> Then you will be able to die
> in step with the God-Man.[45]

The First Week of Lent

Every year, the liturgy for the First Sunday of Lent places before the assembled faithful the temptations of Jesus in the desert—icons painted by Matthew, Mark, and Luke.

In all three, Jesus is in the foreground, alone, marked by the unction of the Spirit received at his baptism on the banks of the Jordan. There is nothing stiff or tense in his face or in his attitude. The gravity of his countenance is equalled by an astonishing serenity, that of a victor in a formidable ordeal. In Matthew's icon, the devil has yielded his place to angels. As for Luke, he has placed in the distance a cross of light around which are visible another condemned man haloed in light, a prostrate Roman centurion, and a crowd of people beating their breasts, and Peter with the cross of his own martyrdom. To tell the truth, we must look with attention in order to distinguish all of these, as if the evangelist had voluntarily left his work unfinished, unless it is part of a diptych or it is one of those canvasses painted on both sides.

As we go deeper into the contemplation of these two icons, we turn to the words, especially to those said by Jesus, written by Matthew and Luke in fiery words, and we find ourselves whispering, "Yes, Lord, you are the Son of God. You alone are Lord. Teach us to say, 'Father, may your will be done.' In you alone are the kingdom, the power, and the glory. Keep us from ever putting God to the test; his Word is enough for us."

The icon signed by Mark is clearly different from the other two: Is it a rough sketch that inspired Matthew and Luke or an intentionally stylized design in which the desert where Jesus stayed forty days has become Paradise again, with tame wild beasts and angels serving the Son of Man? Whatever, the evangelist has depicted the road on which Jesus is going to advance, going ever farther, from one village to the next, announcing the good news of the kingdom of God at hand and preaching conversion.

But each of the three pictures sends us back to passages of Scripture that shed light on them. They offer for our meditation the solidarity of all humans, led into sin through the fault of one person but, more marvelously, redeemed through the obedience of the new Adam, victorious over the tempter (Year A). They place us before the mysteries of the Just One, who saves the future, and of our participation, through baptism, in the death and resurrection of Christ (Year B). Finally, they urge us never to forget that our father was a vagrant Aramean and that all those who invoke the Lord will be saved (Year C).

The icon of the temptation, presented to us every year on the First Sunday, must remain present before our eyes throughout Lent and the paschal celebrations, but neither must we lose sight of it during Ordinary Time; for that is the time of faith—and its trials—day in and day out.

> Lord, with you we shall go to the desert,
> driven like you by the Spirit,
> and we shall eat the Word of God,
> and we shall choose our God,
> and we shall celebrate our Pasch in the desert:
> we shall live in the desert with you.
>
> Lord, we shall go to the desert to be healed,
> driven like you by the Spirit,
> and you will remove sin from our hearts,
> and you will cure our ills,
> and we shall celebrate our Pasch in the desert:
> O living one who generates life!
>
> Lord, we shall go to the desert to pray,
> driven like you by the Spirit,
> and we shall taste the silence of God,
> and we shall be reborn in joy,
> and we shall celebrate our Pasch in the desert:
> we shall walk in God's strength.
>
> Lord, we shall go to the desert toward your cross,
> driven like you by the Spirit,
> and we shall follow your footsteps in the desert,
> and we shall carry our cross,
> and we shall celebrate our Pasch in the desert:
> we shall live the folly of your cross.[46]

From Monday through Saturday

As is the case during Advent—and will be the case in the Easter season— the Missal and the Liturgy of the Hours, during Lent, have prayers and readings proper to each day of the week. In the Missal, the emphasis is on the works and the spiritual attitudes that characterize this period of the liturgical year, that is, penance and conversion.

The Missal and the Lectionary were thoroughly revised following the liturgical reform of Vatican II. Although many prayers, especially the opening prayers at Mass, were borrowed from previous Mass formularies, many other prayers were taken from ancient collections, and all texts were rewritten. As to biblical readings, even though some remained in place—often with verses added or left out—they constitute a new corpus. This is true of both Old and New Testament readings.

The Prayers are appeals to God, asking that his grace help us to live a really Christian Lent, to practice the traditional Lenten works of fasting, prayer, and almsgiving-sharing in the perspective of returning to God and opening ourselves to his salvation, so that the Eucharistic celebration may produce its fruit in us. When we read these prayers one after the other, we easily have the impression that they are repetitious, except for some variations in vocabulary. This is true enough. But precisely, this diversity of expression makes for richness. Besides, their rather general formulation allows everyone to make them their own and to invest the words with a more precise and personal meaning. Far from enclosing us in formulas narrowed down through excessive precision, these diverse prayers are like beacons along the way, and they stimulate our spiritual liberty. Thus, we can say them over and over again without weariness, without repetition.[47]

The opening prayer of Monday immediately expresses what we expect from Lent:

> God our savior,
> bring us back to you
> and fill our minds with your wisdom.
> May we be enriched by our observance of Lent.

This is what Lent is all about: a way of conversion lighted by the law of God constantly meditated and contemplated, as Psalm 119 tirelessly repeats.[48]

This return to God goes along with the "pardon" that he grants us so that our lives may be "sanctified." The "mastery over senses and body," the regulation of "earthly desires," and "self-denial" are inspired by the "desire of finding God" by the search for what is "uniquely necessary." Therefore, there is no room during Lent for self-centered asceticism and tense and joyless efforts. What we expect of this forty-day retreat is "renewal"—rejuvenation.

> Lord,
> may the sacrament you give us
> free us from our sinful ways and bring us new life.
> May this eucharist lead us to salvation.[49]

The Readings from the Old Testament borrow from a different book each day: Leviticus, Isaiah, Jonah, Esther, Ezekiel, and Deuteronomy. Their connection with the Gospel is loose.

First, on Monday, we have two excerpts from the Book of Leviticus (19:1-2, 11-18) that recall the prescriptions of the Law given to Moses: "You shall not steal. You shall not lie. . . . You shall not defraud or rob your neighbor. . . . Judge your fellow men justly. . . . Take no revenge . . ." and so forth. Their formulation in the negative stresses the absolute character of these laws. One of these is particularly remarkable because it is not found in the best known codes, "You shall not curse the deaf, or put a stumbling block in front of the blind."

When all is said and done, these commandments in themselves belong to a rather rudimentary morality. However, something else is in question: we must recognize God's holiness, not only in words, but in acts. The words "I am the Lord" punctuate the terms of this code. And the conclusion is, "You shall love your neighbor as yourself." It is impossible to be more explicit: there is no limit.

In any event, the observance of God's commands is a commitment to his covenant, a human response to divine initiative and grace, a profession of faith shown in acts (Deut 26:16-19—Saturday). Whoever turns toward him obtains forgiveness, as happens to the inhabitants of Nineveh when they heed Jonah's preaching (Jonah 3:1-10—Wednesday). For God does not wish for the death of the wicked but rather rejoices when "he turns from his evil way that he may live." Likewise, from the virtuous he expects perseverance in good deeds (Ezek 18:21-28—Friday). And what God says, God does (Isa 55:10-11—Tuesday).

This week we also read the admirable prayer Queen Esther addresses to God, asking that he give her courage and put on her lips "persuasive words" and change the heart of the redoubtable king—the "lion"—before whom she presents herself on her own initiative in an attempt to have him repeal the decree of extermination aimed at the Jews (Esth C:12, 14-16, 23-25—Thursday).[50]

The Psalms that follow these readings are trustful appeals to God, in which thanksgiving and affirmations of devotion to the Law intermingle. We will want to repeat some of these verses in the course of the day (Pss 19, 34, 51, 138, 130, 119).

The Gospels are taken from Matthew, except Wednesday's, which is taken from Luke. The choice of this last text may surprise us at first sight because "the sign of Jonah" is hardly convincing to us (Luke 11:29-32). The inhabitants of Nineveh converted at the preaching of the prophet who reluctantly fulfilled his task, as we all know. Jesus is "greater than Jonah," indubitably. As for the "queen of the south" who "came from the ends of the earth to hear the wisdom of Solomon"—this is just an old story!

But precisely, we recognize in Jesus the one sent by God. We even know that risen, he is always alive. How, therefore, is it possible that we may be so sluggish when it comes to listening to him? Many persons around us are convinced by the vehement speeches of preachers who arrogate to themselves the title of prophet, whose doctrine is often aberrant and, in spite of what some among them claim, devoid of any support in Scripture. How is it that we, disciples of Christ, remain so insensitive to the call of him whom we know to be the Truth, the Way, and the Life? There is matter for reflection here. "The sign of Jonah" challenges our faith.

The judgment scene described by Matthew leaves no room for escape: talk alone is not enough, acts are needed (Matt 25:31-46—Monday). Lent is a favorable time to test whether our faith is proved by action, effective charity toward the lowly, the poor, the needy, the afflicted. Is not translation into action precisely what is most lacking in Christian discourse?

And what about our prayer (Matt 6:7-15—Tuesday)? Perhaps we are no longer tempted to rehash, to recite endless prayers. Lent invites us to examine the place of prayer in our life. We say the Our Father. The version transmitted to us by Matthew does not say "Forgive us our trespasses as we forgive those who trespass against us" but "Forgive us our debts as we have forgiven those who are in debt to us."[51] There is no opposition between the two formulations. But Matthew underlines that forgiveness of others is not a generous statement of a principle, but a precondition of the forgiveness we ask of God. And Matthew insists, "If you do not forgive others, neither will your Father forgive your transgressions." And we remember those other words of Jesus read this week on Friday: "Therefore, if you bring your gift to the altar and there recall that your brother has anything against you, leave your gift there at the altar, go first and be reconciled with your brother, and then come and offer your gift" (Matt 23-24). The "sign of peace" exchanged before communion is a reminder and expression of this demand. May it never become a rite devoid of meaning!

Another Gospel of this week also speaks of prayer (Matt 7:7-12—Thursday). When we pray, it is our Father we address, this Father infinitely better than all those who on earth hold and honor this beautiful name. With what trust must we not expect from him the "good gift" we ask for!

However, to pray is not only to present a list of requests to God. It is also to knock so that the door may open; to seek so that we may find. To pray, in a word, is the opposite of passivity and lack of commitment.

Finally, we hear two excerpts from the Sermon on the Mount, especially welcome during this time of Lent. Conversion is in no way a superficial attitude: it works in the heart, this interior source of thoughts and intentions. The righteousness that the Bible speaks of and Jesus teaches must not be understood in a legal, still less a legalistic, sense. The "just" are those who obey God's will. Pharisaism is a return to the religious legalism that identifies external conformity to the law with righteousness. This, says Jesus, is a grave deviation, since even though we may walk on rough and austere paths, we do not reach the kingdom when we act in a legalistic manner. And he forcefully affirms that everything is, in truth, decided in the heart. This is not to say that intention is purely and simply equivalent to action, but the former carries the seed of the latter and cannot be regarded as indifferent and without importance (Matt 5:20-26—Friday).

Furthermore, in order to understand the law correctly, we must take its spirit into account, the spirit that the prophets never ceased to make explicit. This is why, even in the synagogue today,[52] the reading of the Law is never separated from that of a prophetic text. The commentary— we could say the homily—follows these two readings. After having recalled the ancient Scriptures—"You have heard that it was said"—Jesus speaks like a prophet and a preacher, but with this authority belonging to him alone: "But I say to you. . . ."

Extending to enemies the love due one's neighbor is certainly in line with the Law, but who could have imposed such an obligation except the Son of God? Not satisfied with simply revealing this command, he, the perfect model for this and all other commands, shows us what it means "to pray for one's enemies."

We find thoughtful relationships with friends among tax collectors and pagans, who even sometimes go as far as forgiving their enemies. If disciples do more than imitating tax collectors and pagans, it is not to appear superior to them through some sort of emulation. Disciples have their model elsewhere: in God, whose sons and daughters they know themselves to be and whose ways of acting they feel bound to follow (Matt 5:43-48—Saturday).

The Liturgy of the Hours is "a source of piety and a nourishment for personal prayer," said Vatican II.[53] For its part, Lent, a potent time for the reorientation of our lives, a great yearly retreat offered to the whole ecclesial community, is a favorable time to give back to prayer its proper place. It is for each person to seek and find the forms and rhythms of prayer. To strive to pray more during Lent is good. But it is much better if the effort made during this time has a follow-up, if it is lived in the perspective of a rediscovery of prayer, lacking which, Christian life withers. More than by its formulas and program, the Liturgy of the Hours in Lent concerns all Christians by offering general orientations one can and must remember.

All the antiphons of the Benedictus (Morning Office) and Magnificat (Evening Office) recall the day's Gospel, from which they borrow—most of the time, verbatim—a key phrase. Prayer is, therefore, born from attentive listening to the word that inspires and guides it. This is a lesson to remember.

The Biblical Readings from Thursday after Ash Wednesday to Saturday of the Third Week are taken from the Book of Exodus.[54] The gathering of the Hebrew people for the first Passover before their liberation from slavery, their wandering in the wilderness, highlighted by so many events and the gift of the Law, all these are evoked by the word "exodus," the title of the second book of the Bible. The Exodus is the birth and the first education of the people of God. The Book of Exodus remains, for the Church as for Israel, the paschal book par excellence. It is indispensable to reread it, year after year, before the celebration of Easter, in order to understand better what Easter signifies and what it announces.

The Patristic Readings of the First Week of Lent are taken from six authors, from the third to the twelfth centuries, and from the Pastoral Constitution on the Church in the Modern World (*Gaudium et Spes*), promulgated by Paul VI on December 7, 1965.

On Sunday, we read an excerpt from a homily by St. Augustine on Psalm 60. The Bishop of Hippo meditates on this psalm in the light of the gospel of Jesus' temptation in the desert.[55]

> . . . We have heard in the gospel how the Lord Jesus Christ was tempted by the devil in the wilderness. Certainly Christ was tempted by the devil. In Christ you were tempted, for Christ received his flesh from your nature, but by his own power gained salvation for you; he suffered death in your nature, but by his own power gained life for you; he suffered insults in your nature, but by his own power gained glory for you; therefore, he suffered temptation in your nature, but by his own power gained victory for you.
>
> If in Christ we have been tempted, in him we overcome the devil. Do you think only of Christ's temptations and fail to think of his victory? See yourself as tempted in him, and see yourself as victorious in him. He could have kept the devil from himself; but if he were not tempted he could not teach you how to triumph over temptation.[56]

On Monday, a homily by St. Gregory Nazianzen is a vibrant exhortation to generous love for the poor. The author begins, however, by enumerating with delight all that we have received.

> Recognize to whom you owe the fact that you exist, that you breathe, that you understand, that you are wise, and, above all, that you know God and hope for the kingdom of heaven. . . .
>
> What benefactor has enabled you to look upon the beauty of the sky, the sun in its course, the circle of the moon, the countless number of stars, with the harmony and order that are theirs like the music of a harp? Who has blessed you with rain, with the art of husbandry, with different kinds of food, with the arts, with houses, with laws, with states, with a life of humanity and culture, with friendship and the easy familiarity of kinship?
>
> . . . In short, who has endowed you with all that makes man superior to all other living creatures?
>
> . . . Because we have received from him so many wonderful gifts, will we not be ashamed to refuse him this one thing only, our generosity? Though he is God and Lord he is not afraid to be known as our Father. Shall we for our part repudiate those who are our kith and kin?
>
> Brethren and friends, let us never allow ourselves to misuse what has been given us by God's gift. If we do, we shall hear Saint Peter say: *Be ashamed of yourselves for holding on to what belongs to someone else. Resolve to imitate God's justice, and no one will be poor.*[57]

On Tuesday, the Gospel at Mass is that of Jesus' teaching on prayer and the Our Father in the version Matthew gives us (6:7-15). We have a homily on the Lord's Prayer by St. Cyprian, bishop of Carthage, who died a martyr in 258, on the Lord's Prayer.

> What prayer could be more a prayer in the spirit than the one given us by Christ, by whom the Holy Spirit was sent upon us? What prayer could be

more a prayer in the truth than the one spoken by the lips of the Son, who is truth himself? It follows that to pray in any other way than the Son has taught us is not only the result of ignorance but of sin. He himself has commanded it, and has said: *You reject the command of God, to set up your own tradition.*

. . . Let the Father recognize the words of his Son. Let the Son who lives in our hearts be also on our lips.[58]

On Wednesday, we have a reading taken from a text by St. Aphraates, often called "the Persian." He was a monk who lived in the fourth century at Mar Mattai near Mosul. He speaks to Christian communities in Syria who are isolated in a Jewish milieu. Recalling the successive covenants granted to Adam, Noah, Abraham, and Moses, he says that all were leading to a new covenant. And here is the covenant God promised to give, "All, from the smallest to the greatest, shall know me." "In this covenant there is no longer any circumcision of the flesh, any seal upon the people."[59]

For Thursday, the Liturgy of the Hours presents an excerpt from a homily on conversion by St. Asterius, bishop of Amasea, in Asia Minor, who died sometime after 400. Through his prophets, God taught penance to his people. He sent John to proclaim conversion and repentance.

. . . Then Christ came himself, and with his own lips cried out: *Come to me, all you who labor and are overburdened, and I will give you rest.* How did he receive those who listened to his call? He readily forgave them their sins; he freed them instantly from all that troubled them. The word made them holy; the Spirit set his seal on them. The old Adam was buried in the waters of baptism; the new man was reborn to the vigor of grace.

What was the result? Those who had been God's enemies became his friends, those estranged from him became his sons, those who did not know him came to worship and love him.

Let us be shepherds like the Lord. . . .

. . . We should not look on men as lost or beyond hope; we should not abandon them when they are in danger or be slow to come to their help. When they turn away from the right path and wander, we must lead them back, and rejoice at their return, welcoming them back into the company of those who lead good and holy lives.[60]

Echoing the Gospel that speaks of the love of enemies, the Liturgy of the Hours has chosen for Friday an admirable passage from Aelred of Rievaulx, an English Cistercian monk (1110-67). He first evokes Christ, who during his passion bore with gentleness and serenity the worst outrages, "the cross, the nails, the lance, the gall, the vinegar" "The perfection of brotherly love lies in the love of one's enemies. We can find no greater inspiration for this than grateful remembrance of the wonderful patience of Christ . . . 'more fair than all the sons of men.'" Then he recalls the prayer that Christ addressed to God, "Father, forgive them," and continues.

> . . . Is any gentleness, any love, lacking in this prayer?
>
> Yet he put into it something more. It was not enough to pray for them: he wanted also to make excuses for them. *Father, forgive them, for they do not know what they are doing.* They are great sinners, yes, but they have little judgment; therefore, *Father, forgive them.* They are nailing me to the cross, but they do not know who it is that they are nailing to the cross: *if they had known, they would never have crucified the Lord of glory;* therefore, *Father, forgive them.* They think it is a lawbreaker, an impostor claiming to be God, a seducer of the people. I have hidden my face from them, and they do not recognize my glory; therefore, *Father, forgive them, for they do not know what they are doing.*
>
> If someone wishes to love himself he must not allow himself to be corrupted by indulging his sinful nature. If he wishes to resist the promptings of his sinful nature he must enlarge the whole horizon of his love to contemplate the loving gentleness of the humanity of the Lord. Further, if he wishes to savor the joy of brotherly love with greater perfection and delight, he must extend even to his enemies the embrace of true love.
>
> But if he wishes to prevent this fire of divine love from growing cold because of injuries received, let him keep the eyes of his soul always fixed on the serene patience of his beloved Lord and Savior.[61]

Finally, on Saturday, the Liturgy of the Hours uses the conclusion of the Introduction—titled "The Situation of Man in the World Today"—to the Pastoral Constitution on Church in the Modern World. It ends with a vibrant profession of faith.

> The Church believes that Christ died and rose for all, and can give man light and strength through his Spirit to fulfill his highest calling; his is the only name under heaven in which men can be saved.
>
> So too the Church believes that the center and goal of all human history is found in her Lord and Master.
>
> The Church also affirms that underlying all changes there are many things that do not change; they have their ultimate foundation in Christ, who is the same yesterday, today and for ever.[62]

This text expresses well the optimism and hope that animate the Church throughout her Lenten journey. In the midst of the ambushes and temptations of this world, the people of God continue their way toward Easter, following Christ, who has already reached the end and, therefore, is present among his own.

The Son of God
in the Glory of His Father

The Journey of Abraham, Father of Believers

Every year, the Second Sunday of Lent commemorates the stage in salvation history marked by the call of Abraham, the father of Jewish, Moslem, and Christian believers. The Book of Genesis devotes thirteen chapters to Abraham's deeds,[1] beginning with his departure from his homeland of Chaldea (Gen 12:1-4a).

To be honest, what is of interest to believers today is not, strictly speaking, Abraham's doings—his biography, his adventures—taken in themselves.[2] What interests them are the roots of their own stories, the way in which God acts toward them and leads them, the answer they must give to God's calls in order to see themselves also actively integrated in this sacred history. Now from all these points of view, Abraham's journey remains and will remain exemplary. What is more, it is a revelation.

Above all things, what is revealed is God's faithfulness and initiative. He set Noah apart and gave him the rainbow as a sign of his covenant (Gen 2:7-9; 3:1-7a—last Sunday); he granted him posterity (Gen 9:18—10:32; 11:10-32) of which Abraham is an offspring.

This sovereign initiative on God's part is expressed by a command that admits of no objection, ''Go forth from the land of your kinsfolk,'' matched by a promise:

> I will make of you a great nation
> and I will bless you. . . .
> All the communities of the earth
> shall find blessing in you,''

after having been scattered following the confusion of tongues at the Tower of Babel (Gen 11:1-9).

The response God expects from Abraham—and from all believers—is an act of faith, hope, and obedience. To tell the truth, these abstract words do not find a place in this story or in any texts of biblical authors. Rather, they record actions, situations in which these virtues, as we call them,

must be put into practice. The case of Abraham is exemplary. "He believed, hoping against hope. . . . He did not doubt God's promise in
unbelief; rather, he was empowered by faith and gave glory to God and
was fully convinced that what he had promised he was also able to do.
That is why 'it was credited to him as righteousness.' But it was not for
him alone that it was written that 'it was credited to him'; it was also
for us" (Rom 4:18-23; see Heb 11:8-12).

From Curse to Blessing
Sacred history begins with a story of disobedience (Gen 2—3) and its consequences punctuated by four curses.[3] In the few verses of this Sunday's
first reading, the words "blessed" and "blessing" are used five times.
The call of Abraham signals a reversal of sacred history. After Noah, Abraham is the father of a new human race: that of believers whom God
blesses.[4]

This blessing will be shared by "all the communities of the earth" which
will stand behind Abraham, the prototype of the believer and of the
blessed one, whose name will become synonymous with benediction.[5]
Abraham is, so to speak, the believer from whom blessing will spread.
In Christ Jesus, and in him alone, all blessings will be recapitulated, as
Paul will write: "Blessed be the God and Father of our Lord Jesus Christ
who has blessed us in Christ with every spiritual blessing in the
heavens. . . . [He had] as a plan for the fullness of times, to sum up
all things in Christ, in heaven and on earth" (Eph 1:3, 10).

It is this faith and hope that Christians celebrate when they remember
Abraham. They entreat God to bless them according to the promise made
to their fathers, "to Abraham and to his descendants forever" (Luke
1:55b).

Lord, let your mercy be on us,
as we place our trust in you.

Upright is the word of the Lord,
and all his works are trustworthy.
He loves justice and right;
of the kindness of the Lord the earth is full.
See, the eyes of the Lord are upon those who fear him,
upon those who hope for his kindness,
To deliver them from death
and preserve them in spite of famine.
Our soul waits for the Lord,
who is our help and our shield. . . .

May your kindness, O LORD, be upon us
  who have put our hope in you.
  (Ps 33:4-5, 18-20, 22)

God's Plan Manifested in Jesus

God's blessing, the object of the promise, was poured out into the whole
universe "through the appearance of our savior Christ Jesus, who de-
stroyed death and brought life and immortality to light through the
gospel." This is the central point of the brief passage we have as a second reading for this Sunday; in the original text, it is one long sentence.
Its poetic composition and theological weight are the more remarkable
as it begins with a simple exhortation: "Bear your share of hardship for
the gospel with the strength that comes from God." As a number of commentators have thought for a long time, perhaps Paul is making use of
a fragment from a liturgical hymn of the first century, which he might
have modified (2 Tim 1:8b-10).

"God saved us and called us to a holy life, not according to our works
but according to his own design and the grace bestowed on us." Therefore, the call to life, to salvation, is absolutely gratuitous; Paul often returns
to this fundamental point.[6] Likewise, he loves to say that salvation rests
upon God's call, answered by us; this is well in keeping with the tradition of the Old Testament, where Abraham is a model of this response
(First Reading).

Paul also speaks several times of the mystery of salvation and election,
long hidden in God's secret design and manifested in Christ Jesus.[7] As
we are familiar with Paul's conception of this mystery, we are surprised
by what we are told in the Second Letter to Timothy. This grace was "bestowed on us in Christ Jesus before time began, but now [is] made manifest." Here, we are no longer dealing with the distinction between the
eternity of God's plan and the historical moment of its manifestation:[8]
the gift made "before time began" has been "now made manifest." We
are accustomed to the idea of the efficacy of God's word: what he says,
he does or will do.[9] Here, Paul goes further, saying that God's hidden
intention is itself effective; his secret project is realized as soon as it is
formed, even if it becomes visible only later.

This manifestation of the efficacious intention of God—his plan—and
of the gift comes about in the preaching of the gospel. What a responsibility for those who are charged with announcing it! "If I preach the
gospel, this is no reason for me to boast, for an obligation has been imposed on me, and woe to me if I do not preach it!" (1 Cor 9:16). "Woe

to you . . . [who] lock the kingdom of heaven before human beings"
(Matt 23:13). But what a grace to be charged with bringing to light what
had been kept secret to be manifested at the appointed time (Mark 4:22).[10]
Whoever wants to do honor to such a responsibility will meet suffering head-on. This is the lot of all those who champion a great cause. But
the gospel—that is the manifestation of the victory of life and immortality over death—requires not only something more, but something else.
We must be personally and totally committed to the realization of salvation, to the point of taking upon ourselves with joy "what is lacking in
the afflictions of Christ" (Col 1:24).[11]

The Transfiguration of Jesus in the Context of Lent

Matthew, Mark, and Luke have placed the transfiguration of Jesus in the
same context: after Peter's confession in Caesarea, the first prediction of
the passion, the words on the condition of discipleship, and the announcement of the Lord's return in the not distant future.[12] Such a strict parallelism in redaction is a rare occurrence. However, no mention is made
of this group of themes on the Second Sunday of Lent. The Gospel of
the transfiguration is proclaimed for itself, or rather, within another framework, that of the celebration of a Sunday in Lent.[13] The passage from
the original literary and redactional context to the liturgical context in no
way does violence to the letter of the Gospels. "With an unerring instinct,
the Lenten liturgy proposes the mystery of Jesus' transfiguration to the
contemplation of the faithful, who are slowly moving toward the feast
of Easter, that is, toward the mysteries—apparently separated but forming a deep unity—of the passion and the resurrection. The liturgy thus
transposes the teaching that the three Synoptic Gospels sought to im-
part."[14] In the liturgy, the Gospel of the transfiguration is proclaimed
to reveal the meaning of the Lenten ascent toward Easter, which the
Church, following her Lord, accomplishes to renew the faith and hope
of the ecclesial community, to stimulate its zeal.[15]

An Anticipated Vision of Christ in Glory

To the Christian community assembled to celebrate the Second Sunday
of Lent, Matthew's Gospel presents a vision of Christ in glory, anticipat-
ing his appearance on the last day (Matt 17:1-9).
Jesus' transfiguration, which the three disciples witness, happens suddenly, on God's initiative. The event takes place on "a high mountain,"
a place to which God descends and humans go up to meet him and which,

in the prophetic tradition, is an evocation of God's manifestation on the last day.[16]

Jesus' "face shone like the sun and his clothes became white as light." According to the Book of Daniel, the just will know such a transfiguration on the last day.

> At that time your people shall escape,
> everyone who is found written in the book.
> But the wise shall shine brightly
> like the splendor of the firmament,
> And those who lead the many to justice
> shall be like the stars forever.
> (Dan 12:1, 3)[17]

Jesus has just announced the return of the Son of Man "in his Father's glory" (Matt 16:27). And suddenly, Peter, James, and John see Jesus resplendent with divine light and whiteness—this same Jesus with whom, only a few moments before, they were climbing the slope; this same Jesus who, soon afterward, will resume in their eyes his usual appearance; this same Jesus whom, later on, they will see disfigured by human outrages and hung on the shameful cross.[18]

The three disciples will bear witness to this vision when the risen Jesus will have been "taken up in glory" (1 Tim 3:16), the glory the Father "gave him" (1 Pet 1:21). The Gospel of the transfiguration illuminates the Lenten pilgrimage of the Church. The tragedy of the cross is not thereby lessened, but it is placed in the perspective of the Easter radiance. The experience of the transfiguration teaches today's Christians, as it taught Peter, James, and John yesterday, that through his death, Jesus has become "the Lord of glory" (1 Cor 2:8) and that his ultimate manifestation is approaching.[19]

Moses and Elijah

The presence of Moses and Elijah, who appear at Jesus' side and converse with him, has never ceased to intrigue commentators of the transfiguration. It is often said they personify the Law and the Prophets.[20] But this interpretation is not unanimous.[21] Some see in Moses and Elijah the two witnesses Revelation speaks of (Rev 11:3-7; see also Deut 19:15). Others cite Jesus' word, "Elijah will indeed come and restore all things; but I tell you that Elijah has already come, and they did not recognize him but did to him whatever they pleased" (Matt 17:11-12). The evangelist adds, "Then the disciples understood that he was speaking to them of John the Baptist" (Matt 17:13).[22] Finally, we can quote from the Book of Malachi.

> Lo, I will send you
>> Elijah, the prophet,
> Before the day of the Lord comes,
>> the great and terrible day.
> (Mal 3:23)

Had not Elijah been taken up into heaven in a fiery chariot (2 Kgs 2:11-13)? As for Moses, who died in Moab and "was buried in the ravine opposite Beth-peor . . . to this day no one knows the place of his burial" (Deut 34:5-6).

If we take into account this ensemble of traditions, the presence of Moses and Elijah appearing at Jesus' side suggests that the transfiguration is a vision of the Lord's glory that will be revealed when he returns.[23] This is a marvelous vision, which Peter, in his ecstasy, wants to last forever, as if the last times have arrived, as if the moment to set up eternal dwellings has already come![24]

Covered by the Shadow of the Luminous Cloud

In response to Peter's proposal, "a bright cloud cast a shadow over them." Light and shadow, the cloud is, in the Bible, "a very special symbol signifying the mystery of the divine presence: it manifests God by veiling him."[25] The Hebrew word designating this luminous shadow—Shĕkhīnāh—first meant "dwelling (tent)." It came to designate the "personal presence of God" and finally became the very name of God. "Then the cloud covered the meeting tent and the glory of the LORD filled the Dwelling. Moses could not enter the meeting tent, because the cloud settled down upon it and the glory of the LORD filled the Dwelling" (Exod 40:34-35). And the angel said to Mary, "The power of the Most High will overshadow you. Therefore the child to be born will be called holy, the Son of God" (Luke 1:35).

But the three disciples are not only spectators of the incandescent transformation of Jesus; they find themselves immersed in the light of the cloud from which a voice is coming, "This is my beloved Son . . . listen to him." He is the new Moses of the new covenant, the one to whom we must listen when he says, "You have heard that it was said. . . . But I say to you. . ." (Matt 5:21-38).

> For, in giving us, as He did, His Son, which is His Word—and He has no other—He spake to us all together, once and for all, in this single Word, and He has no occasion to speak further.
> And this is the sense of that passage with which Saint Paul begins, when he tries to persuade the Hebrews that they should abandon those first manners and ways of converse with God which are in the law of Moses, and

should set their eyes on Christ alone, saying: *Multifariam multisque modis olim Deus loquens patribus in Prophetis: novissime autem diebus istis locutus est nobis in Filio* (Heb 1:1-2). And this is as though he had said: That which God spake of old in the prophets to our fathers, in sundry ways and divers manners, He has now, at last, in these days, spoken to us once and for all in the Son. Herein the Apostle declares that God has become, as it were, dumb, and has no more to say, since that which He spake aforetime, in part to the prophets, He has now spoken altogether in Him, giving us the All, which is His Son.

Wherefore he that would now enquire of God, or seek any vision or revelation, would not only be acting foolishly, but would be committing an offence against God, by setting his eyes altogether upon Christ, and seeking no new thing or aught beside. And God might answer him after this manner, saying: If I have spoken all things to thee in My Word, Which is My Son, and I have no other word, what answer can I now make to thee, or what can I reveal to thee which is greater than this? Set thine eyes on Him alone, for in Him I have spoken and revealed to thee all things, and in Him thou shalt find yet more than that which thou askest and desirest. For thou askest locutions and revelations, which are the part; but if thou set thine eyes upon Him, thou shalt find the whole; for He is My complete locution and answer, and He is all My vision and all My revelation; so that I have spoken to thee, answered thee, declared to thee and revealed to thee, in giving Him to thee as thy brother, companion and master, as ransom and prize. For since that day when I descended upon Him with My Spirit on Mount Tabor, saying: *Hic est filius meus dilectus, in quo mihi bene complacui, ipsum audite* (which is to say: This is My beloved Son, in Whom I am well pleased; hear ye Him), I have left off all these manners of teaching and answering, and I have entrusted this to Him. Hear Him; for I have no more faith to reveal, neither have I any more things to declare. For, if I spake aforetime, it was to promise Christ. . . .[26]

Jesus speaks with the authority of the beloved Son, which he delegated to his Apostles on the mountain in Galilee: "All power in heaven and on earth has been given to me. Go, therefore, and make disciples of all nations, baptizing them in the name of the Father, and of the Son, and of the holy Spirit, teaching them to observe all that I have commanded you. And behold, I am with you always, until the end of the age" (Matt 28:18-20).

The mystery of the transfiguration concerns the entire Church—all Christians! The voice is addressed to us with a particular force during Lent when the insistent call to conversion resounds.

Do Not Be Afraid! Rise!

On hearing the voice coming from the cloud, the disciples "fell prostrate" before him whom Peter calls "Lord." In Matthew's Gospel, these expressions are pregnant with meaning. Indeed, for Matthew, to fall prostrate before Jesus in a gesture of adoration is the attitude befitting the believer. Likewise, anyone who has faith calls Jesus "Lord."[27] In particular, this is the way all will address him on the last day, as Peter does at the transfiguration.[28] This title and this prostration underline the meaning of the vision on the "high mountain": the transfigured Jesus is the risen Lord who will return at the end of time. For disciples living today, between these two manifestations, the attitude and manner of addressing Jesus must be the same as they were for the first disciples.

Finally, how could we forget that when the eleven disciples, assembled on a mountain in Galilee, last saw Jesus on earth, as he was about to send them on their mission before being taken up into heaven, they "worshiped" him? Therefore, the transfiguration clearly has an ecclesial significance. From that time on, the order to be silent is repealed. Moreover, the hour has come to announce, in season and out of season, that Jesus is the Lord, the beloved Son of the Father, close to us and familiar, saying, "Rise, and do not be afraid."

The Light and the Voice Guiding Our Steps

On the road leading to Easter, the Church does not grope its way in darkness. The faith that animates the Church is not a blind trust in God saying to it, "Go forth . . . to a land that I will show you." The luminous cloud that leads it is not only before it. The mountaintop is aglow with it. It illuminates the entire road up to its end where the Lord of glory awaits the Church. Life and immortality shine brightly through the preaching of the gospel. The glory of Christ already enfolds the believers. With the reflection of his light in their eyes, the echo of the Father's voice in their hearts, they walk toward the city that has no need for the light of the sun or of the moon; "for the glory of God [is its] light, and its lamp [is] the Lamb" (Rev 21:23).

> Into what land of solitude,
> forty days and forty nights,
> will you go, driven by the Spirit?
> May it test you and strip you!
> See, the times are fulfilled,
> and God invites you to forget
> your ancient servitudes.
>
> On what incandescent summits
> will you hear the Beloved
> speaking to you through the cloud?

Let him prepare you for his sufferings!
Follow Jesus transfigured:
tomorrow he will be crucified
to ratify the Covenant.[29]

Light and Darkness
on the Easter Road

Take Your Son, Your Only One; You Shall Offer Him Up in Sacrifice
The obedience of Abraham, ready to sacrifice his son at God's command,
is of great importance in the tradition and piety of Jews, Moslems,[30] and
Christians. The biblical account of this episode is remarkably restrained.
Nothing evokes the inner drama of this father, from whom such a
sacrifice[31] is demanded, or of the son. Only Abraham's obedience—
"Ready!"—and God's intervention are described (Gen 22:1-2, 9a, 10-13,
15-18).[32]

For the Old Testament, Abraham behaved in this circumstance as the
complete model of the just one who, with total trust in God, obeys him,
whatever is asked. In Isaac—Abraham's only son—rested the promise of
posterity made to the patriarch. Abraham does not doubt God's faithfulness for a single instant.

> [Wisdom] . . .
> knew the just man, kept him blameless before God,
> and preserved him resolute against pity for his child.
> (Wis 10:5)

> ABRAHAM, father of many peoples
> kept his glory without stain . . .
> and when tested he was found loyal.
> (Sir 44:19-20)[33]

The New Testament has retained the lesson of faith given by Abraham.[34]
It is a text from the Letter to the Hebrews that gave form to the Christian
reading of Abraham's sacrifice.

> By faith Abraham, when put to the test, offered up Isaac, and he who had
> received the promises was ready to offer his only son, of whom it was said,
> "Through Isaac descendants shall bear your name." He reasoned that God
> was able to raise even from the dead, and he received Isaac back as a sym-
> bol. (Heb 11:17-19)

On the basis of this text, most Fathers of the Church have seen in Isaac
the prophetic figure of Christ.[35] This is also why the sacrifice of Abraham

is often represented on frescoes, in particular those of the Roman cemeteries—the catacombs—and sarcophagi.[36]

Eucharistic Prayer 1 (the Roman Canon) places side by side the sacrifice of Abraham and the offering of the Eucharist.

> Look with favor on these offerings and accept them as once you accepted the sacrifice of Abraham, our father in faith. . . .

The *Lauda Sion*, the sequence of the Mass of the Feast of the Body and Blood of Christ, attributed to St. Thomas Aquinas (1225-74), states as a commonly accepted notion that the sacrifice of Isaac prefigures that of Christ.[37] In their celebrations, Christians cannot commemorate the sacrifice of Isaac outside of this perspective. This episode from Abraham's story turns their gaze to the present and the future of a covenant that must benefit "all the communities of the earth."

It remains that faith in the promise must not be taken for granted: it is always put to the test, in one way or another. Sometimes, God seems to contradict himself, to be bent on thwarting the realization of what he has promised. There are times when we have to muster all our trust to continue to walk in the presence of God, who seems to elude us. To cry to God in our distress is not a lack of faith, but is, perhaps, the expression of our "hop[e] against hope."

> I will walk in the presence of the Lord,
> in the land of the living.

> I believed, even when I said,
> "I am greatly afflicted."
> Precious in the eyes of the LORD
> is the death of his faithful ones.
> O LORD, I am your servant;
> I am your servant, the son of your handmaid;
> you have loosed my bonds.
> To you will I offer sacrifice of thanksgiving,
> and I will call upon the name of the LORD.
> My vows to the LORD I will pay
> in the presence of all his people,
> In the courts of the house of the LORD,
> in your midst, O Jerusalem.
> (Ps 116:10, 15-19)

God Did Not Deny His Own Son

The second reading logically follows the first, although it does not mention the sacrifice of Isaac (Rom 8:31b-34).

God did not want Isaac to be sacrificed by his father: he does not want the death of any human. Homicide is abhorrent to him, as the story of Cain attests (Gen 4:1-16). But he "did not spare his own Son but handed him over for us all."

Paul never indulges in theological or mystical considerations founded on abstractions or hypotheses. He does not ask himself whether God could have imagined other ways to save us: God's wisdom is inscrutable and his ways unsearchable (see Rom 11:33-34). We know only what has been revealed of this wisdom. Now it is a fact: God has sent his Son in the flesh (see Rom 1:3), "in the likeness of sinful flesh" (Rom 8:3). This son has been "handed over" to death, like a sinner condemned by the law. But he was not a sinner: he made of his death the supreme act of his love for his Father and for the sinners he had come to save. By dying on the cross he thus conquered death and sin; he broke the connection between the two. This is why death was unable to hold him. He was restored to life; risen, he returned to the right hand of his Father. His victory is that of the whole human race. We all find ourselves, by him and in him, "freed . . . from the law of sin and death. For what the law . . . was powerless to do, this God has done" (Rom 8:2-3). Very simply, God sided with us in a way and with an efficacy no one could have imagined. Such are the facts, such is our faith: God has delivered up his own Son for us all.

Therefore, who can be against us? How can God, who gave us his Son, "not also give us everything else along with him?" Can Christ, who died and rose to save us, condemn us, he who intercedes for us? As far as God and Christ are concerned, our salvation is assured. Far from lulling us to sleep, this certainty keeps us awake because it makes us conscious of our responsibility: this divine work will be operative in us in the measure we live in faith and trust, faithful to God's limitless love.

Transfiguration of the Lord and Resurrection from the Dead

For believers, the manner in which each evangelist records the same facts and the same experiences elucidates their meaning and reveals their reach. This is certainly the case for the three Gospels of the transfiguration. There is no contradiction or even disagreement between them. Nonetheless, they are not identical. This being said, we could be tempted to erase the themes that are not found in all three, even though we might decide to retain some feature easily integrated into this new group. Not only would the result lack any originality, but it would be a fourth narrative, composed neither by Matthew nor Mark nor Luke; it would be not quite a forgery but something other than the Gospel narratives.

Each evangelist's originality is expressed by accents, nuances in the harmony of the writing, by the variation of viewpoints, in a word, by everything that makes for a personal composition. Certainly, we may compare the three stories as a means to better understand what each has meant to say, to emphasize, and so forth. In Year B, the liturgy offers for our contemplation and meditation the transfiguration according to Mark (9:2-10).

The picture of the transfiguration painted by Mark strikes us first by its great economy and its solemnity. Mark says nothing of the transfigured face of Jesus. He reports that "his clothes became dazzling white, such as no fuller on earth could bleach them." Elijah appears along with Moses, and they speak with Jesus, but nothing of their conversation is reported.

It is Peter who takes the initiative of talking. Entranced, but also seized with fright, he proposes to Jesus that he, James, and John set up three tents, "one for you, one for Moses, and one for Elijah." His terror and his joy seem to be caused by his belief that the time of the glorious manifestation of the Lord has come. In any case, his one idea is to make this instant permanent. But, in fact, "he hardly knew what to say" and the vision fades away. "Then a cloud came, casting a shadow over them; then from the cloud came a voice, 'This is my beloved Son. Listen to him.'"

As a response to Peter's words, this voice brings us back to the present of the ministry of Jesus, the ministry of the disciples, and beyond that, the ministry of the Church. The three apostles "suddenly, looking around . . . no longer saw anyone but Jesus alone with them." He is wearing his usual clothes and comes down the mountain with them, just as he had earlier climbed it with them. Then he says one of those words that are calculated to disconcert and make them wonder; "he charged them not to relate what they had seen to anyone, except when the Son of Man had risen from the dead."

They know about the resurrection from the dead: it is part of their creed, as it is of ours; neither they nor we deny it, as do the Sadducees of all times (Mark 12:18). But what has the resurrection to do with the vision they just had, where Jesus "was transfigured before them"? Can the resurrection concern Jesus as it does all other human beings who must pass through death? "Well, yes, Peter, James and John, and all of you, my disciples. In order to understand the transfiguration—and speak of it—you must wait until you have overcome the scandal of my death and have recognized me through paschal faith. Conversely, this transfiguration that you witnessed, you must keep it in your memory for the day when you will see me, on the cross, no longer between Elijah and Moses, but with 'two revolutionaries, one on [my] right and one on [my] left' (Mark 12:27). From the time the secret is revealed (see Mark 4:22), you must never separate death, resurrection, and ascension into the Father's glory. Then you will remember this vision and all the words you will have heard. And you will understand at last.''[38]

As it is related by Mark, the transfiguration leads the disciples to wonder about their faith, their understanding of the mystery of Jesus, and singularly of his passover. Much in the same way as the transfiguration account, the Second Gospel will conclude with the discovery of the empty tomb by Mary Magdalene; Mary, the mother of James; and Salome. "Then they went out and fled from the tomb, seized with trembling and bewilderment. They said nothing to anyone, for they were afraid" (Mark 16:8).[39]

In both cases—and probably not by chance—Mark implicitly says to the reader, "And you, what do you say? Do you understand? What is your faith response? What do you announce to your brothers and sisters? For I hope that by now you are in a position to speak and dare to do so."

The Slow Progress of Paschal Faith

Mark's Gospel is characterized throughout by the slowness of the approach to the mystery, even the danger of misunderstandings, on the part of the closest followers of Jesus. This danger is so great that Jesus seems to hesitate to clearly reveal himself, and sometimes even to regret having done so. Hence, his oft-repeated orders of silence and secrecy.

The Church has not forgotten this lesson. She takes as much time as is needed for the catechumens' first initiation into faith, but she knows that it must be ongoing: far from ending with baptism, it must be unceasingly continued. The liturgy, particularly in Lent, is the place where we find this continuing paschal initiation.[40]

We certainly believe that Jesus died to save us, and that he rose on the third day, according to Scripture; that he went up into heaven, where he is seated in glory at God's right hand, whence he will return to judge the living and the dead. Strengthened by this assurance, we can make our Paul's firm profession of hope our own: "If God is for us, who can be against us?"

However, this beautiful and legitimate assurance in no way justifies any arrogance. The splendor of the transfiguration can only be fleeting here below; the "high mountain" is not the place where Christians and the Church can permanently settle. We live in the time of naked faith, of listening to the Son announced by humans. This is also the time of testing, the time in which we must not cease to lean on the promise, when everything seems not only to contradict the promise but to undermine its foundations, when God himself sometimes seems to forget what he promised.

The stumbling block on the way of faith remains Christ's death and resurrection. If we skip over Good Friday and Holy Saturday, we rob the resurrection of any content and meaning. But if we do not go up to Easter Sunday, we close ourselves to the gift that God has made to us of his Son. In summary, we must always learn, better and better, what "to be raised from the dead" means.

Lent sends each Christian and the entire Church on this long journey of faith. It does not make use of an intense catechesis—the liturgy is not the place for this, despite its catechetical dimension—but of efficacious signs, sacraments, of a grace-bearing symbolic approach; and it leads us on the way of an exodus toward life.

> Today, let us go up the mountain
> On which Jesus will shine forth.
> Who can withstand, O Lord, your light?
> Who will face the cross?
> Today, let us go up the mountain
> On which Jesus will shine forth.
>
> Today, let us remain in the light.
> Jesus Christ will keep us.
> Heal us, Lord, by your wounds,
> Create in us a new heart.
> Today, let us remain in the light.
> Jesus Christ will keep us.
>
> Today, let us walk in the light.
> Jesus will rise.
> Open to us the doors of life,
> Open to us the new times.
> Today, let us walk in the light.
> Jesus will rise.[41]

Second Sunday of Lent—Year C

Glimpses of Easter on the Way of Exodus

The Covenant with Abraham, Father of Believers

Abraham occupies a central place in salvation history.[42] A review of the significant chapters of this history is bound to mention the father of believers. This is what we do every year on the Second Sunday of Lent. After the account of his call (Year A),[43] then of his test of faith (Year B),[44] we now have that of the covenant God concludes with him (Gen 15:5-12, 17-18).[45]

Again, it is the faith of Abraham and his trust in God that are set in relief: he is childless, yet he "put his faith in the Lord," who promises innumerable posterity to him, "Look up at the sky and count the stars. . . . Just so . . . shall your descendants be."

As always—and even today in the liturgy—the promise and the assurance of marvelous things to come are based on the recollection (anamnesis) of the marvelous things God has already accomplished. The departure of the Chaldeans from Ur is the traditional manner of evoking the Exodus also. For the reader who knows sacred history, this is enough to call to mind the years of servitude in Egypt, the liberation from slavery, and the entrance into the Promised Land.[46]

The liturgical anamnesis, a profession of faith in God, who is forever and ever, makes present to us what he has done once and for all, the grace of which reaches us today. It is also a profession of hope in God, who cannot forget. Anamnesis, therefore, is something other than a mere remembrance of the past. Likewise, we find in the Bible the word "remember" addressed to the people; the words "I remember," "I shall remember," spoken by God when he announces a new intervention in keeping with those of the past.

"How am I to know?" To this question God always gives the same answer, "Because I have promised." And Abraham, overtaken by "a trance," sees God perform an old rite of covenant-making, by passing like "a smoking brazier and a flaming torch" between animals that have been split in two. This ritual is singularly expressive. To walk together between the halves of divided animals was like saying, "Let the one who would betray our covenant[47] undergo the fate of these animals!" But here it is God alone who passes between the divided animals! He would cease to be God, he would die as these victims died if he did not fulfill his promise. God commits himself to the covenant that he himself can never break.

"The birds of prey [that] swooped down on the carcasses" and which Abraham drives away could well represent anything that would thwart the covenant and, more precisely, all that would lead humans to doubt God's commitment. Abraham is the accomplished model of the man of faith, and therefore of the just man: he drives away these birds of prey.

This archaic rite that the Book of Genesis mentions here is of considerable significance for today's believers. It reminds them that God's covenant goes back before Sinai. At the same time, it turns their attention to that other "sealing of the covenant";[48] the supreme guarantee of the promise by which he committed himself entirely and in an unheard-of fashion by delivering his own Son for the salvation of all people. Henceforth, it is his cross that stands among us as the pledge of the covenant. It is the mystery of his passion that the Eucharist celebrates every day and makes present anew. It is toward the cross that the dying turn, at the time of the supreme crisis, so that the birds of prey may go away and that they may commend their spirits to God in peace, who has promised the kingdom to the descendants of Abraham, the father of believers.

The Lord is my light and my salvation.

The LORD is my light and my salvation;
    whom should I fear?
The LORD is my life's refuge;
    of whom should I be afraid?
Hear, O LORD, the sound of my call;
    have pity on me, and answer me.
Of you my heart speaks; you my glance seeks;
    your presence, O LORD, I seek.
Hide not your face from me;
    do not in anger repel your servant.
You are my helper; cast me not off.
I believe that I shall see the bounty of the LORD
    in the land of the living.
Wait for the LORD with courage;
    be stouthearted, and wait for the LORD.
(Ps 27:1-2, 7-9c, 13-14)

Already Citizens of Heaven by the Cross of Christ

God has given the promised heritage by the cross of Christ. Already "our citizenship is in heaven," although we still live in the hope of the manifestation of the Lord Jesus Christ, who "will change our lowly body to conform with his glorified body by the power that enables him also to bring all things into subjection to himself." Therefore, this is the time to choose for or against the cross of Christ (Phil 3:17–4:1).

Like many others who followed him, Paul has chosen. His "confidence in flesh" to which he fiercely clung, "whatever gains" he has had, he now considers "a loss," "rubbish,"[49] "because of Christ," that he "may gain Christ" (Phil 3:4-8).

Confident in the covenant, Abraham was ready to sacrifice his son. "Forgetting what lies behind but straining forward to what lies ahead" (Phil 3:13), sacrificing everything, Christians choose the cross of Christ. For "it depends not upon a person's will or exertion, but upon God who shows mercy" (Rom 9:16). Citizens of heaven or of earth? Road that leads to ruin and death or to life? There is no other choice.[50]

Jesus Transfigured

The transfiguration occupies a central literary and theological place in the three Synoptic Gospels. All three versions have about the same number of verses,[51] and there is no notable discrepancy between the three. Each evangelist, however, has his own way of recounting the mystery-event. In their personal styles, we discern characteristics that make us think of other peculiarities, other emphases in their Gospels. We may well expect this to be true of the transfiguration according to Luke, who intends to create an original work in relating events narrated by eyewitnesses (Luke 9:28b-36).[52]

As on the day of his agony, Jesus takes with him Peter, James, and John, in order to go and pray alone. This time, he leads them "up the mountain." Luke worries not a bit about precise topography, which is of no interest to his readers anyway. He is more concerned with the symbolism of places than with the possibility of locating them on a map. This applies to "the mountain." He is not speaking of any hill or of a specific mountain, but of the place to which Jesus would often go to pray. It even seems that "the mountain" is always ready at hand when Jesus seeks solitude for praying (Luke 6:14-2). Besides, in his Gospel and Acts, Luke emphasizes the importance of prayer.[53] Like that at the baptism, the theophany of the transfiguration takes place while Jesus prays.

It seems that the event takes place at night, or at least at dusk, because the apostles are "overcome by sleep" while Jesus prays. Again, a point of similitude with Gethsemane. "Becoming fully awake, they saw his glory and the two men standing with him." These are about to depart; but Peter, desirous to prolong this moment of happiness, wants to set up three tents. "While he was still speaking, a cloud came and cast a shadow over them. . . . Then from the cloud came a voice. . . . After the voice had spoken, Jesus was found alone," and the vision fades away. Here, we are reminded of the narrative of the two men going to Emmaus. "Stay with us," they say and when they recognize him "in the breaking of the bread," they find themselves alone: the vision has vanished (Luke 24:31).

Luke does not mention an order from Jesus, as do Matthew and Mark, but he notes, "They fell silent and did not at that time tell anyone what they had seen." On the third day after Jesus' death, there is no reason to keep silence any longer. "So they set out at once and returned to Jerusalem" in order to tell the eleven apostles and their companions what had happened on the road and how they had recognized Jesus (see Luke 24:33, 35).

The Exodus to Be Accomplished in Jerusalem

Luke describes the metamorphosis of Jesus with much discretion: "his face changed in appearance and his clothing became dazzling white." Moses and Elijah themselves are "in glory." They speak of the exodus of Jesus "that he was going to accomplish in Jerusalem." The Greek word is *exodos*. In his discourse at the synagogue of Antioch in Pisidia, Paul uses the same term to say that John the Baptist prepared the "coming" (*exodos*) of Jesus into the world (Acts 13:24). Entrance into the world, departure from the world, entrance into glory contain a whole Easter symbolism and vocabulary. Besides, the evangelist places the transfiguration just before the great ascent of Jesus to Jerusalem (9:51–19:27). According to Luke, Jerusalem is the place where, in his boyhood, Jesus manifested himself by pronouncing his first recorded words (2:41-52), to which he goes up and where he completes his ministry (19:13–21:38), where he suffers his passion and where he rises (22:1–24:12), where he appears alive to the apostles (24:36-49), from where he ascends into heaven (24:50-52; Acts 1:6-11), where he sends his Spirit to the first community and where Peter gives his first address (Acts 2:1-41), and finally, the point of departure of the mission to all nations (Acts 8:4-8). Attentively contemplated, the transfiguration according to Luke opens onto the whole mystery of the Lord who came into this world, rose from the dead, entered into the Father's glory, and was announced to all nations.

O God, what do I see? The Savior of the world
Hung from a cross, utterly disfigured.
And it is our sins which have thus dishonored
Him who has created heaven, earth, and the seas.

This countenance so fair and full of all graces,
The desire of the most saintly souls,
Resembles the sun and is all transfigured,
For it is obscured by a deep eclipse.

For Elijah and Moses, he has two evildoers,
For heavenly voice, he hears only gibes,
Peter's ecstasy is changed into sobbing.
The sky and all the elements are in pain,
Transfigure, Lord, all our vain comforts,
And turn into tears our hard stony hearts.[54]

In the Context of Lent

Lent is to be understood, celebrated, and lived, like the transfiguration, in the light of the paschal faith of Christians and of the Church on their way to the Easter celebration. Lent is a paschal itinerary, and not just a preparation for the feast; it is a time granted to the Church and to each believer to again purify, renew, vivify their faith in the resurrection. In the measure in which we resolve to undertake this paschal journey, we shall be able to proclaim during the holy night, "Christ is risen!"

We have here a whole concept and practice of Lent, allowing us to give their proper places to penance, reconciliation, and the works pertaining to this liturgical time.

At the Crossroads

From the manger to Easter, the itinerary of Jesus—his exodus—has a twofold character: on the one hand, we have humility, suffering, and death; on the other, light, glory, and life. These latter three are discernible in the former three, if we use the eyes of faith that see through the mystery, thanks to prayer nourished by Scripture. Scripture testifies to the promise God made "to our Fathers, / to Abraham and to his descendants forever" (Luke 1:55). He would cease to be God if he were not faithful to his promise.

The apostles, witnesses of Jesus' agony in Gethsemane, saw him "on the mountain," resplendent in glory, as they have seen him, alive, after the resurrection.

Therefore, we know with certainty where our path leads us with the people of faith. But this exodus, in the blend of light and darkness of our present life, remains a test. At every moment, we must choose anew for or against Christ's cross and refuse to be dominated by earthly things, in order to behave like citizens of heaven awaiting "a savior, the Lord Jesus Christ. He will change our lowly body to conform with his glorified body by the power that enables him also to bring all things into subjection to himself" (Phil 3:20-21).

Lent is the favorable time to look into choices previously made, to correct our itinerary so that we may reach a transfiguration like the one the Son of God chose.

The celebration of the Eucharist—mystery of faith—brings the believer farther along the road to Jerusalem, where the Lord shows himself alive to his disciples, whom he fills with the Holy Spirit so that they may go and announce to the world the good news of salvation.

> We have left
> Our arduous ways
> In order to taste
> Rest, near you;
> Lord, you know
> We seek the Father,
> Teach us to pray.
>
> Shall we know how to watch
> When the flesh is weak?
> The desire for you sustains us
> In faith;
> Lord, we believe:
> You know the Father,
> Show us his beauty.
>
> For an instant our eyes
> Have glimpsed your glory:
> Here you are radiant
> With splendor.
> Lord, our joy,
> You have seen the Father,
> Your face is light.
>
> In the night of times
> Your face was hidden:

The prophets announced
your coming;
Lord, today,
We recognize you
At your Father's voice.

We must continue
To endure trials,
We must go with you
Through other nights;
Lord, Son of God,
Lead us to the Father,
Transfigure our lives.[55]

The Second Week of Lent

The two Sunday pauses of the first part of Lent are marked each year, by the Gospels of the temptation of Jesus in the wilderness and of his transfiguration on the mountain.

During the forty days he spent in solitude, without food or drink, Jesus has faced Satan, victoriously repulsing his assaults with the invincible word—the word, his daily nourishment. Nothing could make him veer away from his total attachment to the Father's will, which he has come to accomplish. Satan will not recover from this initial defeat. By proclaiming the good news of the kingdom and preaching conversion, by working many cures—signs of deliverance from evil—Jesus will go on, unmasking the devil wherever he disguises himself in an effort to keep the advantage over humans that he has held since the deception in the Garden of Eden. When leaving the desert where he overcame temptation, Jesus undertakes his mission to lead humanity on the road of a new and last exodus, all the way to the promised land God has reserved for his own.

On the mountain of transfiguration, Jesus has revealed himself to three disciples in the glory of the resurrection, which all of us will see at his manifestation on the last day. The apostles will keep the memory of this fleeting vision that they did not initially comprehend. After Easter, they will understand that this Jesus, with whom they walked on earth, whom they saw dead on the cross, is the Lord, always living near the Father. When the Spirit will have been given them, they will remember all of his words and will go to announce them to the whole world. On their way, they will meet all sorts of trials (see 2 Cor 11:23-33). Imprisoned, beaten, they will be put to death. But nothing will be able to stop them, because they know that the Lord has triumphed over Satan and that now in his glory, he will welcome them to himself.

These same certitudes animate the life of the Church and believers, not only during Lent but on all the days of their journey, which are all "Days of the Lord." Therefore, when they gather, the people of faith celebrate the exodus of Christ, who by his death entered into the Father's glory, his passover which is also their Passover.

Into what land of solitude,
forty days and forty nights,
will you go, driven by the Spirit?
May it test you and strip you!
See, the times are fulfilled,
and God invites you to forget
your ancient servitudes.

On what incandescent summits
will you hear the Beloved
speaking to you through the cloud?
Let him prepare you for his sufferings!
Follow Jesus transfigured:
tomorrow he will be crucified
to ratify the Covenant.[56]

From Monday through Saturday

On the morrow of the Sunday pause, the Christian community, guided
by the icon of the transfiguration, resumes its weekly Lenten training.

The Missal and the Lectionary present for our prayerful consideration
antiphons that highlight the themes of each day's formulary. Echoing
Peter's words on the mountain, is the opening antiphon for Monday's
Mass: "O LORD, I love the house in which you dwell, / the tenting-place
of your glory" (Ps 26:8). This is meant to encourage us in the combats
of daily life.

The Prayers are those of believers who wrestle with the seductions of sin
and the world, who turn with confidence to God in order to obtain his
pardon and the powerful help of his grace.

Keep us from sin,
and help us to live by your commandment of love.[57]

May the grace of this mystery
prevent us from becoming absorbed in material things.[58]

Lord,
may this communion bring us pardon
and lead us to the joy of heaven.[59]

The themes of these three Monday prayers are tirelessly repeated every
day of the week. However, we should not make the mistake of thinking
that this quest for righteousness entails any preoccupation with self.

God of love,
bring us back to you.
Send your Spirit to make us strong in faith
and active in good works.[60]

The Readings from the Old Testament are successively taken from the books of Daniel, Isaiah, Jeremiah, Genesis, and Micah.

Three of these texts are prayers addressed to God. That from the Book of Daniel is a confession of the sins of the people and of God's mercy (Dan 9:4b-10—Monday).

> But yours, O Lord, our God, are compassion and forgiveness! Yet we rebelled against you and paid no heed to your command, O LORD, our God, to live by the law you gave us through your servants the prophets.

Similarly, the prayer from the Book of Micah exalts God's forgiveness (Mic 7:14-15, 18-20—Saturday).

> Who is there like you, the God who removes guilt
>   and pardons sin for the remnant of his inheritance;
> Who does not persist in anger forever,
>   but delights rather in clemency,
> And will again have compassion on us,
>   treading underfoot our guilt?
> You will cast into the depths of the sea all our sins. . . .

As to Jeremiah, persecuted by those who contrive a plot against him if he mentions his enemies' intentions—"Heed me, O LORD, / and listen to what my adversaries say"—it is not to ask God for their chastisement but for their conversion (Jer 18:18-20—Wednesday).

> Remember that I stood before you
>   to speak in their behalf
>   to turn away your wrath from them.

Elsewhere, Jeremiah contrasts the unhappiness of those who turn away from the Lord and trust "in human beings" to the blessedness of those who put their hope in the Lord. This text has the character of a psalm, closely resembling Psalm 1 (Jer 17:5-10—Thursday).

> Cursed is the man who trusts in human beings,
>   who seeks his strength in flesh,
>   whose heart turns away from the LORD.
> He is like a barren bush in the desert
>   that enjoys no change of season,
> But stands in a lava waste,
>   a salt and empty earth.

> Blessed is the man who trusts in the LORD,
>> whose hope is the LORD.
> He is like a tree planted beside the waters
>> its leaves stay green;
> In the year of drought it shows no distress,
>> but still bears fruit.
> More tortuous than all else is the human heart,
>> beyond remedy; who can understand it?
> I, the LORD, alone probe the mind
>> and test the heart,
> To reward everyone according to his ways,
>> according to the merit of his deeds.

As to Isaiah, he proclaims an oracle of the Lord, who calls to conversion and promises pardon to those who will cease doing wrong (Isa 1:10, 16-20—Tuesday).

> Wash yourselves clean!
> Put away your misdeeds from before my eyes;
>> cease doing evil; learn to do good.
> Make justice your aim; redress the wronged,
>> hear the orphan's plea, defend the widow.
> Come now, let us set things right,
>> says the LORD:
> Though your sins be like scarlet,
>> they may become white as snow;
> Though they be crimson red,
>> they may become white as wool.
> If you are willing, and obey,
>> you shall eat the good things of the land.

In the middle of these prophetic texts, we find an excerpt from the Book of Genesis (Gen 37:3-4, 12-13a, 17b-18—Friday). It is part of the story of Joseph: his brothers sell him as a slave to Ishmaelites. This passage has been chosen because, on this day, we read the parable of the murderous tenants (Matt 21:33-43, 45-46), and because the fate of the only Son is prefigured in it.

The Psalms—or rather the excerpts from psalms—are in harmony with the various readings: appeal to God's mercy, oracle of the Lord addressed to his people, cry of trust in God, recollection of his marvelous deeds, thanksgiving for pardon granted.

> Help us, O God our savior,
>> because of the glory of your name;

Deliver us and pardon our sins
  for your name's sake.
(Ps 79:9—Monday)

Why do you recite my statutes,
  and profess my covenant with your mouth,
Though you hate discipline
  and cast my words behind you?
(Ps 50:16-17—Tuesday)

You will free me from the snare they set for me,
  for you are my refuge.
Into your hands I commend my spirit;
  you will redeem me, O LORD, O faithful God.
(Ps 103:1-4—Wednesday)

Bless the LORD, O my soul;
  and all my being, bless his holy name.
Bless the LORD, O my soul,
  and forget not all his benefits;
He pardons all your iniquities,
  he heals all your ills.
He redeems your life from destruction,
  he crowns you with kindness and compassion. . . .
(Ps 103:1-4—Saturday)

All of these are verses that we will want to repeat in the course of the day, meditate upon for a few moments, or use for a brief evening prayer. Psalm 105, a long poem of forty-five verses, a part of which is read on Friday, recapitulates sacred history from Abraham to the entrance into the Promised Land. As for Psalm 1, which is read on Thursday, it should be known by heart.

Happy the man who follows not
  the counsel of the wicked
Nor walks in the way of sinners,
  nor sits in the company of the insolent,
But delights in the law of the LORD
  and meditates on his law day and night.
He is like a tree
  planted near running water,
That yields its fruit in due season,
  and whose leaves never fade.
[Whatever he does, prospers.]
Not so the wicked, not so;
  they are like chaff which the wind drives away.
Therefore in judgment the wicked shall not stand,
  nor shall sinners, in the assembly of the just.

> For the LORD watches over the way of the just,
>> but the way of the wicked vanishes.

The Gospels, taken from Matthew and Luke, daily form a diptych with the first reading.[61]

When we recognize our sinfulness, we may always turn to God with confidence because in him are "compassion and forgiveness" (First Reading—Monday). We are personally involved in this compassion we appeal to, in this forgiveness we receive, since we must forgive others in the same measure, that is, always and without counting. "Be merciful, just as [also] your Father is merciful. Stop judging and you will not be judged. Stop condemning and you will not be condemned. Forgive and you will be forgiven. Give and gifts will be given to you; a good measure, packed together, shaken down, and overflowing, will be poured into your lap" (Luke 6:36-38—Monday).

Mutual forgiveness is in keeping with the search for justice according to God; this justice establishes relationships between humans that not only exclude all competition, any spirit of domination, but respects the rights of the weakest and most helpless (see First Reading—Tuesday). Going even farther, Jesus gave the example at his last meal with his own (see John 13:1-20) and formulated this general principle (Matt 23:1-12—Tuesday; 20:17-28—Wednesday). "The greatest among you must be your servant. Whoever exalts himself will be humbled; but whoever humbles himself will be exalted" (Tuesday). "Whoever wishes to be great among you shall be your servant; whoever wishes to be first among you shall be your slave. Just so, the Son of Man did not come to be served but to serve and to give his life as a ransom for many" (Wednesday).

"Blessed is the man who trusts in the LORD" (First Reading—Thursday). Such persons will have nothing to fear on the day of judgment. The poor will be there to welcome them: they will take their places near Abraham in the eternal dwellings (Luke 19:19-31, Thursday).

This week ends with two great Gospel texts whose serious teachings must be pondered by the Church as a whole and by individual believers. On Friday, we have the parable of the murderous tenants (Matt 21:33-43, 45-46). Their criminal conduct is insane: to kill the heir in the hope of insuring for themselves the possession of the inheritance. What folly! In fact, the Son was put to death after being sold for "thirty pieces of silver" (Matt 26:15). But instead of depriving him of his inheritance, death allowed him to make it available for a greater number. Such is the work of the Lord, "wonderful in our eyes." "The stone that the builders rejected / has become the cornerstone'' of an edifice more beautiful and more vast.

Finally, on Saturday, we read the parable Jesus told to those who complained, "This man welcomes sinners and eats with them." "A man had two sons. . ." (Luke 15:1-3, 11-32). This Gospel passage is a peak in the revelation of the tenderness and mercy of God, manifested by Jesus and meant to animate his disciples' hearts and inspire their conduct toward brothers and sisters.[62] It assumes its full relief in the context of Lent. All the works of Lent have only one motive and one goal: the fatherly love in God's heart and the love of neighbor. If God welcomes us and opens his arms to us, it is because we are—and remain—his children. Nothing can keep us from returning to him. Furthermore, nothing can gladden us more than the return of our brothers and sisters from far away. Whatever they may have done, whatever the reason for their "conversion" —"Here am I, dying from hunger. I shall get up and go to my father"— we must welcome them without hesitation, like the Father. "We must celebrate and rejoice, because your brother was dead and has come to life again; he was lost and has been found." Any sort of comparison between our brothers' and sisters' behavior and our own would be complaining against God, who takes pleasure in pardoning sin (First Reading).

The Liturgy of the Hours strengthens our spiritual bonds with all members of the Church. For isolated as we may be—even hermits—we live Lent within and with the Church. This communion with fellow travelers—themselves isolated or, on the contrary, members of a religious community—needs a concrete expression. In particular, we will want to use the same readings as the multitude of brothers and sisters who, we know, are all meditating on the same texts from Scripture and the Fathers of the Church, offered to us by the Liturgy of the Hours.

The Biblical Readings continue to be taken from the Book of Exodus, begun on the Thursday after Ash Wednesday (Exod 1:1-22). During this second week, we go through the chapters relating the events that occur between the departure from Egypt after the first Passover up to the promulgation of the Ten Commandments (Exod 13:17–20:17).[63]

The responsories following each of the readings outline the way of a Christian meditation on texts from the Old Testament. However, they do not exhaust a text's meaning and do not aim at delineating an exclusive way of meditating. Rather, they open the field to each person's spiritual freedom.[64] Finally, the prayerful use of responsories teaches us to taste the readings and see them in a Christological, ecclesial way. We could say that without exerting undue constraint, they regulate the spiritual spontaneity and stimulate it by educating it.

The Patristic Readings for this week are not centered on any particular theme. However, on Sunday, we read an excerpt from a homily by Pope Leo the Great (440-61) on the Gospel of the transfiguration.

> The great reason for this transfiguration was to remove the scandal of the cross from the hearts of his disciples, and to prevent the humiliation of his voluntary suffering from disturbing the faith of those who had witnessed the surpassing glory that lay concealed.
>
> With no less forethought he was also providing a firm foundation for the hope of holy Church. The whole body of Christ was to understand the kind of transformation that it would receive as his gift. The members of that body were to look forward to a share in that glory which first blazed out in Christ their head. . . .
>
> In the preaching of the holy Gospel all should receive a strengthening of their faith. No one should be ashamed of the cross of Christ, through which the world has been redeemed.
>
> No one should fear to suffer for the sake of justice; no one should lose confidence in the reward that has been promised. The way to rest is through toil, the way to life is through death. Christ has taken on himself the whole weakness of our lowly human nature. If then we are steadfast in our faith in him and in our love for him, we win the victory that he has won, we receive what he has promised.
>
> When it comes to obeying the commandments or enduring adversity, the words uttered by the Father should always echo in our ears: *This is my Son, the beloved, in whom I am well pleased; listen to him.*[65]

On Monday, we read part of a baptismal catechesis by St. John Chrysostom (ca. 347-407), patriarch of Constantinople, in which he exhorts Christians to recognize in Jesus a new Moses, "God himself [is] . . . our leader and commander." He delights in enumerating the reasons for Jesus' preeminence. Our new Moses has not delivered us from barbarous servitude, but "freed [us] from the much greater slavery to sin." His fellow servants and kinsfolk "could not look on the face of Moses in glory. . . ."

> But you have seen the face of Christ in his glory. Paul cried out: *We see the glory of the Lord with faces unveiled.*
>
> In those days Christ was present to the Israelites as he followed them, but he is present to us in a much deeper sense. The Lord was with them

because of the favor he showed to Moses; now he is with us not simply because of Moses but also because of your obedience. . . .

. . . In those days Moses raised his hands to heaven and brought down manna, the bread of angels; the new Moses raises his hands to heaven and gives us the food of eternal life. Moses struck the rock and brought forth streams of water; Christ touches his table, strikes the spiritual rock of the new covenant and draws forth the living water of the Spirit. This rock is like a fountain in the midst of Christ's table, so that on all sides the flocks may draw near to this living spring and refresh themselves in the waters of salvation.[66]

The figure of Moses and the events of the Exodus have given rise to a whole corpus of patristic literature. On Wednesday and Friday, we read texts by St. Irenaeus (ca. 135-202), bishop of Lyon, in which the emphasis is on the pedagogical character of God's actions.

From the beginning God created man out of his own generosity. He chose the patriarchs to give them salvation. He took his people in hand, teaching them, unteachable as they were, to follow him. He gave them prophets, accustoming man to bear his Spirit and to have communion with God on earth. He who stands in need of no one gave communion with himself to those who need him. Like an architect he outlined the plan of salvation to those who sought to please him. By his own hand he gave food in Egypt to those who did not see him. To those who were restless in the desert he gave a law perfectly suited to them. To those who entered the land of prosperity he gave a worthy inheritance. He killed the fatted calf for those who turned to him as Father, and clothed them with the finest garment. In so many ways he was training the human race to take part in the harmonious song of salvation.[67]

. . . Through the Decalogue he prepared man for friendship with himself and for harmony with his neighbor.[68]

The Liturgy of the Hours also offers two excerpts from homilies on the Psalms, which today are rarely the subject of sermons. Psalm 128—"Happy are you who fear the LORD / who walk in his ways!"—has been commented upon by St. Hilary (ca. 315-67), bishop of Poitiers. We read this on Thursday.

The ways of the Lord are many, though he is himself the way. When he speaks of himself he calls himself the way and shows us the reason why he called himself the way: *No one can come to the Father except through me.*

We must ask for these many ways, we must travel along these many ways, to find the one that is good. That is, we shall find the one way of eternal life through the guidance of many teachers. These ways are found in the law, in the prophets, in the gospels, in the writings of the apostles, in the different good works by which we fulfill the commandments. Blessed are those who walk these ways in the fear of the Lord.[69]

And on Tuesday, we read a passage from St. Augustine (354-430), bishop of Hippo. To Psalm 141, he applies his principle, according to which "[t]his is not my prayer but that of the whole Christ."

> *Let my prayer rise like incense in your sight; let the raising of my hands be an evening sacrifice.*
> This is generally understood of Christ, the head, as every Christian acknowledges. When day was fading into evening, the Lord laid down his life on the cross, to take it up again; he did not lose his life against his will. Here, too, we are symbolized. What part of him hung on the cross if not the part he had received from us? How could God the Father ever cast off and abandon his only Son, who is indeed one God with him? Yet Christ, nailing our weakness to the cross (where, as the Apostle says: *Our old nature was nailed to the cross with him)*, cried out with the very voice of our humanity: *My God, my God, why have you forsaken me?*[70]

Finally, on Saturday, we read a passage from a homily by St. Ambrose (339-97), bishop of Milan, on flight from the world.

> Let us take refuge from this world. You can do this in spirit, even if you are kept here in the body. You can at the same time be here and present to the Lord. Your soul must hold fast to him, you must follow after him in your thoughts, you must tread his ways by faith, not in outward show. You must take refuge in him. He is your refuge and your strength. David addresses him in these words: *I fled to you for refuge, and I was not disappointed.*[71]

Such doctrinal and spiritual richness cannot be summed up; we must make honey from it and feed on it.

> Love the Lord your God with all your heart,
> with all your soul, with all your mind.
> —This is the first and the greatest commandment.

> This is what the Lord your God asks of you:
> to hold him in awe,
> to love him and serve him with all your heart and soul.
> This is the first and the greatest commandment.[72]

From the Third to the Fifth Week of Lent

The first two Sundays of Lent are characterized every year by the Gospels of Jesus' temptation in the desert and his transfiguration according to Matthew (Year A), Mark (Year B), and Luke (Year C).

From the Third Sunday on, this parallelism ends. In Year A, we read, in John's Gospel, three important passages geared to catechumenal initiation: the Samaritan woman (4:5-42), the cure of the man born blind (9:1-41), and the raising of Lazarus (11:1-45). Therefore, in that year, the Church invites us to take a baptismal itinerary from the Third to the Fifth Sunday of Lent.[1]

In Year B, the Gospel readings, again taken from John, deal with the mystery of the death and resurrection of the Lord: the prediction of the raising up of the temple of his body (2:13-25), the end of the conversation with Nicodemus (3:14-21), and the coming of his hour and his trembling at the thought (12:20-31). This itinerary is explicitly paschal.

Lastly, in Year C, the emphasis is placed on the penitential aspect of Lent with a view to forgiveness of sins: Jesus' call to conversion (Luke 13:1-9), the parable of the prodigal son (Luke 15:1-3, 11-32), and the woman caught in adultery (John 8:1-11).

The second readings are excerpts from Paul's letters and, once, from the Letter to the Hebrews.[2] These texts, of great doctrinal and spiritual richness, demand to be reread and pondered.

As to the first readings, they continue to evoke some especially significant stages in the history of salvation.[3]

The Sunday liturgies offer us three itineraries, each having its own characteristics. But neither should we forget the weekday Masses and Liturgy of the Hours that day after day shed light on and guide the progress of the Christian community on its way to the yearly celebration of Easter.

Biblical texts have a particularly important place during Lent, which in spiritual tradition is the time especially devoted to Bible reading. But it is important to understand well in what spirit and in what perspec-

105

tives the Lenten liturgies prepare such a rich and abundant fare for the table of the Word. Certainly the Scriptures have a strong catechetical value. But without spurning this fact, the liturgy selects the readings with another viewpoint: by unveiling the meaning and implications of the mystery, God's word allows us to participate in an active, conscious, and fruitful manner in its celebration in order to live by it day to day. This is why biblical reading and prayer go hand in hand in the liturgy. Both draw us into the dynamics of God's plan and its fulfillment throughout the "Days of the Lord." Lent proves to be the favorable time during which we should apply ourselves to this reading-prayer of Scripture, which endlessly opens us to the wondrous discovery of the infinite dimensions of the mystery in which we share.

Third Sunday of Lent—Year A

Living Water, Gift of God

You Will Not Put the Lord Your God to the Test

The Exodus was a particularly important step in the history of salvation. Then, God's design really took shape and the promise of God to Abraham, "I will make of you a great nation" (Gen 12:2), was concretely realized. It is not surprising to see this event, memorable among all others, often recalled in the Bible not only as the great journey that in days of old brought the people of God from the servitude of Egypt to the Promised Land. The Exodus remains a subject for meditation, always relevant and full of teachings. So many events, revelations punctuated the forty years that Israel spent in the wilderness before crossing the Jordan near Jericho (see Josh 3:1-17)! So many significant facts for the exodus of today's people of God on their way to Easter! So many trials, which we confront as our ancestors did, for whom the time spent in the desert was a time of grumbling and temptations![4] The text read on this Sunday recalls for us one of those circumstances (Exod 17:1-7).

This event is not extraordinary in a desert like that of Sinai: there is no water, and the people suffer from thirst. But let us not see this as an ordinary situation. Moses and the people were embarked on an unusual adventure. It was not a matter of course for them to trust the Lord, even though they generally succeeded in finding water and food in this inhospitable desert. The experience of past marvels done by God was not sufficient for them to confront today's trials without anguish.

"Why did you ever make us leave Egypt? Was it just to have us die here of thirst with our children and our livestock?" This grumbling of the people must have painfully struck Moses' ears and put his own faith to the test. "What shall I do with this people? A little more and they will stone me!" This cry to God is eloquent. Moses, assailed by the murmurings and doubts of the people—"Is the Lord in our midst or not?"—wholeheartedly relies on God, who leads him, and he is unwilling to put the Lord to the test.

Jesus will have the same reaction when, before engaging in his public ministry, he wanted to face the temptations of the desert (Matt 4:7). From that time on, the whole Church and each individual believer follow Christ, the new Moses, during their lives, which is a journey leading to the Promised Land of the kingdom. Meditation on this capital stage in salvation history—the march of the people across the desert of Sinai—resolutely turns us to the present read by the light of the past. Happen what may, let us take care not to accuse the Lord and put him to the test. May there be no Massah and Meribah on our road!

> *If today you hear his voice, harden not your hearts.*
> Come, let us sing joyfully to the LORD;
>   let us acclaim the Rock of our salvation.
> Let us greet him with thanksgiving;
>   let us joyfully sing psalms to him.
> Come, let us bow down in worship;
>   let us kneel before the LORD who made us.
> For he is our God,
>   and we are the people he shepherds, the flock he guides.
> Oh, that today you would hear his voice:
>   "Harden not your hearts as at Meribah,
>   as in the day of Massah in the desert,
> Where your fathers tempted me;
>   they tested me though they had seen my works."
> (Ps 95:1-2, 6-9)

Justified by Faith; Promised to Glory

The life of the Church and believers is from now on an exodus leading us from the world of "this grace in which we stand" to the city where we shall share "the glory of God." This hope cannot disappoint us, because faith, making us just, places us in a new relationship with God and, as a consequence, with others, a relationship of trust and love of which God has taken the initiative, of which the Spirit "poured out into our hearts" is the pledge, of which Christ gave us the proof by dying for us "while we were still sinners" (Rom 5:1-2, 5-8).

What do we have to fear when we have such a proof, such an experience of God's love? How could we doubt God's presence when the Spirit has been poured out into our hearts?

As painful as they may be, the trials of our exodus assume their real meaning. We see in them the travail of giving birth to a new world, the toil of the sowing in view of the harvest.

At the Well of Jacob in Samaria

On its Lenten pilgrimage, the Church tarries near Jacob's well in order to meditate on one of the richest and most endearing passages in the Gospels (John 4:5-42).

The biblical background of this episode is evocative of the patriarchs and full of charm. In this region, Jacob set up camp and an altar to "El, the God of Israel," after his encounter with his brother Esau. A whole tradition of prayer and meditation was attached to Mount Gerizim, prior to the rivalry that arose later between this high place and the Jerusalem Temple. Finally and especially—because today's readers are also particularly sensitive to it—the theme of sources, wells, cool waters springing up is visible all through the narrative. This is certainly a poetic theme, often developed in popular Near Eastern literature; but it is also evocative for anyone who is familiar—even to a small degree—with the Bible.

The Garden of Eden is watered by a stream that "beyond there . . . divides and becomes four branches" (Gen 2:10). Throughout all biblical narratives, the journeys of the patriarchs and their families led them from well to well,[5] which they saluted with shouts of joy:

> . . . so sing to it—
> The well that the princes sank,
>   that the nobles of the peoples dug,
>   with their scepters and their staffs.
> (Num 21:17-18)

Wells and watering sites are places of meeting—or envy—in an arid land. A certain number of memorable encounters took place near a well: Abraham's servant and Rebekah (Gen 24:10-27), Jacob and Rachel (Gen 29:1-14), Moses and Reuel's daughters (Exod 2:15-22).

The problem of water was crucial throughout the whole journey of the people. They expected it to well up by God's grace (First Reading). Similarly, the psalms speak several times of the power of God, on whom the gift of water depends.

Of course, water, spring, and well came to be images of what gives life and justice: the Law, wisdom, the renewal announced by the prophets for messianic times, and in the New Testament the Spirit who vivifies everything (John 7:38-39).

Finally, a still more attentive examination of John's account allows us to faintly discern implicit reminiscences of what we could call "the legend of the well," gift of God that accompanied the Hebrews during their travels and the waters of which were overflowing before Jacob. This legend was more and more embellished in Jewish tradition and exploited in rabbinical commentaries called midrash (explanation) and targum (interpretation).[6]

In summary, the Gospel of the Samaritan woman is composed as a tapestry in which, in order to understand well the main scene, one must not neglect either the warp on which it is woven or the symbolism of the details. We must tarry and consider the background and foreground. Only then can we embrace in one single look the ensemble of a composition whose meaning and wealth remain inexhaustible. This is one of the Gospel passages that do not cease to reveal new perspectives, new depths. We discover these with wonder in the course of our meditation and contemplation of these texts, whatever the way we approach them.[7]

Unpredictable Journey Toward Faith

A first reading of the Gospel of the Samaritan woman could focus on the behavior of the woman at Sychar in order to follow the unpredictable itinerary that led her to faith and caused her to draw after her "many of the Samaritans."

At the point of departure—as so often happens—there is a chance encounter on an often-traveled road, in the course of fulfilling a daily task usually uneventfully accomplished. What is more unremarkable than a weary man sitting at the well and asking for a drink of water? Of course, it is against custom that a Jew should address a Samaritan woman, even to ask for an urgent service. Everything could have stopped there. The woman would have gone home and told of the surprising behavior of that Jew, "He must have been dying of thirst to ask me for a drink, me a Samaritan; of course, I didn't have the heart to refuse him a little water." But this stranger does not say what one expected: a banal word. He speaks of himself giving living water, although he has no bucket for drawing from the deep well: "Who is he or who does he think he is? Since Jacob, the marvel of the waters overflowing by themselves has never occurred again." The traveler seems not to have heard this remark and continues, "Whoever drinks the water I shall give will never thirst; the water I shall give will become in him a spring of water welling up to eternal life."

"Why doesn't this word just make me shrug my shoulders? Why don't I hurry to draw water, give him a drink, and flee as fast as I can from this man talking so strangely? What holds me here, my pitcher in hand? When I catch myself saying, 'Sir, give me this water, so that I may not be thirsty or have to keep coming here to draw water,' I'm not certain I speak only in irony. I feel a sort of unrest, a curiosity I don't recognize."

When the conversation turns more personal—"Go call your husband. . . . I do not have a husband. . . . You are right. . . ."—the woman is really troubled. But perhaps it is still possible to evade by asking a big, general question on a subject—controversial, but less compromising—of theology, of morals, of liturgy. However, Jesus is one of those interlocutors not easily distracted. He calls forth from the innermost depths of hearts certitudes hitherto hidden: "I know that the Messiah is coming, the one called the Anointed; when he comes, he will tell us everything." And the meandering road opens onto the decisive revelation, "Jesus said to her, 'I am he, the one who is speaking to you.' "

The chore of getting water is forgotten, the pitcher left on the ground. It is impossible not to run and share the joy of this incredible encounter with others: "Come to see a man who told me everything I have done. Could he possibly be the Messiah?"

We need the testimony of those who have met the Lord. However, if, in our turn, we believe, it is because "we have heard it for ourselves" and because we have personally recognized in him the Savior of the world.

This reading of the Gospel of the Samaritan woman is not reserved only for those who are preparing for baptism. All of us must, as long as we live, in one way or another, travel at least along some of the stages of this faith itinerary. There are many wells on our road. Sometimes, near one of them, a stranger is waiting to ask us for a drink. Maybe this person is sent by God to help us recollect ourselves and rediscover the face of the Lord, that we have somewhat forgotten. Is it not the Lord speaking to us when the word of God is proclaimed in the assembly where he gives himself as food to his people?

The Living Water Welling Up unto Eternal Life

The preceding reading is useful, but not exhaustive. This passage has a remarkable theological density, expressed, as John is wont to do, through the language of signs, here the sign of living water.

Under any latitude, water evokes life, for which it is indispensable; after a drought, life is miraculously restored by water. Thirsty travelers, exhausted by the hardships of the journey, revive when they find on their way a well or a spring of fresh, pure water. Without water, earth is a desert, where death lies in wait for humans and cattle. The people of God experienced this at the time of their journey through the wilderness, and their history is dominated by the problem of water. Naturally, the symbolism of water holds a particular place among people living in arid regions, but it is familiar also to those living in more temperate areas.

For the prophets, living water is one of the important symbols of the messianic gifts.

> On that day, living waters shall flow from Jerusalem,
> half to the eastern sea, and half to the western sea,
> and it shall be so in summer and in winter.
> (Zech 14:8)

> And the channels of Judah
>   shall flow with water:
> A fountain shall issue from the house of the LORD,
>   to water the Valley of Shittim.
> (Joel 4:18d-h)

> Then he brought me back to the entrance of the temple, and I saw water flowing out from beneath the threshold of the temple toward the east, for the façade of the temple was toward the east; the water flowed down from the southern side of the temple, south of the altar. He led me outside by the north gate, and around to the outer gate facing the east, where I saw water trickling from the southern side. . . . He said to me, "This water flows into the eastern district down upon the Arabah, and empties into the sea, the salt waters, which makes it fresh. Wherever the river flows, every sort of living creature that can multiply shall live, and there shall be abundant fish, for wherever this water comes the sea shall be made fresh. . . . Along both banks of the river, fruit trees of every kind shall grow; their leaves shall not fade, nor their fruit fail. Every month they shall bear fresh fruit, for they shall be watered by the flow from the sanctuary. Their fruit shall serve for food, and their leaves for medicine."
> (Ezek 47:1-2, 8-9, 12)

In sapiential books, living water evokes the wisdom that comes from the assiduous study of the Law: "The teaching of the wise is a fountain of life" (Prov 13:14); "The words from a man's mouth are deep waters,/ but the source of wisdom is a flowing brook" (Prov 18:4). Wisdom is a large stream flowing from the Law; the wise person is like a "rivulet from the stream" (Sir 24:28).

From allegorical commentaries to mystical interpretations, the Well—here we must capitalize the word—is the gift of God, the mysterious source that is no longer in a particular place but accompanies the people of the covenant and is always ready for those who come to it. The dialogue with the Samaritan woman is put in this context and continues a long tradition; this dialogue reaches its peak when Jesus reveals the mystery of his person, "If you knew the gift of God. . . ."

It had been said that God is "the source of living waters" (Jer 2:13; 17:13). Isaiah had announced, "With joy you will draw water / at the fountain of salvation" (12:3; see 55:1). And Jesus declares, "Whoever drinks the water I shall give will never thirst; the water I shall give will become in him a spring of water welling up to eternal life." Therefore, he reveals himself as the one who fulfills the promises by giving freely the water of life to thirsty humans, to "the one who wants it" (Rev 22:17), as the shepherd who leads God's people "to springs of life-giving water" (Rev 7:17).

But Christians who today read the Gospel of the Samaritan woman know that the revelation does not stop there. Indeed, John reports another word of Jesus: "Let anyone who thirsts come to me and drink. Whoever believes in me, as scripture says: 'Rivers of living water will flow from within him' " (7:38). And the evangelist comments, "He said this in reference to the Spirit that those who came to believe in him were to receive" (7:39).

This interpretation by John himself shows what fullness of meaning is contained in the old biblical image of living water, which Jesus uses when speaking with the Samaritan woman. This meaning becomes richer and richer as revelation and its understanding progress in the Church.

The liturgy exploits this wealth of meaning. The Gospel of the Samaritan woman was read on the first Sunday of the original three-week Lent, during which the initiation, both collective and catechetical, of catechumens accepted for baptism took place.[8] This text has, indeed, a clear and pronounced baptismal and paschal flavor, in addition to the character of a faith itinerary. This meaning and scope appear to anyone who does not read this Gospel passage as the simple record of a news item, as the edifying narrative of the encounter between Jesus and a woman of Samaria. We must read it, or rather meditate it, in the spirit of the evangelist who wrote it. The context of the Lenten liturgy helps us to see and rediscover the undying relevance of this great text.

Worshipers of the Father in Spirit and in Truth

Source of wisdom and truth, which he received from the Father and which he gives through the Spirit to those who believe in him, Jesus inaugurates a new worship. This worship is not valid only in a given place to the exclusion of all others. The true worshipers of the Father are those who worship him in union with the Christ-Truth, those whose adoration is inspired by the Spirit of truth communicated by Christ.

There is no condemnation here of external worship to the benefit of a worship which would be "in Spirit" because totally internal, without external expression, regulation, or inspiration. Prayer, and singularly liturgical prayer, owes its value to the fact that it is objectively addressed to the Father "through our Lord Jesus Christ, his Son, our Lord and God, who lives and reigns with him and the Holy Spirit." The offering of worship is adoration "in Spirit and in truth" because it is done

> Through him,
> with him,
> in him,
> in the unity of the Holy Spirit. . . .

The Real Food of the One Sent by God

If he had wanted to report only a story of conversion—however rich in teaching—John would not have inserted the dialogue between Jesus and his disciples coming back from the town where they had gone for food. At first sight, this dialogue seems to break the continuity of the narration.[9] However, it is not a stopgap and even less a digression but, on the contrary, a key to the reading of this passage and an invitation to understand it well.

First of all, we notice that the way the disciples are led into the mystery parallels that used with the Samaritan woman. The same method introduces them to the heart of the revelation.[10] The disciples find Jesus where they had left him. But they are surprised to see him conversing with a woman—this just was not done. However, they refrain from asking him questions. As the Samaritan woman leaves, they unpack their purchases and—nothing more normal—invite Jesus to eat, since this is why they had gone shopping. Besides, he must need food, since he is so tired that he has waited for them rather than accompany them.

But instead of enjoying the picnic, Jesus says to them, "I have food to eat of which you do not know." The disciples conclude that someone must have brought him something to eat. Then comes the clear revelation, "My food is to do the will of the one who sent me and to finish his work."

Once more Jesus has recourse to a symbol of the wisdom tradition. In the same way as water and wine, bread, the staple for human beings, symbolizes the gift of wisdom coming from the Law.

He who fears the Lord will do this;
 he who is practiced in the law will come to wisdom. . . .
[She will]
Nourish him with the bread of understanding,
 and give him the water of learning to drink.
(Sir 1, 3)

Wisdom has built her house,
 she has set up her seven columns;
She has dressed her meat, mixed her wine,
 yes, she has spread her table.
She has sent out her maidens; she calls
 from the heights out over the city:
"Let whoever is simple turn in here;
 to him who lacks understanding, I say,
Come, eat of my food,
 and drink of the wine I have mixed!
Forsake foolishness that you may live;
 advance in the way of understanding."
(Prov 9:1-6)

This wisdom coming from the assiduous study and practice of the Law is not just a doctrine, and still less a lifeless principle. It is participation in divine Wisdom, who was by God's side as his artisan,

when he established the heavens . . .
 when he marked out the vault over the face of the deep;
When he made firm the skies above,
 when he fixed fast the foundations of the earth;
When he set for the sea its limit
 so that the waters should not transgress his command. . . .
(Prov 8:27-29)

"She governs all things well" (Wis 8:1). The gift of wisdom is therefore made to humans as a principle of action in the service of God's will and design.

To do the will of the Father is why Jesus came "down from heaven" (John 6:38): this is his raison d'être, his food, his life.

This word of Jesus answers the question in the disciples' minds, and it reveals the significance of this episode: "I was speaking with this woman to do the will of him who sent me, to do his work!"

At this point, how can we help but remember the great prayer pronounced when "his hour had come to pass from this world to the Father" (John 13:1), "I glorified you on earth by accomplishing the work that you gave me to do" (John 17:4). At the moment of entering his passover, Jesus claims one single thing as a reason for asking the Father to glorify the Son (John 17:1): he has never said or done anything except in obedience to God's will.[11] Such a total, vital conformity between the wills of two persons suggests a total union, a unity of life. God's will "is the exclusive food of the Son, thanks to which he is what he is."[12]

Already the Fields Are Ripe for the Harvest

Without any transition, Jesus passes from his own work to the task incumbent on his disciples. He has just pronounced a word of capital importance for the understanding of the meaning and magnitude of his obedience to God's will. It seems that the disciples pay scant attention to it and make a remark—unconnected with what was just said—on the aspect of the surrounding fields, "In four months the harvest will be here." Without giving way to discouragement on account of such inattention to his words or such lack of comprehension, Jesus builds on this remark to bring the disciples back to the mystery he is revealing to them.

"Look up and see." The formula occurs several times in the Old Testament to mean the economy of the end of times: right now, one listens; then, one will see. The phrase invites the disciples to "see," in faith, invisible supernatural realities or what is certain to happen, since God promises it.

> To whom can you liken me as an equal?
> says the Holy One.
> Lift up your eyes on high
> and see who has created these. . . .
> (Isa 40:25-26b)

> The Lord said to [Abraham]: "Look about you, and from where you are
> . . . ; all the land that you see I will give to you and your descendants
> forever."
> (Gen 13:14-15)

> Up, Jerusalem! stand upon the heights;
> look to the east and see your children
> Gathered from the east and the west
> at the word of the Holy One.
> (Bar 5:5; see Isa 49:18; 60:4)

Jesus speaks in the same way. He invites the disciples to see, in faith and hope, "the fields ripe for the harvest." The Samaritan woman and the many inhabitants of Sychar who receive his words are its first fruits. In the Father's field there are many workers. Each one has a special task;

they all benefit by the labor of others. However, the workers must always remember that they have been sent by Christ. He himself is the sower, and also the seed, the wheat kernel fallen to the ground. The Gospel of the Samaritan woman thus opens up onto the situation and missionary activity of the Church, characteristic of the end times.

Thirst for the Living God
The Lenten journey gives the Church at large and each believer the double experience of a thirst no well on earth can quench and the water that springs up from the heart into eternal life.[13]

> The patriarchs had their wells: Abraham had his, Isaac his, Jacob, I think, also. Taking these wells as a point of departure, travel through the Scriptures searching for wells and arrive at the Gospels. You will find the one near which our Savior rested, after the exertion of the journey, when the Samaritan woman came to draw water. Then he explains the virtues of the well—or the wells—in Scripture and, comparing the diverse waters, reveals the secrets of the divine mystery. For it is said that those who drink the waters of the earthly well will still be thirsty, but in those who will have drunk the waters given by Jesus "a spring of water [will well] up to eternal life" (John 4:14). In another passage of the Gospel, there is no longer a question of spring or well but of something more important: "Whoever believes in me, as Scripture says:
> 'Rivers of living water will flow from within him' " (John 7:38).
> Therefore, you see: those who believe possess more than sources, but rivers; in any case, both sources and rivers bring eternal life, not the mortal one.[14]

The liturgy is the privileged place where these living waters well up, abundant and varied, when the word of God is proclaimed. The Spirit awakens adoration, prayer, and thanksgiving in believers' hearts. The Lord gives himself to his people as food under the signs of bread and wine. But it is everyone's responsibility to make sure that these life-giving waters can spring up: "The wells of our souls need a well digger; they must be cleaned, freed from everything earthly so that the water tables of rational thoughts that God has placed there may produce streams of pure and sincere water. As long as dirt blocks the water tables and obstructs them, the secret current, the pure water cannot flow."[15]

Lent is the favorable time to do this great yearly work while singing:

> If you knew the gift of God,
> if you believed in him who is speaking,
> you would know the Father in Spirit and truth;
> leave behind the well of Samaria

and come to drink the living water out of the Rock:
Jesus Christ.

Lord, give us this water
that I may not be thirsty again!

In you is the source of life,
in your light we behold the light.

Keep those who have known you in your love,
keep all sincere hearts in your justice.[16]

To Believe in Jesus, the One Who Is Sent

David, God's Elect

When recalling the main steps in salvation history, the biblical authors could not fail to mention the election and anointment of David (1 Sam 16:1, 6-7, 10-13a).

David! At the mere mention of this name, a host of memories crowds upon us: the combat of the young warrior who, armed only with a simple slingshot, conquered the giant Goliath; the exploits against the Philistines, which aroused the jealousy of Saul; the friendship with Jonathan and the heartrending mourning after the death of this faithful companion; the passion for Bathsheba and the plot hatched to get rid of Uriah, the husband standing in the way. And, also, the repentance of the king after the crime; the dance before the ark; the psalms attributed to David, who is also credited with inventing musical instruments to praise God.[1] But above all, David is the founder of the dynasty from which the Messiah, whom he prefigures, will be born.

The hope of Israel constantly recalls the promises made to David, promises God cannot go back on.

> I have made a covenant with my chosen one,
>   I have sworn to David my servant:
> Forever will I confirm your posterity
>   and establish your throne for all generations.
> I will not violate my covenant;
>   the promise of my lips I will not alter.
> Once, by my holiness, have I sworn;
>   I will not be false to David.
> (Ps 89:4-5, 35-36)

As for the prophets, they announce the coming of a new David, whose rising they foresee. Thus, Isaiah, in a well-known text, reminds us during Midnight Mass at Christmas,

For a child is born to us, a son is given us;
  upon his shoulder dominion rests.
They name him Wonder-Counselor, God-Hero,
  Father-Forever, Prince of Peace.
His dominion is vast
  and forever peaceful,
From David's throne, and over his kingdom,
  which he confirms and sustains
By judgment and justice,
  both now and forever.
The zeal of the LORD of hosts will do this!
(Isa 9:5-6; see Mic 5:1-3)

Recalling these promises and prophecies, the New Testament and early Christian preaching will announce that Jesus is the awaited son of David.[2]

Born in Bethlehem, "the city of David" (Luke 2:4), he was not different from others in human eyes. But God anointed him with the Spirit and made him known as his chosen one by those who listen to his voice and follow him.

The Lord is my shepherd; there is nothing I shall want.

The LORD is my shepherd; I shall not want.
  In verdant pastures he gives me repose;
Beside restful waters he leads me;
  he refreshes my soul.
He guides me in right paths
  for his name's sake.
Even though I walk in the dark valley
  I fear no evil; for you are at my side
With your rod and your staff
  that give me courage.
You spread the table before me
  in the sight of my foes;
You anoint my head with oil;
  my cup overflows.
Only goodness and kindness follow me
  all the days of my life;
And I shall dwell in the house of the LORD
  for years to come.
(Ps 23)

Once Darkness, Today Light

"To sum up all things in Christ, in heaven and on earth," such is the eternal plan that God has been pursuing forever. He gave the mission of fulfilling this plan to his Son, the new David, over whom John the

Baptist saw the Spirit descend and rest at Jesus' baptism (John 1:34). Those who, in faith, welcome God's elect and are regenerated in the baptismal bath, become light and must henceforth live as "children of light." Such is Paul's pressing exhortation that the liturgy has us listen to on this Fourth Sunday of Lent in Year A (Eph 5:8-14).

When we have become light, we know "what is pleasing to the Lord"— "every kind of goodness and righteousness and truth"—and we do it with joy. What a pity, indeed, if the "children of light" should ever return to "the fruitless works of darkness"! Equipped to unmask "these things," Christ's disciples will not let themselves get caught by their delusive glamour.

This exhortation assumes its full meaning when we remember that in the early Christian era one of the most beautiful of the traditional names for baptism was "illumination" (*photismos* in Greek). It is at that moment, indeed, that the believer becomes light in Christ. This is why, Paul says, that at the instant when the neophytes emerged from the baptismal waters, the whole congregation sang,

> Awake, O sleeper,
> and arise from the dead
> and Christ will give you light.
> (Eph 5:14)

Wonderful Paul! Down the centuries, his preaching keeps all its force and all its freshness. This is due to the fact that he envisions daily Christian life, faith, and celebration of the sacraments within the unity of one single mystery: the plan of salvation, revealed to believers, in which they participate, thanks to holy rites and to everyday life that is led in the light of the gospel under the guidance of the Spirit.

A Blind Beggar on Jesus' Path
After the Gospel of Jesus, source of living water, here is that of the one sent by God opening the eyes of a man born blind (John 9:1-41).

A long meditation on one of Jesus' "signs," this passage occupies an important place in John's Gospel, and singularly in the "Book of Signs,"[3] where the rather short narrative of what Jesus did is flanked by long discourses. However, the composition of the Gospel of the man born blind is different. The healing itself is very briefly reported in three verses. But it provokes a whole series of reactions and questions that give to this passage the proportions of a discourse. Furthermore, Jesus intervenes very little: in the beginning, for the cure, and at the end, for short addresses to the healed man first, then to the Pharisees. However, he remains in the foreground all the time. For it is he who is subjected to a trial through the various questionings imposed on the man and his parents. We must, therefore, read and reread this passage with as much care as John used in writing it.

This text lends itself to readings on several levels. The first one is that of diverse reactions sparked by a healing. The style here is remarkable, lively, captivating. But by the end of the passage, we cannot help thinking that the evangelist did not write this story only to report the counterpoint of bystanders' behavior following a miracle worked by Jesus. Of course, we could draw valuable lessons from his cure, especially in the field of apologetics: if Jesus was able to open the eyes of a man born blind, it was because he came from God. Nevertheless, the interest of such a reading would remain quite superficial.

More interesting is the reading focusing on the way in which the story plays with opposite words like "knowledge" and "ignorance." The blind man—who, by the way, has not asked for anything—passes from ignorance about Jesus to recognition of his identity. The man's parents know that their son was blind, that he has been cured; but they do not know what happened. Finally, the Pharisees, assured in their knowledge, find themselves charged with culpable ignorance. In the same way, the text plays with the words "blind" and "sighted." The man born blind becomes capable of sight, not only in the literal meaning of the term, but also in a spiritual sense: his eyes open to faith. Others, enjoying normal vision, are blind when it comes to discerning spiritual realities. We are also struck by the titles attributed to Jesus—light, the one sent, prophet, Son of Man, Lord—that appear according to a progression following that of the passage from darkness to light. Finally, we hear the accusations against the cured man and Jesus, who are charged with being sinners, then the accusations of Jesus against his accusers, who are blind persons whose sin remains.

This reading is not only interesting but profitable. It spontaneously becomes meditative and leads all of us to question ourselves about our so-called knowledge and ignorance and about the meaning given to the titles attributed to Jesus, to take sides in the proceedings against him. In doing so, we discern more and more the great theological depth of this text, which is not mere news coverage. And we look at the reading again to follow it to a deeper level.

The Coming of Light into the Darkness

From the beginning of his Gospel, in the introduction improperly called "prologue," John speaks of the coming of God's Word into the world as that of the light which enlightens everyone and which the darkness can refuse to accept (see 1:5, 9-10). The cure of the man born blind shows Jesus in the exercise of this mission—this work (see 5:17), for which the Father sent him. Such is the meaning of the miracle. There is no place here for questions about the origin or the causes of the man's condition, as Jesus meets him on his way. "Rabbi, who sinned, this man or his parents?"[4] The question is whether or not we recognize in Jesus "the light of the world," and this is a question that remains asked of all readers of the Gospel. But how is Jesus the light? How can we recognize him?

The answer is found in John's Gospel, given by Jesus himself. To those who say, "If you are the Messiah, tell us plainly," Jesus retorts, "The works I do in my Father's name testify to me" (10:24-25). These works are a greater testimony than any human can give, even John the Baptist himself (see 5:36). Jesus often comes back to this point, going as far as saying, "If I do not perform my Father's works, do not believe me; but if I perform them, even if you do not believe me, believe the works, so that you may realize [and understand] that the Father is in me and I am in the Father" (10:37-38; see 14:11). Truly, the works he accomplishes are the decisive credentials that show him to be the one sent by the Father as the Light of the world. They are perfectly coherent with all that the Bible reveals about God. Those who do not see must ask themselves whether or not they are blind.

The Coming of Jesus into the World to Ask the Question Again

First of all, it is believers who must critically look at themselves and unceasingly question themselves anew. They have the Scriptures, which the Church today offers them in plenty. How do they read them and hear them in the liturgy and preaching? To seek confirmation for their ideas, even their prejudices? To accept the challenge the Scriptures bring when they unmask the "works of darkness," which to their shame the "children of light" perform (Second Reading)? These are serious questions that all of us must regularly face to avoid falling imperceptibly into a tragic blindness. The saints became saints because they never ceased to allow themselves to be questioned by Christ and the Gospels. Without such searching, tepidity threatens. Neither cold nor hot. This can appear to be "honest mediocrity" to human eyes. But it is written in Revelation that God spits the lukewarm out of his mouth (see Rev 3:15-16), those who do not resolutely act according to the truth (see John 3:21).

Together with being a principle of action pleasing to God, the light of Christ enables us to recognize good wherever it is, to unhesitatingly identify it and, finally, to see God at work in it. But we often refuse to do this, or we dare not express our opinion. Thus the parents of the cured man. They cannot deny that this man is their son, that he was born blind, and that he has recovered his sight. But they are evasive when asked, "How does he now see?" "We do not know how he sees now. . . ." Not uncommonly, we hide behind such a statement of ignorance through fear of what could be the consequences of giving testimony. We fear getting involved in a deeper and deeper commitment. We usually do not go as far as denying the very possibility of God's intervention. But silence becomes complicity when we should speak: it gives free play to those who reject God's intervention and contributes to entrenching the timid in their timidity. Who will describe the ravages caused or fostered by a timorous neutrality?

From Blindness to Faith

The man Jesus met was very simply cured of his blindness: a little mud applied to the eyes, afterwards washed off in the Pool of Siloam, and upon returning, he could see. By contrast, it is only little by little, progressively, that his inner eyes were opened, that he was brought to faith. Obviously, the evangelist wants to rivet his readers' attention on this gradual way of recognizing the Lord. In fact, this is an itinerary that believers never cease to follow.

> You heard a great mystery. Ask someone, "Are you Christian?" He or she answers, "I am not," if the person is a pagan or Jew. If the answer is "I am," you pursue the questioning. "Are you a catechumen or a full-fledged believer?" If the answer comes, "Catechumen," he or she has been anointed, but not yet washed. But anointed in what way? Ask and you will hear the answer; ask in whom that person believes; by the very fact the person is a catechumen, the reply will be, "In Christ." And now I address myself to both faithful and catechumens. What did I say about saliva and mud? That it is the sign of the Word made flesh. This the catechumens understand; but having been anointed is not enough; let them hasten to the bath if they desire the light.[5]

John makes no mention of anything the blind beggar might have done to attract Jesus' attention. But who could say why, one day, one makes a gesture, dares one step, that will set in motion a whole chain of events?

Must we not recognize, in the end, that we unknowingly were moved by an initiative of God?

Often the change that happens surprises not only relatives and acquaintances, but also its beneficiary. However, we must admit it, "It is really me." How did this happen? Very simply and yet in an extraordinary manner. By reflecting on events and also by answering the queries of people, we become more and more aware, and our faith grows more and more explicit.

At this level of reading, the theological significance of the Gospel of the man born blind appears; it is a sort of illustrated treatise of the journey toward faith, under the action of grace from beginning to end; the summit is reached when we prostrate ourselves and confess, "I believe, Lord, you are the light of my eyes."

Liturgical Background and Sacramental Significance

Jesus met the man born blind after he "went out of the temple area," to which he had gone for the feast of Tabernacles (see John 7:2, 10).[6] For a whole week, there was great merrymaking in Jerusalem, to which pilgrims flocked. During the ceremonies, all waved the *lulab*, a palm frond to which were attached branches of myrtle and willow, while holding citrons[7] in their other hand.

The end of the harvest, especially if it had been good, the booths erected in gardens or on terraces gave a special ambience to this week marked with songs and dances, celebrations, and sacrifices in the Temple. But it was also the commemoration of the entrance into the Promised Land with a strong increase of hope for the coming of the Messiah and the end times. Therefore, it is not surprising that heated discussions were going on concerning Jesus, whose teachings in the Temple took on a singular relief and aroused fresh controversies (see John 7–8). It is in this liturgical context that the great messianic revelation of Jesus is set: "Let anyone who thirsts come to me and drink. Whoever believes in me, as scripture says:

'Rivers of living water will flow from within him' " (7:37-38).
"I am the light of the world. Whoever follows me will not walk in darkness, but will have the light of life" (8:12).

These words were pronounced on each day of the feast, while the priests went to draw water from the fountain of Siloam and solemnly carried it to the Temple in a golden pitcher; then they poured it on the corner of the altar at night, when the courtyard of the women was brilliantly illuminated.⁸ Such is the original liturgical context in which, according to John, the "sign" of the blind man's cure must be placed. But Christian readers of the Gospel cannot read this passage—especially on a Sunday of Lent—without thinking of the catechumenate and baptism. Like a catechumen, the blind man, once cured, goes toward the progressive recognition of him who opened his eyes. This recognition advances in rhythm with the questions asked, which are not unlike those of the old "scrutinies."⁹ Finally, this Gospel reminds the baptized that they will have to testify to their faith at the risk of being rejected by some or henceforth ignored by others.¹⁰

Following Christ, the Light of Our Eyes

By celebrating Christ, the Light of the world, the Fourth Sunday of Lent, Year A, calls Christians and the entire Church to a new impetus in their journey following the Lord.

We may say of some people that they are lights, because their doctrine, their wisdom, their teachings, and their examples shine like beacons on the road, or because they attract and fascinate us. But it is in the proper and not in the metaphorical sense that we speak of Christ when confessing that he is the Light of the world, "Light from Light," because "True God from True God."

In him and through him, believers become "children of light" and can, like him, perform works that are pleasing to God. It is a marvelous transformation that turns a blind person into one who lives by light and is called to walk from light to light.

> Blind of heart from birth,
> I am coming to you, Light of the world:
> touch my eyes and wash me in the fountain
> where the Spirit dispels the darkness of sin.
>
> *May I see the splendor of your glory!*
> *May I live as a child of light!*
>
> I love you, Lord, my strength;
> I call upon the Lord, I am saved.
>
> You are my light, Lord,
> my God, enlighten my darkness.
>
> Formerly you were darkness,
> now, in Christ, you are light.¹¹

Jesus, Resurrection and Life

I Will Open Your Graves and Have You Rise from Them

When it speaks of the Exile, biblical tradition evokes the great deportation of the inhabitants of the kingdom of Judah who lived in Mesopotamia (Babylon) from 597 to 538 B.C. From scattered data in several books of the Bible especially,[1] historians can give us information on the living conditions and activities of the exiles. We also learn that the time of the deportation to Babylon was a period of intense literary and theological activity: the writing of parts of the Pentateuch, the definitive edition of Deuteronomy, and a re-reading of earlier prophets.[2] But, above all, the Exile has remained in biblical memory the great trial, the punishment for sin, where God revealed himself in all his holiness, even in the midst of the nations, and in his unshakable faithfulness.[3] For this reason, this stage in sacred history is recalled during Lent.

Ezekiel, the priest and prophet, was among the deportees. He is, among all the prophets, the herald of God's faithfulness and power, which the vicissitudes of history cannot hold in check. When everything seems lost, when the visible guarantees of the covenant have disappeared—dwelling in the Promised Land, the Davidic dynasty, the Temple—God remains faithful and capable of creating a new future for his own. He will open the tombs that hold them imprisoned; he will lead them out (Ezek 37:12-14).[4]

The liberation from captivity is guaranteed by the word of the Lord. This is one of the principal lessons of Ezekiel's oracles: "You shall know that I am the LORD." In one form or another, this affirmation is repeated eighty-six times in the book of this prophet. And this is what we will essentially remember from this reading: nothing can cause us to doubt the promises of the Lord, who will deliver his people since he has committed himself to it.

With the Lord there is mercy, and fullness of redemption.

Out of the depths I cry to you, O LORD;
  LORD, hear my voice!

Let your ears be attentive
  to my voice in supplication:
If you, O LORD, mark iniquities,
  LORD, who can stand?
But with you is forgiveness,
  that you may be revered.
I trust in the LORD;
  my soul trusts in his word.
My soul waits for the LORD
  more than sentinels wait for the dawn.
More than sentinels wait for the dawn,
  let Israel wait for the LORD,
For with the LORD is kindness
  and with him is plenteous redemption;
And he will redeem Israel
  from all their iniquities.
(Ps 130)

Under the Power of the Spirit, Not the Flesh

What God had promised, he marvelously realized in Jesus Christ, unique Savior of all people, without distinction, and through the Spirit given to believers. Still marked by sin and subject to death that is its consequence, they have the assurance that their mortal bodies will find life again. The liberation brought by Christ goes that far (Rom 8:8-11).

The strong and concrete doctrine of this text rests on the antithesis of flesh and spirit.

For Paul, the flesh designates the human world stained by sin, the world under the yoke of death. The spirit, on the contrary, evokes the divine world in which humanity is assumed by Christ, the spiritual world engendered by God in Jesus' resurrection. The flesh is human nature, body and soul, closing in upon itself and its sin. The spirit is a force of new life given to the believer by the Spirit of the risen Christ. If we keep this distinction in mind, the text becomes clear.

There is no visible difference between people, whether believers or not: their being and their life are subject to the same laws of human nature, to the same hazards affecting them in body and soul; all are traveling toward bodily death. However, the believers' condition is fundamentally—albeit invisibly—other. The Spirit gives them the possibility of living free of sin, "although the body is dead because of sin." This same "Spirit of the one who raised Jesus from the dead" will give life to their mortal bodies. Such is, in all its realism, the mystery of salvation as it unfolds in each person, but only in the measure in which we strive to become what we are. It is the same for our Christian condition as for our human condition: we are humans, but we must, at every moment, assume our human condition; we are, through Christ and in the Spirit, new creatures, but only in the measure in which, at every moment, we die and rise with Christ. Once more, Paul shows how theology and morality are intimately connected. When we speak of "Christian being," we are led to discerning what is "Christian acting." The conduct of Christians is nothing other than their faith lived out.

The Last "Sign" of Jesus and His Glorification

In John's Gospel, as in the Lenten Lectionary of Year A, the raising of Lazarus is the last "sign" that Jesus works in order to manifest the glory of the Father and announce his supreme personal glorification at his passover (John 11:1-45).[5]

For John, Jesus' miracles—and his works in general—are "signs." For, while glorifying the Father, these actions give us intimations of the true identity of the one who does them, and as a consequence, they aim at enkindling faith.[6] We have here genuine theophanies that point to the supreme manifestation of the cross, the glorification, the "elevation" of the Son of Man (John see 12:23, 31). From his open side will gush forth blood and water, signs of the fecundity of Christ's death, which is the source of life for those who, lifting their eyes to him, believe like John, the faithful witness (see 19:34-37).

If the evangelist devotes such space to the raising of Lazarus,[7] it is because it prepares us to understand well the meaning of the Lord's passion. An attentive reading reveals this intention. Jesus has escaped the hands of those who wanted to stone him and has withdrawn beyond the Jordan to the place where John had first baptized (see 10:39-40). Now he returns to Judea—Bethany is "near Jerusalem, only about two miles away"—because the hour has come when the Son of Man is to be glorified.[8]

Jesus leaves "to awaken" his friend from death, knowing full well that his Father always listens to his prayer. He assures Martha that her brother Lazarus will come back to life. However, he is "perturbed and deeply troubled," and he weeps. Emotion surges again when he reaches the tomb.

"See how he loved him," some witnesses say; others, "Could not one who opened the eyes of the blind man have done something so that this man would not have died?" A good number of commentators and preachers have also seen in the emotions and tears of Jesus the expression of the deep friendship that bound him to Lazarus and his sisters. They like to highlight the fact that he was filled with the feelings common to all humans. Some even go so far as to interpret Jesus' reaction to his friend's death as the expression, equally human, of his trouble at the absurdity of death.

Despite its interest and the lofty developments to which it can give rise, this reading is probably not the one that corresponds to John's intent.[9] For we notice that he speaks of a similar "trouble" in Jesus four other times. When Philip mentions the Greeks who want to see him, Jesus says, "The hour has come for the Son of Man to be glorified." And he adds, "I am troubled now" (12:23, 27). When "his hour had come to pass from this world to the Father," (13:1) during the meal he was taking with his disciples, "Jesus was deeply troubled and testified, 'Amen, amen, I say to you, one of you will betray me' " (13:21). But, although the prospect of his passion troubles him, Jesus does not hesitate, and with full lucidity he assumes his vocation: "What should I say? 'Father, save me from this hour'? But it was for this purpose that I came to this hour" (12:27). And he asks his disciples not to let themselves be troubled by the prediction of his death (see 14:1, 27).

In his account of the passion, John does not speak of Jesus' agony in Gethsemane. It is hinted at here, in the Gospel of the raising of Lazarus, which is a sign not only of mastery over death given by the Father to the Son of Man, but also of the glory that his own resurrection will make manifest on Easter.

But other details do not escape attentive readers; these details show how much the reality signified by the raising of Lazarus goes beyond the sign. People had to remove the stone that closed the tomb where Lazarus was laid. "On the first day of the week, Mary of Magdala came to the tomb early in the morning . . . and saw the stone removed from the tomb" (20:1). Lazarus came out "tied hand and foot with burial bands, and his face was wrapped in a cloth"; he had to be untied so that he could move. The linens used in Jesus' burial remained there; Peter and John saw "the cloth that had covered his head, not with the burial cloths but rolled up in a separate place" (20:7). No one had to intervene either to roll away the stone or to free Jesus from his bonds.

Lastly and most importantly, Lazarus was called back to life only for a while. It even seems that he had been dead for a long time when John wrote his Gospel; for he speaks of him as of someone unknown to his readers, since he identifies him as the brother of Mary and Martha. In contrast, Jesus came out of the tomb to live forever.

Truly, the raising of Lazarus is the sign that prefigures the definitive triumph of Jesus on the cross, God's glory, and the glorification of the Son victorious over death, who "awakens" believers, making them pass, already here below, to the life that bodily death cannot touch.

I Am the Resurrection and the Life. Do You Believe This?

The raising of Lazarus is the ultimate and decisive sign worked by Jesus. A variety of features show that it must be understood in the perspective of the "hour" of Jesus that will see his glorification and make manifest the Father's glory. This all-important text is especially appropriate to the Sunday before Passion Sunday in Year A, after the Gospels of the living water and the man born blind. The liturgical context—in harmony with that of John's Gospel—points to a symbolic understanding, replete with meaning, of this great deed in Jesus' life. This is an event-sign to which each of us must try to relate, an event-revelation that requires from each of us a personal answer. "I am the resurrection and the life. . . . Do you believe this?" No one in the Christian assembly can evade this question.

The other miracles John reports are habitually followed by a discourse that explains the meaning of the sign just worked.[10] Nothing of the sort here, but only a certain number of declarations made as the action develops. "This illness is not to end in death, but is for the glory of God, that the Son of God may be glorified through it." "If one walks during the day, he does not stumble, because he sees the light of this world. But if one walks at night, he stumbles, because the light is not in him." "Lazarus has died. And I am glad for you that I was not there, that you may believe." This sort of composition has been likened to the words of a commentator explaining the unfolding of a liturgy,[11] arousing the attention, spurring the curiosity, and provoking the reflection of the assembly.

And so we find ourselves led to the dialogue with Martha and to the culminating point of the revelation, which confers meaning on the sign. "I am the resurrection and the life." This supreme declaration of Jesus is followed by the ever-resounding question, "Do you believe this?"

> Jesus said to Martha, "Your brother will rise." The answer was ambiguous. He did not say, "I am going to raise up your brother now," but, "Your brother will rise." Martha answered, "I know he will rise, in the resurrec-

tion of the last day. Of that resurrection I am sure; of this, unsure." Jesus told her, "I am the resurrection. You say, 'My brother will rise on the last day.' It is true; but he who will raise him up then can also raise him up now." He said, "I am the resurrection and the life." Listen, my brothers and sisters, listen to what he is saying. Assuredly, the hope of all those present was to see Lazarus, dead for four days, come back to life: let us listen and let us be raised up. How many in this assembly are laboring under the weight of habit. Perhaps among those present here there are some of those impure ones who sully themselves in infamous pleasures and to whom someone will say, "Do not do this, lest you perish"; and they answer, "We cannot snatch ourselves from our habits." O, Lord, raise these people up! "I am the resurrection and the life," he says, the resurrection because the life.[12]

From Death to Life

Since it entered into the world, death, together with sin that is its cause, puts its imprint on everything. For all that, death cannot defeat the God of life and of the living. God delivers his people from their graves—the grave of deportation, for instance—as soon as they turn from their sin. Indeed, from the beginning, he has promised that death will not have the last word. "I have said it, and I will do it," he says over and over again.

This promise accompanies that of a savior whom prophets, sent by God, announced in order to teach humankind "to hope for salvation."[13]

"And the Word became flesh. . . ." "Through him was life. . . ." "But to those who did accept him he gave power to become children of God, to those who believe in his name, who were born not by natural generation nor by human choice nor by a man's decision but of God" (John 1:14, 4, 12-13).

Of this power and this mission, Jesus gave signs, among which the raising of Lazarus stands out. Through this sign, he showed that he himself was the resurrection and the life, and he declared, "Whoever believes in me, even if he dies, will live and everyone who lives and believes in me will never die."

This process of moving toward life is started at baptism, in which we are born to faith. Still under the law of death, we can and we must, animated by the Spirit who vivifies us, lead a life free of the control of mortal flesh, with the assurance of one day sharing in the Lord's resurrection.

Such a certainty must not, however, cause us to forget the inescapable step of the cross. Christ, resurrection and life, has gone through it with us. The raising of Lazarus had as its immediate consequence the condem-

nation of Jesus to death; he freely gave his life so that we might live forever. Like Thomas, we say, "Let us also go to Jerusalem to die with him,"
and with him to rise.

> The Master of life approaches the tomb:
> "Lazarus, wake up from among the dead!
> And you, buried in sin,
> see and believe I am the resurrection."

> *If we die with you, Lord,*
> *with you, we shall enter life.*

> I exalt you, Lord,
> you who raise me up.

> At night, come tears,
> At dawn, cries of joy.

> If the dead do not rise,
> Christ has not risen either.[14]

From the Third
to the Fifth Week—Year A

From the Third to the Fifth Sunday, Year A, the Lenten itinerary of the Church is marked by three major texts from John's Gospel. They remind us that Jesus is the living water that wells up into a life-giving source within each believer, the light that opens the eyes of those who were born blind, the resurrection and the life of those who believe.

This revelation is set within the dynamics of salvation history, the main stages of which cannot be forgotten, in particular the long march of the people, whose thirst God quenched with water out of the rock; the election of David, Jesus' ancestor; the innumerable manifestations of the unflagging faithfulness of God, who always does what he says.

This history is still that of today, having reached, with Christ and through him, its decisive phase. Through Christ, God has made us righteous and has given us, by faith, access to the world of grace, in which we are established. Hope does not disappoint, which helps us to wait to have a share in God's glory, because the Holy Spirit has been poured out in our hearts by God. At the appointed time, while we were incapable of anything, he sent his Son to save, by his death, the sinners that we were (see Rom 8:1-2, 5-8). Having become light, children of light, we can walk in full security, doing what is pleasing to God (see Eph 5:8-14). Although our body is destined to die, we are no longer under the sway of the flesh. "The Spirit of the one who raised Jesus from the dead will give life to your mortal bodies" (Rom 8:11).

This itinerary opens onto vast vistas. Based on the biblical texts proclaimed at Mass, the whole of revelation is uncovered and made more distinct. In the foreground, Jesus stands out in a light that shows him more and more clearly to be the Son of God, accomplishing the Father's work. On the horizon, the passover of Christ is delineated, and toward it the Church journeys and prepares for the solemn celebration.

This paschal itinerary proves to be eminently sacramental, baptismal. We cannot travel along it without constantly referring ourselves to baptism. The catechumens will receive it, and the accompanying Christian community will remember it.

So if it happens that by rendering thanks to God for what he has already done for his people, becoming more conscious day by day of what faith and the reception of the signs of faith imply, we are constantly impelled to become what we are in Christ, through the Spirit. Then we will be able to readily enter the yearly celebration of Holy Week and Easter.

In Three Days I Will Raise Up the Temple of My Body

The Law of the Lord, the Way of Freedom

Every Sunday of Lent commemorates one of the main events of salvation history. The giving of the Decalogue on Sinai is, among all others, a notable fact in this history (Exod 20:1-17). The Decalogue—also called the Ten Commandments (Deut 4:13; 10:4)[1]—is the fundamental law that regulates the moral life of the people. Jesus recalled several of its precepts (Matt 19:16-22; Mark 10:17-22; Luke 18:18-22). St. Augustine made them the framework of his teaching on Christian morality. The condensed and easily memorized formulation of God's commandments has been, in successive ages and even up to the present day,[2] the basis of catechesis and of the exposition of Christian conduct toward God and others. The Decalogue is, therefore, a venerable biblical text, even if several of its precepts are found in earlier nonbiblical traditions.[3]

The way that God designates himself in order to establish his authority immediately captures our attention: he is he who freed his people from slavery. His law is addressed to humans whom he has willed and continues to will free. They are not subject to blind and obscure powers "in the sky above or on the earth below or in the waters beneath the earth." He who speaks, speaks with unveiled face, saying "Me," "I." He addresses a "You." We have here the whole spirituality of the desert.

> In the desert, I seek your face,
> in the desert, your bread nourishes me.
> I am not afraid to walk in your footsteps.
> Your living water gushes forth
> to quench my thirst.
>
> *Espoused to you in justice,*
> *espoused to you in love,*
> *in faithfulness,*
> *I shall know*
> *as I am known.*

In the desert, I hear your Word,
in the desert, far away from the din,
the memory of your Law comforts me.
O hidden God,
you want to speak to my heart.

In the desert, I draw in your breath,
in the desert, the Spirit dwells.
It is the force which, in the morning, impels me.
It is the fire
which, at night, goes before me.[4]

He is a "jealous" God. This qualifier might surprise us, but it must be remembered that the Bible readily resorts to the image of marriage to describe the covenant between God and his people.[5] God is jealous because his love cannot bear the unfaithfulness or the indifference of his own. This is confirmed by what follows: God says he is "inflicting punishment for their fathers' wickedness on the children of those who hate me, down to the third and fourth generation; but bestowing mercy down to the thousandth generation on the children of those who love me and keep my commandments." There is no common measure between love and wrath: in contrast to his love, God's wrath does not last forever.

"You shall not take the name of the LORD, your God, in vain." The holiness of God is involved here; it is blasphemy to take the Lord's name with the intention of associating it with an evil action.[6] This is far-reaching. How can we invoke, name, God in prayer and afterwards harm others? What a scandal when those who have been sanctified by the invocation of the Name prove to be evildoers and by their conduct lead others to blaspheme God!

As to the seventh day, it is presented here as the weekly release from the servitude of daily work by which all must benefit: male and female servants, immigrants, and even animals. The rest of the seventh day is an act of worship rendered to God, who has given freedom to his people. Memory of this liberation is made in a particularly explicit way at the time the first fruits of the harvest are presented with the words: "Then you shall declare before the LORD, your God, 'My father was a wandering Aramean who went down to Egypt. . . . When the Egyptians maltreated and oppressed us, imposing hard labor upon us, we cried to the LORD, the God of our fathers, and he heard our cry and saw our affliction, our toil and our oppression. He brought us out of Egypt with his strong hand and outstretched arm, with terrifying power, with signs and wonders. . .'" (Deut 26:5-8). At the same time, this remembrance inspires the right conduct toward strangers inhabiting the land: "You too must befriend the alien, for you were once aliens yourselves in the land of Egypt" (Deut 10:19). "You shall not oppress an alien; you well know how it feels to be an alien, since you were once aliens yourselves in the land of Egypt" (Exod 23:9).

It is truly a law of liberty that God has promulgated, whose application would change many things in the world. In any country, who are the citizens whose ancestors have not been immigrants into the land they occupy today and strangers in the land they fled? It has been a long time, perhaps, and we have forgotten. All the more reason to often repeat, "My father was a wandering Aramean . . . an alien."

God's commands are "tools for good works,"[7] revelations of the Lord, "words of eternal life."

> *Lord, you have the words of everlasting life.*
>
> The law of the LORD is perfect,
>   refreshing the soul;
> The decree of the LORD is trustworthy,
>   giving wisdom to the simple.
> The precepts of the LORD are right,
>   rejoicing the heart;
> The command of the LORD is clear,
>   enlightening the eye;
> The fear of the LORD is pure,
>   enduring forever;
> The ordinances of the LORD are true,
>   all of them just;
> They are more precious than gold,
>   than a heap of purest gold;
> Sweeter also than syrup
>   or honey from the comb.
> (Ps 19:8-11)

Folly and Weakness of God; Supreme Wisdom and Strength

All through sacred history, God shows himself to be disconcerting in his initiatives, as well as in his choice of bringing about his plans. His way of acting is so contrary to human wisdom and calculation that the temptation not to follow him on this path is sometimes great. This often happened, particularly when he asked his people to rely on him instead of trusting alliances with powerful people or the guarantees of a diplomacy that negotiates and accepts compromise. The prophets had tried hard to remind the people of what failures human wisdom and reckoning had met with in the past; still, the people returned to these means again and again. But why speak of the past? Today still—and it will probably always be the case—it remains very difficult to believe in the strength of weakness, in the wisdom that looks like folly. Only love allows us to understand in a small way God's conduct—his optimism, his propensity toward unbounded and ever renewed trust, his unceasing calls to freedom and not to constraint—and the secret of the efficacy of such means. For love is weakness and folly because it does not seek to impose any dominion and because it gratuitously offers itself. But it is an unalterable force because it can resist anything; and it is supreme wisdom because it alone understands everything. And God is love.

Love cannot be shown by reasoning; it is shown, period. It does not impose itself; it is received when we open ourselves and respond to its offer. It exposes itself—painfully—to refusal. Such is the love of God, who risked his Son for the salvation of the world. "We proclaim Christ crucified," Paul says simply (1 Cor 1:22-25).

In opposing weakness and strength, folly and wisdom, Paul does not question the validity of either the messianic expectation of Israel or the quest for meaning pursued by Greek philosophy. If those were devoid of value and grandeur, there would be no scandal of the cross. The strength-weakness and folly-wisdom of God belong to a level of absolute transcendence because God is the Totally Other. His power and his wisdom are revealed and work in and through weakness and folly because he has no need for the external means of strength and wisdom, he, the All-Powerful, Wisdom itself. The cross is paradoxical power and wisdom—folly and even scandal—because through it God realizes his design of salvation and justice, because in Jesus crucified he gives himself totally and personally while remaining totally himself.

Henceforth, it is impossible to domesticate God or Christ, to imprison them in the grip of human strength and wisdom. The cross is there, at the heart of all realities, in the Church, in apostleship; it is "stumbling block" and "foolishness" that only faith makes us recognize as "power" and "wisdom" to which the Spirit gives us access.

The Sign of the Temple Cleansed by Jesus
The four Gospels report that one day Jesus chased the merchants and money changers from the Temple.[8] John's Gospel sees in this a sign to be understood by faith, and it attests to the reflection of the early Church on this event. Therefore, it is important, especially during Lent, to read

this Gospel passage from the viewpoint and in the spirit of John when he wrote it down (John 2:13-25).

The reading of this text requires great attention, because it uses an ensemble of biblical data and themes: the Temple, its significance and its future; the Messiah; the salvation of Israel and the nations; the end times. But, through all this, the focus is on the person of Jesus and his mystery. The evangelist wanted us to remember this episode so that we might believe that Jesus is the Christ, the Son of God, and that by believing in him we might "have life in his name" (20:31).[9]

In the Bible, the Temple is the sign of God's presence amid his people, as well as of salvation in progress. It is from the Temple that the light and glory of the Lord shine forth, that the water giving life to all creation springs up (see Ezek 47:1-12). Destruction and reconstruction of the Temple are always connected with the dispersion and reunification of God's people, with the salvation of the nations that ascend to Sion in pilgrimage (see Isa 2:2-3; Mic 4:1-3).[10] The prayer of the psalms attests to this place and significance of the Temple in the religious vision of the people of the Bible.

> O God, the nations have come into your inheritance;
>   they have defiled your holy temple.
> (Ps 79:1)
>
> O God, we ponder your kindness
>   within your temple.
> (Ps 48:10)
>
> May we be filled with the good things of your house,
>   the holy things of your temple!
> (Ps 65:5)
>
> For your temple, in Jerusalem,
>   let the kings bring you gifts.
> (Ps 68:30)

Notwithstanding all of the above, the people were waiting for a new temple, expected to come down from heaven on the day when God would definitively reside among his people. This would happen with the coming of the Messiah, who would cleanse the Temple.

The veneration of the edifice of stone, center of worship, special place of the only true God, and symbol of his glory, thus opened onto wide spiritual horizons under the impulse of the prophets' preaching, particularly during the Exile. On foreign soil, the people had experienced God's presence, unconnected with a sacred enclosure: "Though I have removed

them far among the nations and scattered them over foreign countries—
and was for a while their only sanctuary in the countries to where they
had gone. . ." (Ezek 11:16). This experience of exile and prophetic
preaching fostered the rise of a temple spirituality that has continued to
develop to this day.

> Thus says the LORD: . . .
> What kind of house can you build for me;
>   what is to be my resting place?
> My hand made all these things
>   when all of them came to be. . . .
> (Isa 66:1-2)

These words are not meant to authorize any contempt for the buildings
in which the assembly gathers for the proclamation of the Word, prayer,
and praise of the Lord. But a word of caution is in order against formalism, against a conception and practice that would ignore the fact that
temples are signs. Finally, what is important is spiritual worship, worship "in Spirit and truth" (John 4:24).

The action of Jesus must be placed in this context. In some way, he
acts out a parable.[11] The disciples will understand this and understand
it today by remembering the prophet's prediction, "On that day there
shall no longer be any merchant in the house of the LORD of hosts" (Zech
14:21). "Zeal for your house consumes me" (Ps 69:10).[12]

But the Gospel does not stop here. It reports a mysterious word of Jesus
that will make sense only later on.

The Body of Christ, the True Temple

In driving out merchants and money changers, Jesus acts as a prophet
assured of his authority. Those who are the first witnesses of this vehement manifestation of zeal for God's house understand its significance.
We can sympathize with their reaction, "What sign can you show us for
doing this?" But it does not matter. What interests us is Jesus' answer,
"Destroy this temple and in three days I will raise it up." We must admit that this word in itself is quite enigmatic. If he is talking about "this
Temple" from which he has just expelled merchants and money changers,
Jesus only opens himself to mockery, "This temple has been under construction for forty-six years, and you will raise it up in three days?" In
effect, this is absurd. What does he mean? What is this irrefutable sign
of his authority? John hastens to explain, "But he was speaking of the
temple of his body." And immediately he adds that the disciples remem-

bered these words of Jesus and deciphered their meaning "when he was raised from the dead."

In fact, the verb "to get up again"—*egeirein* in Greek—is used to mean "to bring to life again" in the technical Christian vocabulary. But the significance of this word of Jesus is due not only to the use of a Greek word with two possible meanings.[13] John says that the disciples, remembering after the resurrection what Jesus had said, "came to believe in the scriptures and the word Jesus had spoken."

Today's Christians are even better off. They have at their disposal the writings of the New Testament and, in particular, John's Gospel. At the beginning, the evangelist wrote:

> And the Word became flesh
> and made his dwelling among us,
> and we saw his glory,
> the glory as of the Father's only Son,
> full of grace and truth.
> (John 1:14)

Jesus worked signs that manifested this glory: thus the raising of Lazarus (11:4-40). Finally, there is this quite explicit text in Revelation, "I saw no temple in the city [the heavenly Jerusalem], for its temple is the Lord God almighty and the Lamb" (Rev 21:22).[14]

The major sign, that which justifies what Jesus did and gives authority to his words, the sign that reveals him as Son of God, is his resurrection. But all signs, and in particular this one, demand a total commitment that the Lord can trust.

Signs and Faith

"While he was in Jerusalem for the feast of Passover, many began to believe in his name when they saw the signs he was doing. But Jesus would not trust himself to them because he knew them all, and did not need anyone to testify about human nature. He himself understood it well" (John 2:23-25).

Several times, John inserts in his Gospel a similar summary. "Jesus did this as the beginning of his signs in Cana in Galilee and so revealed his glory, and his disciples began to believe in him" (2:11). "After the two days, he left there for Galilee. . . . When he came into Galilee, the Galileans welcomed him, since they had seen all he had done in Jerusalem at the feast; for they themselves had gone to the feast" (4:43, 45). "Now many of the Jews who had come to Mary and seen what he had done began to believe in him. But some of them went to the Pharisees and told them what Jesus had done. So the chief priests and the Pharisees convened the Sanhedrin and said, 'What are we going to do? This man is performing many signs. If we leave him alone, all will believe in him, and the Romans will come and take away both our land and our nation' '' (11:45-48).

What is treated here is the subject of signs and the faith they produce in some people, while they provoke hostility in others. In the last two cases, they are further connected with the Passover: the one that Jesus had celebrated, the other that he is going to suffer because, precisely, his deeds arouse faith in too great a number of persons. Therefore, signs are intended to produce faith, but they do not force it. It is even possible that a first movement of acceptance be short-lived. But we must go to the end, to faith in Jesus himself, who is, by his death and resurrection, the ultimate sign toward which all other signs are directed.

As for Jesus, he has no need of signs to know what is in the human heart. He has direct knowledge of it, like God, "who fashioned the heart of each, / he who knows all their works" (Ps 33:15), who "knows the thoughts of men" (Ps 94:11).

Eyes on Christ, Wisdom of the Living God

There is a great risk for religion to drift toward a joyless conformism to moral precepts imposed by a redoubtable All-Powerful or based on the so-called "natural law," object of endless discussions and controversies. The commandments that God decrees at Sinai are the charter of a people freed from slavery. It is a covenant contract assured of unfailing faithfulness that the Lord proposes to his people, entreating them to become wholeheartedly attached to him.

Even when they turn away from him, God, in his mercy, does not abandon the humans whom he loves, going so far as to send his own Son to save the world, the Son who delivered himself to death. A crucified Messiah! This is scandal and folly in human eyes. And yet it is the supreme wisdom and strength of a God who is love. In his Son, dead and risen, he makes of believers, by the Holy Spirit, the temple where he resides.[15]

To believe is to recognize in Jesus the Wisdom of the living God and to walk in his footsteps, remembering both his words and the signs he worked.

God prepared for himself
a dwelling among humans,
he has set the stone
and lighted the fire.
Today,
he multiplies the bread
and joins our hands together:
now our hearts are but one.

God with us, God in us,
we are the body of Christ!

Here is the promised land
where the human assembly
knows the love of God.

Here is the festive space
where the human family
gives a face to God.

Here is the house of peace
where those who share
receive the gift of God.

Here is the open temple
where those who adore
become witnesses of God.[16]

Christ Raised on the Cross, Sign of God's Love

God: Slow to Anger, Rich in Mercy

Holy God cannot tolerate sin; he abhors it. He becomes indignant when he sees it committed, especially by those who have freely entered a covenant with him and whom he has surrounded with his kind and protective love. But he holds back his anger. Always ready to forgive at the first sign of repentance, he does not abandon those who turn away from him. On the contrary, without waiting or becoming weary, and never hesitating to take the first step, he sends them messengers to beg them to return. This has been so since the beginning, since original sin: the whole of sacred history attests to this faithfulness of God, of which certain striking events are exemplary illustrations. The exile to Babylon is among these, as well as the manner in which the trial ended. Therefore, it is not surprising that the authors of Chronicles evokes these facts in concluding their theological meditation on the checkered history of the faithfulness of Israel, to whom God never ceases to manifest his mercy (2 Chr 36:14-16, 19-23).[1]

These events are part of sacred history; therefore, we cannot show a lack of attention to them. Nevertheless, the truth is that today's readers are less interested in the material facts than in their religious significance. Biblical authors such as the authors of Chronicles already strove to disclose the theological interpretation of the reported facts. Thus, they opened the way to a reading of past events rich in teaching applicable to the present. This is why the Church still recalls the mercy of God, who has unceasingly renewed covenants with human beings, teaching them through the prophets "to hope for salvation."[2]

Repentance and Forgiveness, Objectives of Punishment

There is a logical connection between sin and punishment for sin. Who, indeed, would God be if he were to remain indifferent to the abominations committed against the commandments he has decreed, the charter of justice and liberty? What is to be said about a covenant that God would see broken without reacting? Crime, sacrilegious practices, profanations committed with impunity scandalize us.[3] However, there is a problem.

On the one hand, who can unquestionably declare that such and such a misfortune is a punishment for sin? Jesus, one day, reacted against this simplistic interpretation devoid of any nuance. The disciples were asking, "Who sinned, this man or his parents, that he was born blind?" Jesus answered, "Neither he nor his parents sinned; it is so that the works of God might be made visible through him" (John 9:2-3, Fourth Sunday of Lent—Year A). We must, therefore, guard against hasty judgments, especially in particular cases.[4]

The authors of Chronicles are certainly convinced that the Exile and the ruin of the Temple were God's punishments. But they refer to the preaching of the prophets—Jeremiah and Ezekiel in particular[5]—whom God, without waiting or becoming weary, sent to his people to warn them and urge them to conversion. Not only did they not want to listen to them, but they persecuted them.[6]

The authors also point out that the Exile and destruction of the Temple had no value or justification in themselves. Happening when "the anger of the LORD against his people was so inflamed that there was no remedy," the punishment, like the exhortations of the Lord's messengers, had for its goal the conversion and forgiveness of those who had done evil. And as we speak of a punishment imposed by God, the expected result was not uncertain. A king—Nebuchadnezzar—was the instrument of God's punishment (Jer 25:9). Another king—Cyrus—was the instrument of salvation. It is the Lord, the authors say, who inspired Cyrus to put an end to the Exile. This king of Persia even acknowledged, in his edict, that God had "charged [him] to build him a house in Jerusalem."

Although such a reading of history is foreign to us, and it is a delicate thing to do with discernment, nonetheless, this passage from Chronicles is no less stimulating today, especially during Lent. It quickens our faith and our hope in God, the Savior. It motivates our trustful and constant prayer. This prayer joins, in particular, the entreaties of those who are bent under the weight of injustice and oppression, the consequence of sin, but we shall keep ourselves from saying—or thinking—that this sin deserved this punishment.

Let my tongue be silenced, if I ever forget you!

By the streams of Babylon
  we sat and wept
  when we remembered Zion.
On the aspens of that land
  we hung up our harps,
Though there our captors asked of us
  the lyrics of our songs,
And our despoilers urged us to be joyous:
  "Sing for us the songs of Zion!"
How could we sing a song of the LORD
  in a foreign land?
If I forget you, Jerusalem,
  may my right hand be forgotten!
May my tongue cleave to my palate
  if I remember you not,
If I place not Jerusalem
  ahead of my joy.
(Ps 137:1-6)

Saved by Grace Because of Faith

God's mercy shows itself throughout sacred history. Punishment for sin itself is the expression of this mercy. When God resorts to it, it is because he has exhausted all other means apt to provoke conversion, and he acts always in view of being able to grant pardon. He hides himself so that he will be sought, patiently awaiting the moment when he will show himself again. This infinite mercy and love—without measure or end—God has shown to us in Christ Jesus (Eph 2:4-10).

Love of the Father, salvation through Christ: all prefaces to the Eucharistic Prayer express this outline. And it is with a prayer of thanksgiving according to the same model that Paul begins his Letter to the Ephesians.

> Blessed be the God and Father of our Lord Jesus Christ, who has blessed us in Christ with every spiritual blessing in the heavens, as he chose us in him, before the foundation of the world, to be holy and without blemish before him. In love he destined us for adoption to himself through Jesus Christ, in accord with the favor of his will, for the praise of the glory of his grace that he granted us in the beloved.

God, our Father, loves us so much that despite our unfaithfulness, he continually shows us new riches of his love and mercy. With Christ, this revelation reaches its summit. For "we were dead in our transgressions" and, through him, dead and risen for us, salvation has been given "by grace," by faith, without any act on our part to merit it. But we must say more. We were dead: God "brought us to life with Christ"; he created us anew "for the good works that God has prepared in advance, that we should live in them."

This way of "good works" is that of daily conduct, but also that of the Pasch of Christians following Christ. Even now we are risen with him, even now "our citizenship is in heaven" (Phil 3:20) where we reign with him. We can, with the Acts of the Apostles (1:1-6), distinguish the resurrection and the ascension of the Lord as two moments of his passover, but without forgetting that, in reality, there is one single paschal mystery, as Mark's and Luke's Gospels show (Mark 16:19; Luke 24:50-51).[7] Having passed from death to life at baptism, Christians, by dying to sin everyday, advance toward their full resurrection, they already live "in the heavens in Christ Jesus." The second phase of this paschal mystery will be realized as surely for them as for the Lord:

> I will give the victor the right to sit with me on my throne, as I myself first won the victory and sit with my Father on his throne. (Rev 3:21)

The Son of Man Lifted Up for the Salvation of Believers

Even outside its literary context—at the end of the conversation between Jesus and Nicodemus—the passage from John's Gospel read on this Sunday is of great spiritual and theological importance. Besides, several of its elements concur with and complete what the other two readings say (John 3:14-21).

"And just as Moses lifted up the serpent in the desert, so must the Son of Man be lifted up, so that everyone who believes in him may have eternal life." In John's Gospel, the lifting up of the Son of Man refers to Jesus on the cross.[8] The cross is thus seen as the supreme manifestation—the epiphany—of the glory of Christ because it marks the hour of the Lord's victory over evil, because at that moment the obedience of the Son, who receives the Spirit from his Father, shines forth (19:30).

The recalling of the bronze serpent raised up by Moses is meaningful. The Lord had sent venomous serpents to the Hebrews as punishment for sin. Those who had been bitten by them would not die if they looked upon the serpent on the pole (Num 21:6-9). Thereafter, to have life, we must raise our eyes to the crucified one (John 19:37) in order to obtain eternal life through him.

This "looking upon" is part of John's vocabulary of faith. And when he speaks of eternal life, it is an already present reality that he designates: "Whoever hears my word and believes in the one who sent me has eternal life and will not come to condemnation, but has passed from death to life'' (5:24); ''Whoever believes in the Son has eternal life'' (3:36; see 6:47); ''Whoever possesses the Son has life'' (1 John 5:12).

God's Love and Judgment

''God is love'' (1 John 4:16). He showed his love for us by sending his only Son into the world so that we might live through him (see 1 John 4:9). ''God did not send his Son into the world to condemn the world, but that the world might be saved through him.'' We could not say more strongly or clearly that the intent of God, when sending his Son, is exclusively salvation; that, as a consequence, judgment and eventual condemnation do not proceed from his initiative or action. These two propositions—affirmative, then negative—reinforce each other to express the same truth. But then how can we still speak of judgment? The mention of the bronze serpent helps us find the beginning of an answer. It was raised in order that those who looked upon it would recover. As a consequence, those who did not do this condemned themselves, in spite of the intervention of God and Moses, his servant. Likewise, Christ was given to the world by the Father and raised up on a cross. However, we have here only the beginning of an answer, an analogy.

Christ is the true Light that came into the world in order to enlighten everyone and, by making them children of God, to confer salvation on those who receive him. But it is up to each person to receive him, to come into his light rather than remain in the darkness (1:1-14). No one can escape this personal choice. The coming of the Son of God into the world, the decisive battle between light and darkness, obliges each one to take sides right now.

In fact, John's Gospel has the form of a suit against Jesus, one in which we must choose our side; it is impossible to remain neutral. Either we recognize in Jesus light, truth, and life, and we welcome salvation, or we refuse Christ by preferring darkness, evil deeds, death: in this case we find ourselves—voluntarily—judged.

The Path to God's Love Always Open

God created human beings free and, by entrusting the universe to them, offered them life in his friendship. Misled by the enemy, they broke this covenant, as we might call it, to which they had been parties. But God, for his part, did not go back on his word. He made the world so that all creatures might be filled with his blessings and might rejoice in his light.

> Even when he disobeyed you and lost your friendship
> you did not abandon him to the power of death,
> but helped all men to seek and find you.
> Again and again you offered a covenant to man,
> and through the prophets taught him to hope for salvation.[9]

The mission of those sent by God consisted especially in warning people that by leaving the way traced by God, they were running headlong to their ruin. But they spurned those words and mocked the prophets. There was no longer, then, any remedy: having chosen the wrong path in spite of God's repeated warnings, human beings knew unhappiness. God resolved to punish them to elicit repentance and conversion. In fact, during the years of the Exile, he continued to send them prophets; he patiently led them to come back to their senses, to reread the Law he had given them, to better understand its meaning and its importance, and even to discover that in a foreign land God remained present in the midst of his people, who were learning to render him a more spiritual worship since there was no longer any temple. Thus, the Exile proved to be the opportunity for a renewal of the covenant; and the time of punishment, a period of considerable purification and progress for the religion of the people, from whom God, rich in mercy, never withdrew his love.

Finally, it was his own Son that he sent into the world to be our Savior.

> In fulfillment of [God's will]
> he gave himself up to death;
> but by rising from the dead
> he destroyed death and restored life.[10]

Whoever looks up at the cross recognizes the great love with which God has loved us and the totally gratuitous nature of salvation. Whoever believes in Christ "lifted up" and stays on the road planned for us by God "will not be condemned."

> If hope has made you walk
> farther than fear,
> you will raise your eyes.
> Then you will be able to hold firm
> until you reach the sun of God.
>
> If anger caused you to clamor for justice for all,
> your heart will be wounded.
> Then you will be able to struggle
> along with the oppressed.

If weakness made you fall along the way,
you will know how to open your arms.
Then you will be able to dance
to the rhythm of forgiveness.

If destitution made you search in the hungry night,
you will have an open heart.
Then you will be able to give
the bread of poverty.

If suffering made you shed tears of blood,
you will have cleansed eyes.
Then you will be able to pray
with your brother on the cross.

If sadness has made you doubt
on one evening you felt abandoned,
you will know how to carry your cross.
Then you will be able to die
in step with the God-Man.[11]

Fifth Sunday of Lent—Year B

"Seeing" Jesus

A New Covenant

Christians readily speak of New Testament, the New Covenant. This latter expression is found only once in the part of the Bible we call the Old Testament, in the passage from the Book of Jeremiah read on this Sunday (Jer 31:31-34).

Afterwards, Ezekiel,[1] then the anonymous prophets of the Exile or the period immediately following,[2] spoke of an eternal covenant, probably from the perspective of this text from Jeremiah. Moreover, it is the longest quotation from the Old Testament found in the New: the Letter to the Hebrews quotes it in its entirety (8:8-11).

Paul considers himself a "minister of a new covenant" (2 Cor 3:6, 14).

Finally, every time the Eucharist is celebrated, we hear the words pronounced by Jesus himself at the Last Supper, as reported by Luke (22:20) and Paul (1 Cor 11:25) and summed up in the Eucharistic Prayer: "This is the cup of my blood, the blood of the new and everlasting covenant. . . ."

It is henceforth impossible for us to read apart from these perspectives the text from Jeremiah offered to us by the liturgy of the Fifth Sunday of Lent. What is more, we are seriously challenged by it to know what we are and what we must be as Christians.

"I Will Be Their God, They Shall Be My People"

"I their God; they my people." This formula vividly and strongly expresses the mutual relationship established by the covenant that the two partners commit themselves to live and develop. This definition is not new, it is true.

> You are all now standing before the LORD, your God—your chiefs and judges, your elders and officials, and all of the men of Israel, together with your wives and children and the aliens who live in your camp, down to those who hew wood and draw water for you—that you may enter into the covenant of the LORD, your God, which he concluded with you today under this sanction of a curse; so that he may now establish you as his people and he may be your God, as he promised you and as he swore to your

fathers Abraham, Isaac and Jacob. But it is not with you alone that I am making this covenant, under this sanction of a curse; it is just as much with those who are not here among us today as it is with those of us who are now here present before the LORD, our God.
(Deut 29:9-14)

We find this definition elsewhere in Jeremiah[3] and in the prophets that followed him.[4] This formulation has also been likened to that of marriage or adoption: "She is my wife and I am her husband from this day and forever"; "I am his father and he is my son."[5] In fact, Jeremiah, like Hosea, expresses the relationship between God and his people by using terms and images of betrothal and marriage (2:2; 3:1-3) or of the relationship between father and children (3:4; 31:20). "No longer will they have need to teach their friends and kinsmen how to know the LORD. All, from least to greatest, shall know me." "To know" means, first of all, to recognize who are the others, therefore, at the same time, to accept in principle and respect in fact the duties, the obligations resulting from the relationship one has with others, whether children, servants, or kindred. But "to know" also evokes the most intimate and total community of life and love.

The New Initiative of the God of the Covenant

Because he led them out of Egypt, God had rights over his people; but they broke the covenant of the Lord by shaking off their yoke and refusing the service they owed (2:20). Through his prophet, God gave numerous calls to conversion.

> Return, rebel Israel, says the LORD,
>   I will not remain angry with you;
> For I am merciful, says the LORD,
>   I will not continue my wrath forever.
> Only know your guilt (3:12-13).

Of course, there was, under Josiah, at the beginning of Jeremiah's ministry—in 622—the solemn renewal of the covenant when, after the "discovery" of the Book of the Law,[6] the entire people formally promised to observe it (2 Kgs 23:1-3). But these great professions of faithfulness had no more effect than the successive resolutions we make, though with a sincere heart. The result was a sort of legalism that could only disappoint God. Hosea, in his time, had already deplored the legalism and the superficial character of the conversions of Israel.

> Your piety is like a morning cloud
>   like the dew that early passes away.

For it is love that I desire, not sacrifice,
and knowledge of God rather than holocausts (6:4, 6).[7]

The human heart is complicated, even sick (see Jer 17:9). Otherwise, people would see the scandalous contradiction between their worship and their conduct outside the Temple. God becomes indignant over this, "How can you say, 'This is the temple of the LORD! the temple of the LORD! the temple of the LORD!' and continue with all your abominations?" (see Jer 7:4-10). Truly, it is the human heart that must be changed, and only God can work this transformation, "If you allow me, I will return, / for you are the LORD, my God" (Jer 31:18). This is what God does by taking the initiative of a new covenant.

The Law in the Heart in Times Past

The newness of this covenant consists in this: hereafter—"the days are coming"—God will lead his people by a law written upon everyone's heart, not on tablets of stone or in a book. This way of speaking is unusual because, ordinarily, it was said that God had "set [the Law] before" the people (Jer 9:12; Deut 4:8; 11:32; 1 Kgs 9:6; Jer 44:10). Now, he will cause the law to be intimately connected with everyone, to be within everyone's heart (see Ps 40:10). In a word, all will find themselves personally taught like the prophets.

This intimate union with God—"All . . . shall know me"—and with God's will has for a foundation and condition the remission of sins, "I will forgive their evildoing and remember their sin no more." The covenant at Sinai was connected to the deliverance from the bondage in Egypt. The new covenant will be written upon the heart—"a new heart"—if it is first freed from sin.

Create a clean heart in me, O God.

Have mercy on me, O God, in your goodness;
  in the greatness of you compassion wipe out my offense.
Thoroughly wash me from my guilt
  and of my sin cleanse me.
A clean heart create for me, O God,
  and a steadfast spirit renew within me.
Cast me not out from your presence,
  and your holy spirit take not from me.
Give me back the joy of your salvation,
  and a willing spirit sustain in me.
I will teach transgressors your ways,
  and sinners shall return to you.
(Ps 51:3-4, 12-15)

Dying Is Costly

Two sentences of an extraordinary density, rich on account of their paradoxes, make up the second reading of this Sunday preceding Passion (Palm) Sunday of Year B (Heb 5:7-9).

"In the days when he was in the flesh, [Christ] offered prayers and supplications with loud cries and tears to the one who was able to save him from death. . . ." Facing his death, Jesus did not behave as an impassive hero. The agony at Gethsemane attests both to his consciousness of his impending sacrifice and his resolute obedience to the Father.[8] But the brevity of the narrative, the way in which he rose and woke his apostles when the band coming to arrest him was nearing (Matt 26:46; Mark 14:42) could make us believe otherwise: what strength, what self-mastery!

The Letter to the Hebrews seems to say that the prospect of his death was painfully present to Jesus' mind, if not every day of his mortal life, at any rate often, and that it inspired his "prayers and supplications" to God. He offered them "with loud cries and tears." At Gethsemane, he said, "My Father, if it is possible, let this cup pass from me,"[9] immediately adding, "Yet, not as I will, but as you will" (Matt 26:39).[10] Here the author of Hebrews simply reminds us that God "was able to save him from death." But he adds, "He was heard because of his reverence." What did Jesus ask in his prayer that was granted him? Certainly not to escape death, because then he would not have been heard. Neither did he ask to rise again because he never doubted his Father, whom he always regarded as the God of the living, not the dead (see Mark 12:18-27). Did he not rather ask to be freed from anguish when faced with death?

Certainly, Jesus accepted to give himself up to death.[11] "This is why the Father loves me, because I lay down my life in order to take it up again. No one takes it from me, but I lay it down on my own. I have power to lay it down, and power to take it up again. This command I have received from my Father" (John 10:17-18). But this determination, this resolute and confident obedience, the assurance of being raised on the third day, did not render Jesus unfeeling. On the contrary, the perfect man that he was, endowed with a perfect sensibility, must have felt an unprecedented anguish before death—and death on a cross—before the horror waiting for that he did not evade. Is not the dread of what is to come more tormenting than the reality?

In fact, his prayer was heard. Luke suggests it, "And to strengthen him an angel from heaven appeared to him" (22:43). He showed a marvelous—divine—serenity on the cross. But the anguish was still there, "My God, my God, why have you forsaken me?" (Matt 27:46). But he died commending his spirit into the Father's hands. Everything was accomplished, was resolved in peace. Several witnesses were deeply impressed, "Truly, this was the Son of God" (Matt 27:54; Mark 15:39).

The Son's Costly Obedience, Cause of Eternal Salvation

"Son though he was, he learned obedience from what he suffered; and when he was made perfect, he became the source of eternal salvation for all who obey him." "Son though he was." In his quality of Son, he was fully in accord with the Father's will. But, in his humanity, he "learned" from experience what it costs to obey when obedience is crucifying, a word that, for him, was not just a way of speaking. This seems surprising since we have learned that Jesus did not know sin through having committed it. But is this the only and best way to really know the burden of sin?

> Only the blind of spirit believe that evil is known to those wretches alone who let themselves, little by little, be devoured by it, who at the end of their mournful labors have known only sin's precarious pleasures, its dull melancholy, its obscure and sterile rumination. Oh vain fall, oh cries never to be heard by the living, cold messengers of the shoreless night. If hell has no answer for the questioning dead, it is not because it refuses to answer (for rigorous, alas, in observance, is the imperishable fire), but it is because hell has nothing to say, will say nothing eternally.
>
> Only a certain purity, a certain simplicity, the divine ignorance of saints, catching evil off its guard, can penetrate its thickness, penetrate the thickness of immemorial deceit. To know man's truth one must, through a miracle of compassion, embrace his pain, and what does it matter whether one knows its impure source or not? "All I know about sin," the Saint of Ars would say, "I have learned from the lips of sinners." And what had he heard, the venerable and sublime child, among all those shameful confidences, all the inexhaustible babble, but the groan and death rattle of spent passion that in the end breaks the hardest hearts. And can any understanding of evil equal insight into pain? Is there anything that can go beyond pity?[12]

Obedience to God is an interior conformity to his will; it was perfect, unique, in Jesus, the Son of the Father. But this obedience is also a personal and concrete commitment to do what God's will requires; this is the test and the measure of obedience; Jesus "learned [it] from what he suffered." "Becoming obedient to death, / even death on a cross" (Phil 2:8), he is the perfect human and the cause of salvation for all those who follow him on the way opened by his teaching and obedience. To believe is to say "Yes"—Amen—to God through Jesus Christ our Savior.

The Request of Pagans Who Want to See Jesus

John presents the end of Jesus' ministry within the framework of a week that begins "six days before Passover," in the same way he had shown the beginning of Jesus' ministry within the framework of an inaugural week.[13] When we read the whole Gospel, we cannot fail to notice this literary structure, and we must then ask ourselves what the evangelist wants to convey by it. However, the deep and objective meaning of what Jesus did and said remains intact even outside the editorial context. This is the case for the Gospel passage of this Sunday (John 12:20-33).[14]

"Now there were some Greeks among those who had come up to worship at the feast. They came to Philip, who was from Bethsaida in Galilee, and asked him, 'Sir, we would like to see Jesus.' Philip went and told Andrew; then Andrew and Philip went and told Jesus." These Greeks are pagans belonging to the category of foreigners who were called "those who worship (or fear) God." Their faith and sympathy for Judaism fell short of full integration into the Jewish people by the rite of circumcision, by contrast with the "proselytes," who were also of pagan origin. They are the prototype of all others—pagans "fearing God," "proselytes" or not—who later on will be eager to hear the gospel and actively disposed to accept it.[15]

These Greeks want to "see" Jesus. If they simply wanted to catch a glimpse of him, they could easily have satisfied their desire; Jesus does not hide himself. The reader of John's Gospel knows that the verb "to see" is often used in a quasi-technical sense and then means "to believe."[16] The perfect model of the believer is the disciple who, having entered the empty tomb on Easter day, "saw and believed" (John 20:8). Therefore, the request of these God-fearing persons is one of faith.

That they address themselves to Philip, who is from Bethsaida, can be explained by the fact that this companion of Jesus speaks Greek. "Philip went and told Andrew; then Andrew and Philip went and told Jesus." These details give us food for thought. Since they are God-fearing, these Greeks have gone beyond the boundaries of paganism, thanks to their discovery of Judaism. They have certainly heard of Jesus; perhaps they have witnessed his triumphal entry into Jerusalem. Therefore, it is not surprising that they want to go farther. Does not their asking Philip to see Jesus suggest that access to faith is gradual? In any event, it is a theologically founded fact. Even in the case of sudden illumination, personal though it may be, the adherence to God and Christ by faith takes place within a people, within the Church, and through their mediation. To see Jesus, one must be led to him by an apostle. The testimony of those who lived at his side shows him to us and we cannot do without it. Hence, the necessity of apostolic writings, especially the Gospels, transmitted by tradition, of which parents, teachers, catechists, preachers, and other believers are, for each one, the close witnesses, the immediate bearers.

The Pagans' Access to Faith and the "Hour" of Jesus

Rather curiously, the story of the Greeks' coming to see Jesus stops short: nothing is said either of how Jesus received their request, transmitted by Philip and Andrew, or of what became of these God-fearers. This is not the first instance of such an abrupt end. In the narrative of the encounter between Jesus and Nicodemus, we first have a dialogue (see John 3:1-10). Then Nicodemus disappears. The evangelist next reports a teaching of Jesus in the form of a monologue that could have taken place without Nicodemus' presence (see 3:11-21). Therefore, there is no reason to ask questions or to imagine what the evangelist did not deem worth saying. The paths of faith are open to pagans, as proved by the Greeks who want to see Jesus. This is the fact. What follows is the explanation, the commentary placed in the mouth of Jesus himself.

The pagans' access to faith is connected to the "hour" of Jesus and reveals that it has come. This hour, mentioned several times in the Fourth Gospel,[17] toward which we walk from the beginning (see John 2:4), which Jesus never loses sight of, is that of the glorification of the "Son of Man."[18] It is the hour of his passover—passion, death, resurrection, ascension— for which Jesus came, for which he longs, though fearing it (see John 12:13, 27); the hour when he will draw all human beings to himself (see John 12:32).

Then, at that hour, everyone will be able to see Jesus lifted up on the cross and, looking at him, obtain eternal salvation.

The Grain of Wheat Fallen to Earth

Then comes a little parable whose terms and themes are familiar to readers of the Gospels.[19] The general meaning of this parable is clear. The grain of wheat designates Jesus, who by his death becomes the standing tree from which everyone can receive the fruit of life. What an extraordinary abundance! Through the death of one is gained the salvation of an innumerable multitude. We spontaneously, and rightly, think of the parables of the sower and the seed[20] and the mustard seed.[21] A text from the Book of Daniel also comes to mind. It speaks of a tree that Nebuchadnezzar saw in a dream. According to Daniel's interpretation, it signifies that the king's "rule extends over the whole earth" (4:19). This same image can be taken to mean the tree of the cross on which the Lord was lifted up and which gives fruit in abundance to feed all people. "I saw a tree of great height at the center of the world. It was large and strong, with its top touching the heavens, and it could be seen to the ends of the earth. Its leaves were beautiful and its fruit abundant, providing food for all. Under it the wild beasts found shade, in its branches the birds of the air nested; all men ate of it" (Dan 4:7-9). It is from the height of the cross planted in the center of the earth that Christ draws all people to himself. It is at this hour that he becomes the king of the universe.

In order to share in the glorification of Christ, to be where he is, disciples must follow Jesus by showing a determination similar to his, must go to the point of losing their lives, must detach themselves from their lives "in this world" to "preserve [them] for eternal life." The four evangelists have kept the memory of what Jesus says here and have recorded this sentence in almost identical terms.[22] It is impossible to erase this saying, to announce Jesus' hour without echoing it.

"I Am Troubled . . . Father, Glorify Your Name"

John's Gospel shows Jesus always and everywhere active throughout his passion: he stands upright and resolutely, freely walks toward his hour; he peacefully commends his spirit to God, without a cry, after having said, "It is finished" (19:30). But this peace and serenity have nothing in common with insensibility. At Lazarus' grave, Jesus could not hide that he was "perturbed and deeply troubled" (11:33).[23] How could he not have been more perturbed and more deeply troubled at the moment of facing his own death? John was with the other apostles in Gethsemane and even in the group of three that Jesus chose to be nearest to him when he was praying in the garden (see Matt 26:37). It is the memory of this agony that is evoked here, in another context and with a different presentation.[24] Although "troubled," Jesus does not hesitate. He does not ask his Father to deliver him from this hour, since it is for this hour that he has come. He simply says, "Father, glorify your name." A full, complete, and active adherence to the will of him who sent him, Jesus' prayer shows his clear perception of the mystery. His passion glorifies the Father because it forcefully reveals the power of his love that saves the whole of humankind.

The Glorification of the Father—Yesterday, Today, Tomorrow

"Then a voice came from heaven, 'I have glorified it and will glorify it again.' " It is not for Jesus but for us that this voice, never stilled, is heard. Every word of God, pronounced once for all, remains forever.

God has already glorified his name: the signs worked by Jesus have shown it—from the first, that of the water changed into wine at Cana (2:1-11), up to the last, the raising of Lazarus (11:1-44). The narratives of these two signs, which flank all the others, explicitly mention Jesus' hour (see 2:4) and the manifestation of the glory of God, by which the Son must be glorified (see 2:11; 11:4). For John, the cross is the transfiguration of Jesus: the voice from heaven is heard on the eve of the passion.

The Father will be glorified in his Son at the hour of the passover of death and resurrection (see 17:4-5, 17-24). This glory will also burst forth through the works accomplished by the disciples (see Acts 4:21) and in the conversion of pagans (see Acts 11:18).

Decisive Importance of the Hour

" 'Now is the time of judgment on this world; now the ruler of this world will be driven out. And when I am lifted up from the earth, I will draw everyone to myself.' He said this indicating the kind of death he would die."

These few lines are packed with meaning. Many teachings on the mystery of the Lord's passover and many topics for concrete reflections on choices that cannot be evaded are contained in them. The verbs used are a first indication of this richness of meaning: "to judge," "to lift up," "to draw," "to indicate," as well as the emphatic repetition of "now."

To say that the judgment of the world is already taking place in the present means two things. On the one hand Satan, "the ruler of this world," leader of all those who do evil and oppose God, is definitively conquered and "driven out," condemned, expelled into darkness. On the other hand, at the hour of Jesus, a boundary line is established between those who stand on the side of the Lord and the others.[25] Lifted up on the cross, Jesus draws all human beings to himself—his two arms are open—but all do not allow themselves to be drawn.[26]

New Covenant, Eternal Covenant

"I will place my law within them, and write it upon their hearts." With these words, God announces and promises a new covenant that will not be subject to the fluctuations of the human will. How shall this be? Where will God find these persons who, in full freedom, will bind themselves to him in faith? What initiative is he going to take to turn into reality this immense hope raised by his promise?

These questions find their answers in Jesus, his Son, sent into the world. He has conformed himself to the Father's will with all the fibers of his human heart, learning and showing to what point obedience to God can and must go. By dying on the cross, he has driven out the ruler of this world who since the beginning has been striving to prevent human beings from living in harmony with God, themselves, and their brothers and sisters.

Grain of wheat fallen into the earth, he has risen, tree of life laden with fruit. Lifted up on the cross, he is forever the sign and source of salvation for all those who look to him with faith and follow him into the glory God reserves for them. He is the head of the people of the new and eternal covenant in his blood poured out for all as atonement for the sins of all.

> The grain of wheat falling to the ground,
> it will sprout, hidden in the furrow;
> the grain of wheat falling to the ground,
> vital force, promise of harvests.
>
> The grain of wheat, its dying hour has come:
> if it does not die, the grain remains alone;
> the grain of wheat, its dying hour has come:
> if it dies, the grain will bear fruit.
>
> Lord Jesus, your death is a baptism;
> streams of life well up from your cross;
> Lord Jesus, your death is a baptism
> and your Spirit transfigures us into you.[27]

Third Sunday of Lent—Year C

Today, If You Hear His Voice

Faithful to His Promise, God Guides History

The scene reported in the passage from the Book of Exodus read on this Sunday is among the most famous in the Bible. It tells of an important phase in salvation history, Moses' call, to which the revelation of the divine name was associated in the definitive redaction of the book.[1] As it is found in the Lectionary, the text emphasizes this revelation by placing it within the continuum of earlier revelations (Exod 3:1-8a, 13-15).[2]

Born in Egypt, raised by Pharaoh's daughter, Moses had received a well-rounded education and did not share the conditions of his Hebrew brothers and sisters, subjected to heavy labors. But in his heart, he had remained one of them and did not hesitate to kill an Egyptian who mistreated a Hebrew. As word of this spread, he was forced to flee and take refuge "in the land of Midian" (Exod 2:15), where he resumed the nomadic existence of his ancestors and renewed contact with the traditions of the patriarchs.[3] While he was leading the flock of his father-in-law across the desert, Moses received the gift of a theophany: "He came to Horeb, the mountain of God.[4] There an angel of the LORD[5] appeared to him in fire flaming out of a bush. . . . The bush, though on fire, was not consumed."[6]

"This remarkable sight"—a bush on fire yet not consumed—aroused Moses' curiosity and can still capture our imagination. But the Bible does not describe a theophany for its own sake. What counts, what we must remember, is the word that is pronounced.

He "who dwells in the bush" (Deut 33:16) styles himself "the God of Abraham, the God of Isaac, the God of Jacob." This is no mere way of speaking. At the time of his appearance at Shechem, God had said to Abraham, "To your descendants I will give this land" (Gen 12:7). Later on, during a night vision, God told him: "Know for certain that your descendants shall be aliens in a land not their own, where they shall be enslaved and oppressed for four hundred years. But I will bring judgment on the nation they must serve, and in the end they will depart with great wealth" (Gen 15:13-14).

162

Isaac, too, had a vision during a time of famine: "Do not go down to Egypt, but continue to camp wherever in this land I tell you. Stay in this land, and I will be with you and bless you; for to you and your descendants I will give all these lands, in fulfillment of the oath that I swore to your father Abraham" (Gen 26:2-3).

During his famous dream in which he saw "a stairway [resting] on the ground, with its top reaching to the heavens," Jacob heard the Lord say to him, "I, the LORD, am the God of your forefather Abraham and the God of Isaac; the land on which you are lying I will give to you and your descendants" (Gen 28:13). Then in another night vision in Beer-sheba, God said: "I am God, the God of your father. Do not be afraid to go down to Egypt, for there I will make you a great nation" (Gen 46:3).

Now, God is saying to Moses: "I am the God of your father . . . the God of Abraham, the God of Isaac, the God of Jacob. . . . Come, now! I will send you to Pharaoh to lead my people, the Israelites, out of Egypt."

We notice these endless moves from country to country, which political or economic events coerced the patriarchs and their clans to undertake, a complex and circuitous story of the origins and formation of a people. But through it all, we notice the continuity of the masterly plan of God, which he reveals to Abraham, Isaac, Jacob, and Moses. Nothing is able to hold in check the promise of the God of history.

He Is Called "I Am"

"God replied [to Moses], 'I am who am.' Then he added, 'This is what you shall tell the Israelites: I AM sent me to you. . . . the LORD . . . God. . . . This is my name forever. . . .'"

Whatever may be the importance of this solemn and explicit revelation of the divine name, must we conclude from it that the divine name was totally unknown up till then and that Moses had no knowledge of God's identity? One thing is certain: the Bible has kept for us the witness of traditions, according to which God had been invoked from the beginning under the name of Yahweh (see Gen 4:26),[7] which was then used throughout the history of the patriarchs.[8] It is a question for exegetes and other specialists; it concerns the use of the diverse traditions found in the Pentateuch.[9] By contrast, the narrative of the revelation of the divine name to Moses concerns, even today, all believers: What do they say when they name God?[10]

The expression here translated by "I am who am" is not clear. Sometimes it is understood as a refusal on the part of God, who would judge

Moses' question—and ours—improper and, as a consequence, would register his objection by saying "I am who I am."[11] Such a refusal would deprive us of the possibility of invoking God under a name that we could not know unless he revealed it. Furthermore, this answer fits poorly with what follows; for God speaks twice again, and what he says expresses the meaning of the name Yahweh by again using the verb "to be."

Sometimes the translation "I am who I shall be"[12] has been proposed, which comes down to saying, "Who am I? You will see—you will learn to know me—by what I shall do."[13] It is true, in fact, that God reveals himself gradually as salvation history unfolds. Faithful, merciful, and finally Father of our Lord Jesus Christ, who sends his Spirit. But we cannot be content with this interpretation, although it is pertinent and deserves to be remembered.

By saying, "I am who am," the Lord sets himself over against the so-called gods who are not (see Isa 43:10). Therefore, he can name himself "I am" in the absolute sense, that is, "Yahweh"[14] or "the Lord." Henceforth, we shall speak of him by saying "He is."[15] To invoke him is to remember the marvels he has worked for his people by delivering them from slavery and, at the same time, it is to ask him with confidence to renew these marvelous deeds for us today. This is why he says, "This is my name forever; / this is my title for all generations."

Such is God: the All-Other, the All-Powerful, who possesses being to the point of being designated by it—I AM is his name. Hence, the steadfastness of his attributes—faithfulness, tenderness, justice, love—which we use to invoke him.

The Lord is kind and merciful.

Bless the LORD, O my soul;
  and all my being, bless his holy name.
Bless the LORD, O my soul,
  and forget not all his benefits;
He pardons all your iniquities,
  he heals all your ills.
He redeems your life from destruction,
  he crowns you with kindness and compassion. . . .
The LORD secures justice
  and the rights of all the oppressed.
He has made known his ways to Moses,
  and his deeds to the children of Israel.
Merciful and gracious is the LORD,
  slow to anger and abounding in kindness.

For as the heavens are high above the earth,
    so surpassing is his kindness toward those who fear him.
(Ps 103:1-4, 6-8, 11)

Let Those Who Believe Themselves Strong Beware of Falling

The Lenten liturgy commemorates with particular insistence the main steps of salvation history, especially that of the Exodus. This recalling is not meant simply to place before the assembled Christians some memorable facts of the past enshrined in the Bible. Neither is it meant to evoke earlier experiences in order to buttress or illustrate a moral discourse. The steps of salvation history selected by the liturgy are, above all, revelations of God's actions and initiatives, of the way in which the faithfulness of him who names himself "I Am" pursues his saving plan and fulfills it, of his patience, of his mercy. They convey to us the calls that God unceasingly addresses to his people. They project their light on Christ and his mission, on the Church, God's people walking toward the Jerusalem on high. Salvation history unfolds without interruption. The faithful of every age must enter into it by making a response to God's call, basically a similar commitment made throughout the centuries, and by not stumbling upon obstacles that in one way or another seem to be similar throughout history. The case of the Exodus is particularly representative, as Paul says (1 Cor 10:1-6, 10-12).

Paul considers two elements: the cloud and food and drink. At the crossing of the Red Sea, this cloud that preceded the people moved to their rear in order to protect the Hebrews from Pharaoh's army (see Exod 14:19-20). And during the journey through the desert, the whole people benefited from the gift of the manna and the water that Moses caused to gush forth from the rock (see Exod 16).

All, Paul says, "were baptized . . . in the cloud," when it moved, "and in the sea," when they crossed it. Indeed, by passing in this manner through the cloud and the sea, the Hebrews escaped their slavery, and God then made them into a new people. Now baptism is "illumination" and "immersion" in water, from which one emerges free from sin. When one thinks of it, the appropriateness of the analogy is inescapable.[16]

The Old Testament already regarded the manna and the water in the desert as gifts of God sent from heaven (Neh 9:15). The manna was celebrated as a wonderful food.

> . . . You nourished your people
>   with food of angels

and furnished them bread from heaven,
  ready to hand, untoiled for,
endowed with all delights and conforming
  to every taste. . . .
blended to whatever each one wished.
(Wis 16:20-21)[17]

Jesus himself compared the manna to the other heavenly bread, the "true" bread that gives life to the world. He proclaimed: "I am the living bread that came down from heaven; whoever eats this bread will live forever; and the bread that I will give is my flesh for the life of the world. . . . Whoever eats my flesh and drinks my blood has eternal life. . . . This is the bread that came down from heaven. Unlike your ancestors who ate and still died, whoever eats this bread will live forever" (John 6: 51, 54, 58). The Church recognizes in the body and blood of Christ the food and drink on the way of her own journey through the desert.

What is more surprising to us is the affirmation that the rock from which the Hebrews drank water "was the Christ." But in the rabbinical literature with which Paul was familiar, this rock of the desert had become a rock unlike any other; it accompanied the people on their march, with them climbed the mountains and descended into the valleys, stood in front of the door of the meeting tent, and was constantly available to furnish the necessary water.[18] Moreover, as his point of departure, Paul always focuses upon Christ and his own Christian experience to find prefigurations in the signs and events of the past.[19] For all through salvation history God had as his focus Christ, in whom and through whom he acted.

Having said this, Paul concludes: the drama of the past must not be repeated; all these graces and interventions of God must not be fruitless. This is all the more serious today because we are nearer to the end times. Let us faithfully walk behind Christ, victorious over all temptations. Let us be confident, but not presumptuous. Let us rely on the Lord and not on our own strength. What would be the use of having been baptized, of receiving the spiritual food, if, walking at a snail's pace, we were to stumble on the obstacles of the way?

The Urgency of Conversion and God's Patience

We sometimes catch ourselves dreaming of immanent justice . . . for others, being scandalized not to see certain crimes immediately punished by God, interpreting as divine chastisement the misfortunes of certain persons, calling God to account when we ourselves are afflicted by trials we deem undeserved and, finally, looking for those responsible for the catastrophes we have endured. It is true that evil begets evil, but the dominion of sin is too general for us to attribute responsibility only to certain persons, as if others—including ourselves—had no part in it. And above all, we must not forget that God is never in any way the author of misfortune; he offers only life; he does only good. To keep this in mind does not imply a certain fatalism that resigns itself to the absurdity of the world and humankind, whose endless whims create a continual threat for the peace, harmony, and security of the earth and its inhabitants. Neither should we give up seeking the causes of misfortunes while despairing of finding any means to prevent them (Luke 13:1-9).

Some Galileans were massacred by Herod. Why and under what circumstances? For us it matters little. Eighteen persons were killed by a falling tower. Were these victims more culpable than other people? That is not the question, Jesus answers, and, by the same token, categorically refuses any pretension to blame God—his justice or his carelessness or his powerlessness—for any catastrophe whatever. If we speak of sin, it is to recognize that we are all sinners. We must apply ourselves to our own conversion. For sin is the great misfortune, irremediable if we do not turn away from it.

"Repent!" Continuing what the prophets and John the Baptist had said, Jesus voices an urgent appeal with a new authority. It is also the call of the Church at all times, and with renewed force during Lent.

God is patient; he cannot bring himself to cut down the barren tree, cannot stop hoping that it might show signs of bearing fruit after receiving special care. It is God's patience that grants a delay to give the sinner a last chance to be converted and bear fruit. It is God's patience that, far from justifying negligence, must make the sinner conscious of the urgency of conversion. God does not tire, does not lose patience . . . ever. For "it may bear fruit in the future." But he is powerless before those who refuse to yield to the unceasing calls of his kind solicitude and grace.

Who Then Is God?

The more we enter the mystery of God by the light of revelation, the more its height, breadth, and unfathomable depth appear (see Eph 3:18). He told his name to Moses: I AM. We, too, use the verb "to be" to identify ourselves, but never alone in the absolute sense; we must always have it followed by something that will complete it. We are conscious of being able to say "I" when speaking of ourselves in the past and in the present, while envisioning our future. But there are many changes in us and in the past we evoke. There is great fragility in our present, in this "I" unable to withdraw by itself from the many slaveries that hold it captive. As to the future, we can say nothing about it with any assurance. I am always I, and yet I constantly change. I am subject to unceasing fluctuations in all the domains of this "I"; it even happens that I doubt, that I do not recognize myself in who I was yesterday or in who I am today. When I hear God say, "I AM," I grasp something of the meaning of the name, but I must add that he is not in the same way as I am. Hence the dizziness caused by "negative" theology, which recognizes God as the All-Other.

> Tell them
> what the wind says to the rocks,
> what the sea says to the mountains.
> Tell them
> that an immense goodness
> suffuses the universe.
>
> Tell them
> that God is not what they believe,
> that he is a wine one drinks,
> a shared banquet
> at which all give and receive.
>
> Tell them
> that he is a flute player
> in the midday light;
> he comes near then flees
> leaping toward the springs.
>
> Tell them
> that only his voice
> could teach you your name.
>
> Tell them
> his face is full of innocence
> his tranquility and his laughter.
> Tell them
> that he is your space and your night,
> your wound and your joy.
>
> But tell them too
> that he is not what you say
> and that you know
> nothing of him.[20]

But God has not only said his name, which illuminates his mystery while veiling it from our eyes, incapable of bearing his light; he has also revealed himself by what he did and what he never ceases to do. He shows himself—as our experience verifies—faithful and reliable, slow to anger and full of mercy, patient and always ready to trust, to trust again. We have here a beginning of the unending litany of God's attributes, of the visible manifestations of what he is.

Throughout history, God has manifested himself in order to reveal to human beings the way of salvation and, when they have strayed, to urge them to return to this way of life.

Far from ever despairing of humankind, God sent his own Son to preach conversion one last time and to pour out into the world the Spirit, source of all fruitfulness.

This Son, who had a human name, spoke like God, saying like him, "I AM": the Bread of life, come down from heaven (John 6:35, 41, 48, 51), the Light of the world (8:12), the Door (10:9), the Good Shepherd (10:11-14), the Resurrection (11:25), the Way, the Truth, the Life (14:6). And even, "If you do not believe that I AM, you will die in your sins"; "When you lift up the Son of Man, then you will realize that I AM"; "Amen, amen, I say to you, before Abraham came to be, I AM" (8:24, 28, 58).

This is why, and in what sense, we call him THE LORD.

> God, beyond all that is created,
> we could only call you
> the Unknowable.
> Blessed are you for the other voice
> that knows your Name,
> that comes from you,
> and gives to our humanity
> the power to render thanks.
>
> You, whom no one has seen,
> we see you sharing
> our sufferings.
> Blessed are you for having shown
> on the beloved face
> of Christ offered to our eyes,
> your immense glory!
>
> You, whom no one has heard,
> we are listening to you, word hidden
> in the place where we are.
> Blessed are you for having sown

in the universe destined for holiness
words that speak today
and fashion us!

You, whom no one has touched,
we caught you:
the Tree is standing ready
deep in the earth!
Blessed are you for having placed
in the hands of the smallest ones
this Body where nothing can hide
your fatherly heart![21]

Fourth Sunday of Lent—Year C

God Invites Us to the Feast of His Forgiveness

Manna in the Desert and Passover in the Promised Land

The crossing of the Jordan at the end of the years of wandering through the desert and the entrance into the Promised Land mark an important date in the history of God's people; they are also events forever written in holy history. The first reading of this Sunday recalls these events very briefly, but in a way that helps us to understand them (Josh 5:10-12).[1]

The entrance into the Promised Land puts an end to the wanderings in the desert and inaugurates the settling of God's people: the manna no longer falls; the people eat the fruits of the earth. It is also the fulfillment of the promise first made to Abraham,[2] and often renewed afterwards,[3] of a land on which to settle. All this proves the faithfulness of God and the constancy with which he efficiently pursues his plans.

But we will particularly note the liturgical character given to the reported events. The crossing of the Jordan resembles a procession. The ark proceeds first, carried by twelve men, one for each tribe. When the priests set foot in the waters of the Jordan, the marvel of the Red Sea is repeated and the people cross dry-shod. Twelve stones are set up as a memorial. Then the rite of circumcision follows. After the men are recovered, Passover is celebrated in the evening as on the night the people left Egypt (Josh 3:1–5:12).

On the day after "they ate of the produce of the land" and in that year "they ate the yield of the land of Canaan."

For Christians, this text has sacramental and singularly Eucharistic connotations. The passage through baptismal waters has led them to the bank of the Promised Land. The Eucharist gives them a pledge of eternal life, "I am the bread of life. Your ancestors ate the manna in the desert, but they died. . . . Whoever eats this bread will live forever" (John 6:48-49, 51). New Moses, Christ is also the new Joshua,[4] who opens to his disciples access to the kingdom. Every Eucharist is a stop during which we celebrate the Passover by recalling with thanksgiving the marvels of God.

171

Taste and see the goodness of the Lord.

I will bless the LORD at all times;
  his praise shall be ever in my mouth.
Let my soul glory in the LORD;
  the lowly will hear me and be glad.
Glorify the LORD with me,
  let us together extol his name.
I sought the LORD, and he answered me
  and delivered me from all my fears.
Look to him that you may be radiant with joy,
  and your faces may not blush with shame.
When the afflicted man called out, the LORD heard,
  and from all his distress he saved him.
(Ps 34:1-7)

A New Creature in a New World

All images—the crossings of the Red Sea and the Jordan, the entrance into the Promised Land, the manna—are only weak illustrations of the reality of God's work accomplished by Christ and the resulting situation for believers; Paul describes them both in vigorous terms (2 Cor 5:17-21).

"So whoever is in Christ is a new creation: the old things have passed away; behold, new things have come." We have to repeat several times these very simple expressions so that their force may be progressively revealed. "New creation . . . new things. . . ." Little by little, thanks to the light of scriptural reminiscences, their richness and depth appear, along with their very concrete meanings.

The Book of Isaiah contains these words of the Lord, "See, I am doing something new" (43:19).

Lo, I am about to create new heavens
  and a new earth;
The things of the past shall not be remembered
  or come to mind (65:7).

These promises concerned the immediate future: the end of the Exile, an exodus more marvelous than the first one. But the oracle also had in view a more remote future: it announced God's intervention in messianic times and, still beyond, the new universe which will be established at the end of time, and which was contemplated by John in his vision written in the Book of Revelation: "Then I saw a new heaven and a new earth" (21:1). But the process is already begun, "behold, new things have come" at the center of which humankind is placed as "a new creation." Indeed, the redemption worked by Christ, in whom "were created all things in / heaven and on earth" (Col 1:16), is a restoration of the whole universe.[5] Whoever believes in Christ is born again, is saved "through the bath of rebirth / and [renewed] by the Holy Spirit" (Titus 3:5), and becomes a "new person" (Eph 2:15; Rom 6:4).[6] What is spoken of here is a reshaping of the whole being and not a mere moral and spiritual renewal: "new world," "new creation."

To be sure, a decisive step in salvation history has been taken. The world and humankind are henceforth on a definitive level and in a definitive state. There will be no other beginning, no other "creation." The destiny—the "end"—is now rightly and definitively reoriented.

God Has Reconciled Us to Himself in Christ

"And all this is from God, who has reconciled us to himself through Christ . . . God was reconciling the world to himself in Christ. . . ."

"To reconcile" means "to restore to friendship or harmony." The Greek verb used by Paul has a more dynamic meaning: to change, to move from one state to another.[7] This reconciliation establishes with God—and at the same time with others—new relationships as we pass from a state of hostility to one of friendship: "Indeed, if, while we were enemies, we were reconciled to God through the death of his Son, how much more, once reconciled, will we be saved by his life" (Rom 5:10). Therefore, salvation is, at it were, the normal sequel of this change of situation, of state.

The gospel is the good news of this reconciliation acquired by Christ and in him offered to all. The apostles are the preachers of this good news. They exercise the ministry of reconciliation. Ambassadors of Christ, they address to all this urgent appeal: "In the name of Christ, allow yourselves to be reconciled to God."

The Sinless Christ Identified with Sin

"For our sake he made him to be sin who did not know sin, so that we might become the righteousness of God in Him." What striking contrasts! Christ, we know, was "holy, innocent, undefiled" (Heb 7:26). No one could ever charge him with sin (see John 8:46).[8] So how can Paul say that God "made him to be sin"?[9] How are we to understand such a paradox bordering on contradiction in its very terms, and so shocking? Undoubtedly, we must first remember that God willed that his Son—who freely accepted this mission—be in full solidarity with sinful humanity and in full subjection—inasmuch as possible—to the consequences of sin: pain, contempt, death. The reality of the incarnation goes so far as to identify

Christ with sin. But Paul does not say that this identification makes Christ a sinner.

Being in solidarity with sinful humanity, Christ was able to make it share in his obedience, his righteousness (see Rom 5:11) manifested by his death on the cross of evildoers: "This man was innocent beyond doubt" (Luke 23:47).

For our part, we become "the righteousness of God in him." This does not mean that we are transformed into "the righteousness of God," but that we receive its effects in the measure of our capabilities, of our openness to this gift. For if Christ has erased for all people the debt of their sins, they do not remain any less debtors to whom the debt has been remitted—forgiven debtors. There is a similarity between Christ's identification with the sin he has not committed and our freely bestowed identification with "the righteousness of God."[10]

Sharing the Joy of the Father Who Finds His Son Again

Through Christ, sinful human beings have "become the righteousness of God." By his words, his acts, his attitude toward them, Jesus concretely showed how God welcomes them. He does not remain aloof and distant when waiting for their return, urged on them by the prophets he sent: he goes to meet them. And when he finds those who had wandered far away from him, he rejoices and invites his own to share in his joy. Luke—who has been called the evangelist of God's mercy and joy—has grouped three parables of Jesus that emphasize this joy of God.[11] We read the third of these on this Sunday of Lent (Luke 15:1-3, 11-32).

Rightly so, the Lectionary takes up the two verses that open chapter 15 of Luke's Gospel: "The tax collectors and sinners were all drawing near to listen to him, but the Pharisees and scribes began to complain, saying, 'This man welcomes sinners and eats with them.' " This sentence has not only a literary and redactional interest.[12] It tells us to whom Jesus addresses these three parables, and why. We must therefore read and hear them with this "declaration of intent" in mind: the three parables respond to the recriminations formulated by some concerning Jesus' conduct. The answer to these bitter and accusatory complaints is found in an identical way in the first two parables: "Rejoice with me because I have found" what I had lost.

The same invitation resounds, only more developed, more urgent, in this Sunday's parable. We no longer are dealing with some man who finds his lost sheep or some woman who finds her lost coin. The parable dramatizes the story of a father who finds his younger son again. Then, immediately, everything else comes to a stop and he organizes a feast: "But his father ordered his servants, 'Quickly bring the finest robe and put it on him; put a ring on his finger and sandals on his feet. Take the fattened calf and slaughter it. Then let us celebrate with a feast. . . .'" They begin to celebrate without even waiting for the older son, still out in the fields. Surely he will not delay for long; he can then join in the rejoicing, which in any case is nowhere near ending.

The older son indeed comes back. However, not only does he recriminate against his father, but he grows very angry, not understanding that "now we must celebrate and rejoice" because of his brother's return. The lesson is obvious: we must share in God's joy when he finds one of his children who was lost.

But the parable does not stop here. It is important to study the three characters of this story.

The Older Brother

The older brother is the most transparent character; he directly represents those to whom the parable is directed.[13]

Back from work, he hears the sounds of a feast; he asks what is going on and, upon learning the cause of this rejoicing, flies into a rage and refuses to set foot in the house. The narrative does not accuse him. This first movement is not held against him: it is quite understandable.

Since he does not want to come in, his father goes out to entreat him; overwhelmed by anger, the older son pours out his heart in an aggressive and somewhat rude manner. But what he says is true: this grievance reminds us of the reaction, at pay time, of the workers hired first for the grape harvest, "This is not fair" (see Matt 20:12). He goes even further, in effect accusing his father of outrageous ingratitude.

The terms used by the older son define a certain religious ideal: "to serve" (God) with perseverance ("all these years"), being careful not to break any commandment ("not once did I disobey your orders"). This ideal—ours?—lacks neither greatness nor merit. But precisely: What is the foundation of such a relationship to God? Servile fear? In any case, this service of God does not seem to be inspired by love, and appears foreign to what a freely given service is. Conscious of being a good "servant" of his father, does not the older son think that he has rights that have been denied him? Upon hearing these complaints, and understanding the mentality they reveal, Christians cannot avoid questioning themselves. If they understand so well the older son's reaction, is it not because they somehow forget Jesus' word on the attitude that befits those who have done all that God has commanded them (see Luke 17:7-10)?[14]

It is not the misconduct of his younger brother that scandalizes the older son and risks making him deviate from his own way of acting. He despises sinners: "Your son," he says, speaking of his brother with as much disdain as the Pharisee of another parable, who, seeing the man standing at a distance and praying in the Temple, says, "This tax collector" (see Luke 18:9-14).[15]

What scandalizes the older son is his father's behavior. If this is how things stand, what advantage is there for the just? What good is it to exert oneself to faithfully observe the commandments?

The Younger Son

The portrait of the younger son is not flattering. It pretty well corresponds to the idea of the sinner entertained by Pharisees of all times. The young man leaves for a faraway country, a pagan land, no doubt. There he leads a profligate life, the only one imaginable in such circles. He finds himself reduced to tending swine—what a disgrace!—and even to envying the swine the food they receive. In a word, the very image of the sinner fallen to the depths of human and spiritual depravity.

When he finally takes the time to think and decides to return home, he does not express the least bit of remorse for his conduct or for the heartache he has caused his father: he is starving here; at least at home he will have his share of the abundance of bread the servants receive. Moreover, the beautiful sentence he prepares to speak seems calculated to mollify a justly angry father so that he will obtain from him a portion of the servant's bread.

There is really not the slightest idealization of the sinner in this parable. In no way can we see in "the prodigal son" a model of repentance and conversion. Anyhow, the return of a repentant sinner has never shocked any Pharisee. On the contrary, the conversion of a penitent rather confirms Pharisees and other law-abiding persons in their conception of faithfulness and religion.

The Father

Obviously, the central character of the parable is the father.[16] It is at him that we must keep looking. It is by pondering his words and conduct that we shall learn the principal lesson of the parable by which Jesus explains his actions: they are in harmony with the conduct of God, whose image this father is.

"While he was still a long way off, his father caught sight of him, and was filled with compassion. He ran to his son, embraced him and kissed him." He does not listen to the little speech his son begins to recite. He has only one concern: to clothe him with the best robe and quickly prepare a feast "because this son of mine was dead, and has come to life again; he was lost, and has been found." This degree of excitement and agitation lively expresses the eagerness of the father, who forestalls any word or actions on his son's part. We can imagine him saying, "You are here; this is enough; let us celebrate your return; we will talk of all this later." This is Jesus' response to those who grumble, "This is how God is," Father among all fathers, "from whom every family in heaven and on earth is named" (Eph 3:15).

> Whom must we recognize in this father? God, of course: no one is father as he is, no one is benevolent as he is. This is why he will welcome you— you who are his child, even if you have wasted what you had received from him, even if you arrive naked—because you have come back, and he will rejoice over your return more than over the wisdom of his other children.[17]

"My son, you are here with me always; everything I have is yours." This is all he says to his angry son. "No, I am not doing you any wrong. You are and remain my older son. But my heart is big enough for me to love your brother too, without taking anything away from my love for you. You have to understand that we must celebrate and rejoice. Enter wholeheartedly into the joy of the feast!"

Did the older son hear this last invitation of his father, or not? What was finally his response? The parable says nothing about it; it remains open, incomplete. It is for each one of us to decide what this older sibling—who we all are—does.

The Immeasurable Love of the Saving God

The pasch celebrated in each Eucharist is a memorial of the infinite love God manifests to sinners. In Jesus Christ, this Father transforms believers into new creatures and leads them into the promised land of a new world. We cannot celebrate this memorial without being filled with a total confidence in this God who, for us, has identified his Son with sin. Nothing, therefore, can take us away from God's love or his fatherly care, not even our sin and the consciousness we have of it. Nothing can ever weaken our hope of salvation, whether for ourselves or for our brothers and sisters who are sinners.

But this confidence entails demands assumed with joy. We are—or we shall become—truly children of this Father only by sharing his love for all his children even—and especially—those who have gone far away and live in sin. With how much greater reason shall we eagerly share God's joy when one of his children, our brother or sister, comes back home.

Obedience to commandments and faithfulness to God's service owe their value to the love which inspires them and which they translate into actions. Then they have their immediate reward in the joy of hearing God tell us, "My child, 'you are here with me always; everything I have is yours.'"

> No lost child unforgiven who seeks him,
> no one has strayed too far for God;
> let tears come, bringing a new birth,
> joy of returning to the Father.
>
> No wound too deep for his healing hand,
> nothing is lost for God;
> let grace come, bringing a new life,
> flame surging from the embers.
>
> No darkness devoid of hope for light,
> nothing is finished for God;
> let dawn come, in which love rises,
> song of Easter morning.[18]

Fifth Sunday of Lent—Year C

God's Mercy, Our Hope

Salvation History: Present and Future

On every Sunday in Lent, the Liturgy of the Word evokes one of the important steps of salvation history. This Sunday, the evocation is set in the perspective of the end of time, called eschatology (Isa 43:16-21).

In the oracle proclaimed by the prophet, God, once more,[1] speaks as the Creator of everything, his people, heaven and earth (see Isa 45:18). The Hebrews first experienced creation in their own creation as a people chosen for salvation. Starting from there, they came to understand that God created the universe and humankind to save them, a thing he could do by reason of his omnipotence. The first creation was the beginning of salvation history, throughout which God will not cease to create: a people, a new people and, finally, new heavens and a new earth.[2] This constant intervention by God has known peaks, moments when it was manifested with more brightness: thus, the crossing of the Red Sea at the Exodus, when "he [opened] a way in the sea . . . [and led] out chariots and horsemen, a powerful army . . . snuffed out and quenched like a wick." Well, all this is nothing—"Remember not the events of the past, / the things of long ago consider not"—when compared to what he will do at the close of history, a new world. Desert or wasteland will no longer exist; all nature and the wild animals themselves will "honor" their creator.

To be truthful, God speaks of this future in the present tense, "I am doing something new." By contrast, the future is used to evoke, in images, the manifestations of this newness. It is because "it springs forth" already, and we would have to be blind not to notice. "Do you not perceive it?" asks God.

As for the people whom the Lord has formed for himself, today, as yesterday and every day, they sing God's praises. When they see this new world, they will repeat the praises.

Therefore, there is continuity between the present time of salvation history and the newness of the world to come. On the one hand, we can—and must—perceive today the seeds of what will happen. On the other hand, the "new hymn" (Rev 14:3) that will be sung in the heavenly city will repeat the praise that God's people already address to him. We could even say that to sing today the glory of God is an apprenticeship for singing the heavenly songs: "Holy, holy, holy Lord! Hosanna in the highest! Alleluia!"

The prophet's oracle thus emphasizes the unity of salvation history, its dynamism and expansion, the transcendence of its completion. However, we must correctly understand that salvation does not unfold in linear fashion, as do connected historical events. It is from the outset, and more and more as it goes on, qualified by its End; it possesses a dimension that is called eschatological, that is to say, related to the end of time and the ultimate manifestation of the Lord. During the life they lead here below, despite toils and weariness, the Church and believers walk in joy, their eyes fixed on the horizon, the end of their journey.

> *The Lord has done great things for us;*
> *we are filled with joy.*
>
> When the Lord brought back the captives of Zion,
>   we were like men dreaming.
> Then our mouth was filled with laughter,
>   and our tongue with rejoicing.
> Then they said among the nations,
>   "The Lord has done great things for them."
> The Lord has done great things for us;
>   we are glad indeed.
> Restore our fortunes, O Lord,
>   like the torrents in the southern desert.
> Those that sow in tears
>   shall reap rejoicing.
> Although they go forth weeping,
>   carrying the seed to be sown,
> They shall come back rejoicing,
>   carrying their sheaves.
> (Ps 126)

Only One Thing Counts: Running Toward the Goal

Paul describes this progressive advance toward the goal by a comparison familiar to him: the race of athletes.[3] Such a way of speaking allows Paul to describe the spirit, the demands, and the basis of the exhilarating dynamism of Christian life (Phil 3:8-14).

To become Christian is to know Christ Jesus, our Lord. In the Bible, and according to the religious Hellenistic vocabulary, this knowledge implies communion. Far from being simply an intellectual[4] way of knowing, it is love and total self-giving, a union that is intimate and without reserve. The meaning and importance of this knowledge are expressed especially by Hosea and Jeremiah. ''For it is love that I desire, not sacrifice, / and knowledge of God rather than holocausts'' (Hos 6:6).[5] To know God is to share the effective love he bears for the poor and unfortunate, to practice, like God, what is right and just (see Jer 22:15-16).[6] To know Christ is to be one with the ''power of his resurrection'' by being united with him in suffering and death in order to rise with him.

None can acquire such knowledge by themselves: it is a gift of God beyond all gifts, without comparison to any other gift, ''the supreme good.'' Thus, Paul has joyfully left behind the ''gains'' he used to enjoy, regarding them now as rubbish, together with whatever he could have outside of this knowledge-communion.[7] Faith and union with Christ are supreme gifts; to dispose ourselves to receive and keep them, we must renounce everything else, everything that recently gave us or could give us any assurance, which is now perceived as illusory. For the righteousness that faith brings comes from God himself, and he knows us as righteous only in Christ Jesus. We are speaking of divine righteousness. A righteousness coming from ourselves would be a hopeless attempt at entering into communion with God.

But Paul tells us that this faith and assurance—this gift—does not let us be inactive; the ''already'' of salvation must not make us forget the ''not yet.'' ''It is not that I have already taken hold of it or have already attained perfect maturity, but I continue my pursuit in hope that I may possess it, since I have indeed been taken possession of by [Jesus]. . . . I for my part do not consider myself to have taken possession. . . . Forgetting what lies behind but straining forward to what lies ahead, I continue my pursuit toward the goal, the prize of God's upward calling, in Christ Jesus.''

We could not better express the dynamism of Christian life, the determination with which, in joy and hope, humans, seized by Christ, looking toward him alone, run to meet him.

> You have made us for you, Lord,
> and our hearts are restless
> until they dwell in you.[8]

I Judge No One

Whereas the Gospels of the other Sundays in Year C are always taken from Luke, this one, on the Fifth Sunday, is from John: the well-known episode of the woman caught in adultery whom Jesus did not condemn (John 8:1-11).

It is enough to read or hear this passage from the Fourth Gospel to be struck by its similarity of tone and perspective with the Gospels proclaimed on the preceding two Sundays: the call to conversion (Luke 13:1-9—Third Sunday) and especially the parable of the prodigal son (Luke 15:1-3, 11-32—Fourth Sunday). We feel we are still in Luke's Gospel. In fact, exegetes think it likely that this passage was written by Luke and later inserted into the Fourth Gospel, where it is the perfect illustration for this word of Jesus, "I do not judge anyone" (8:15).[9] Whatever the case, we have here the indisputable witness of one evangelical tradition of Jesus' life,[10] an integral part of the good news of God's mercy proclaimed in words and actions by the Lord himself.

Jesus Teaches after Praying

Luke noted that in the last days he spent in Jerusalem before his passion, "during the day, Jesus was teaching in the temple area, but at night he would leave and stay at the place called the Mount of Olives. And all the people would get up early each morning to listen to him in the temple area" (21:37-38). This retreat into solitude was certainly not inspired only by the legitimate and necessary need for rest. Several times, Luke notes that the Lord withdrew alone, apart, and often on a hill, to pray during the night.[11] There is nothing surprising, then, in Jesus doing the same thing every day of the last week spent in Jerusalem before his passion. More than ever, he felt it necessary to reserve such moments of encounter with the Father,[12] in order to draw from him the strength he needed and to discern what he must absolutely teach during these few days still at his disposal.[13]

Therefore, once more he is sitting in the Temple,[14] where he is teaching "all the people" crowding upon him to listen to him. "All the people," that is, the multitude of lowly folks and simple hearts, eager to hear God's word.

An Insidious Question of Life or Death

This peace is suddenly disrupted by the arrival of a group of "scribes and . . . Pharisees"[15] pushing and bringing forward in front of Jesus a woman just caught in adultery.[16]

"In the law,[17] Moses commanded us to stone such women. So what do you say?" It is a question of life or death: immediately for the woman;

and also for Jesus, since, the evangelist says, "they said this to test him, so that they could have some charge to bring against him." Indeed, if Jesus answers "Stone her, since the Law commands it," he will be seen by all as an impostor, first of all by the people "hanging on his words" (Luke 19:48). They will say, "He was preaching mercy and here he is condemning to death a woman without having listened to her, which is contrary to the Law.[18] Young Daniel showed more wisdom. When the two elders appointed as judges that year summoned Susanna, testifying that they had surprised her in the act of adultery, Daniel questioned them and convicted them of false testimony. But how can Jesus let them stone her without verifying the grounds for the accusation?"[19]

If, on the contrary, Jesus says to pardon her, he makes light of the Law; and in the event the sin is proved, he becomes its accomplice by casually absolving the woman. And people could then tell him, "How can you acquit this woman of a sin deemed very serious by the Law?" In either case, his teaching on the demands of his message would thus be stripped of all credibility, even with the ordinary people. The snare is a perfect one: whatever answer he gives, Jesus is caught.

Throw the First Stone If You Are Without Sin

We can admire the way in which Jesus, once more, foils an insidious ploy.[20] But, beyond this, there is a lesson to learn. To those who put the question to him, Jesus first of all opposes a silence during which all must be holding their breath and which they undoubtedly interpret in different ways, some perhaps with satisfaction, as a sign of embarrassment. "Jesus bent down and began to write on the ground with his finger." What did he write? As the Gospel does not tell us, we are sorely tempted to guess it, or rather to imagine it. But what is the use? It is futile even to wonder at the meaning of this gesture and even more to hypothesize on what Jesus was writing on the ground.[21] One thing is certain: Jesus' attitude and gesture do not express any contempt or lack of interest for this woman—her sin, her fate—or any lack of appreciation of the seriousness, the gravity of the question put to him. For this question concerns the woman standing in the middle of all, it concerns those who, asking themselves the question sincerely and in good faith, await a response from the Master, and finally, it concerns Jesus himself.

"Jesus bent down" to write on the ground, thus avoiding looking at those who questioned him about the woman, at those surrounding him. Is not this delicacy and discretion of Jesus an invitation addressed to the readers and hearers of the Gospel? Joining in Jesus' silence, we shall take advantage of the brief pause to reflect on how his words might strike a responsive chord in our hearts regarding the situation.

"Let the one among you who is without sin be the first to throw a stone at her." This is a direct and clear allusion to the Law: it prescribed that the one who denounced a crime thus give the signal for the stoning (see Deut 13:9-10; 17:7). But let us not be mistaken about the meaning of Jesus' answer. It does not mean that, because we ourselves are sinners, we are forbidden to render justice or pronounce a sentence. But it urges all of us to scrutinize our intentions. In France, it is required today that witnesses in criminal cases take an oath to speak without hatred. And we could have other motivations equally invalidating—in conscience—when we clamor for the punishment of a guilty person. Finally, Christians must remember Jesus' word on the wooden beam and splinter (see Luke 6:41-42). Conscious of being sinners, we must strive to reconcile, as much as possible, justice and mercy. Because he was without sin, Jesus could come close to sinners without being contaminated by their sin, and he could show mercy without in the least making compromises with evil, without failing to recognize its gravity. The same is true of genuine saints. While vigorously denouncing sin, they show admirable mercy toward sinners. Moreover, because of their holiness, they convey to sinners a strong demand for conversion in the very act of granting them pardon in God's name.

"They went away one by one, beginning with the elders." Sometimes we hear it said that the older ones left first because, having lived longer, they were burdened with more sins. This is one explanation. We could retort, however, that their leaving before the others demonstrates wisdom and better self-knowledge. But what is the interest of these rather unkind judgments either on the older set or the younger? Since again Jesus lowers his eyes and keeps silent, let us take advantage of this moment of recollection to humbly confess our sin—without comparing ourselves to anyone—by giving thanks to the one who, being without sin, can and wants to obtain pardon for us.

Misery and Mercy, Face-to-Face

Jesus "was left alone with the woman before him." St. Augustine has remarkably expressed the meaning of this silent and dramatic face-to-face that the woman must have experienced with intense emotion, not knowing yet what was going to happen to her: "*Relicti sunt duo, miseria et mis-ericordia.*" "Only two were left, misery and mercy."[22]

"Then Jesus straightened up and said to her, 'Woman, where are they? Has no one condemned you?' She replied, 'No one, sir.' " These are the only words the sinner pronounces. Probably, in her turn, she dares to look up at Jesus when he says to her, "Neither do I condemn you. Go [and] from now on do not sin any more."

> What does this mean, Lord? Do you approve sins? Nothing of the sort. Listen to what follows, "Go, and, from now on, do not sin any more." The Lord has condemned too, but the sin, not the person, for if he approved sins, he would say, "I shall not condemn you either, go, live as you see fit, sure of being pardoned, no matter how great your sin. . . ." He did not say this, but " 'Neither do I condemn you'; however, reassured as to the past, be on your guard for the future; I have erased your faults; keep my commandments in order to receive my promises."[23]

The story, which from beginning to end is sparingly told but filled with great dramatic tension, ends here. What became of the woman? The Gospel does not tell us, as it did not say what the older son had finally done in the parable of last Sunday. This encounter between Jesus and a woman caught in the very act of adultery leads us to examine our own attitudes toward our brothers and sisters guilty of serious sin, as well as our own reactions when our misery meets with the mercy of God in the Gospels or in the sacrament of penance and reconciliation.

A Path in Our Desert

The liturgy of the Fifth Sunday admirably brings to a close the Lenten itinerary of conversion we have walked in Year C, under Luke's guidance.

Whatever the efforts and renunciations we must consent to—the "gains" of former days—it remains that to be converted is to turn with joy and trust to the Father, always ready to receive us; to the mercy of God, always offered, revealed by Christ in words and actions. To be converted is to start on the road of righteousness that does not come from us, but from faith in Christ, in whom God will recognize us as righteous, whatever our sins may be, even if the whole world condemns us. Through Christ, God makes of us "a new creation." The efficacious word of salvation is pronounced over us, "Neither do I condemn you. Go [and] from now on do not sin any more."

> Will you throw the stone
> at those whom I welcome and do not condemn?
> I desire love,

learn its justice;
have you forgotten my cross?

You do not want the death of sinners,
but that they may live.

Lord, how many are my oppressors,
many those who say of my soul:
no salvation for it in its God.

If you remember sins, Lord,
who then will be able to stand?
But with you is forgiveness,
I love you and I hope.

I give you thanks, God, my Master,
with all my heart,
for your love for me is great,
you have drawn me from the depths of my misery.[24]

Jeremiah—Prophet in a Time of Crisis and Conversion

Is Jeremiah a biblical figure of Lent? Bossuet, the great bishop of Meaux in France, has enumerated the many traits by which the prophet of Anathoth announces Christ and traces a program for Lent.

> The prophet shows Zion its return. Looking farther, he announces her deliverer: this new David, whose reign will be eternal; this man of perfect wisdom, who will be enclosed and carried in a woman's womb. And he also foretells the new covenant that, through him, God will conclude with the redeemed people.
>
> Raise your voice, O Jeremiah! You a prophet sanctified from the womb, you a virgin prophet, figure of a great prophet, who also will be a virgin and son of a virgin. Sing for us the mercies of our God. Reproach us with our lack of gratitude, make us blush for our crimes. Give us the example of humility, patience, and meekness. Before our eyes, go again into your horrid prison, a figure of Christ's tomb; then, come out of it, a figure of his resurrection. Show us his persecutions in yours.
>
> And we, Lord, waiting to meditate at greater length on the mysteries of your passion and triumphant resurrection, we shall prepare ourselves by contemplating with faith the prophets who prefigured these mysteries.[1]

The stature of Jeremiah was such that Jesus' contemporaries compared him to this great prophet (see Matt 16:14). It has been written of him that had he not existed, "religious history would have taken a different turn . . . there would not have been any Christianity."[2]

A prophet for a time of crisis, since he came "to root up and to tear down, / to destroy and to demolish," he whom the Lord used as a hammer to strike the whole world and even his own people, was also sent "to build and to plant" (Jer 1:10). Thus, he became, in his own time, as well as for all times, the great artisan of that interior religion that would flourish among "the poor of the Lord" and would find expression in the prayer of many a psalmist. We certainly will not waste our time during Lent if we frequent Jeremiah through a fruitful *lectio divina*.

It is a fact that the rich palette of Lenten biblical readings hardly gives Jeremiah the place he seems to deserve.[3] The Lectionary prefers to make us attend to the testimony of the whole of Scripture rather than to that of one single writer. The limits and method of this brief essay are determined by the recognition of the above fact. Excellent studies have been devoted to Jeremiah in recent years; we can only refer readers to them.[4]

Without abandoning the liturgical Lectionary, we may attempt to compare on certain points the prophet's work, the Letter to the Hebrews, and the Book of Exodus. To explain Scripture by Scripture, to ponder in prayer the Christological meaning of the Bible, which, St. Augustine said, is "pregnant with Christ"—is this not the very manner in which the liturgy proceeds to help us contemplate the mysteries of salvation? Is it not also, thanks to words borrowed from the very Word of God, to give life to the Christian way of being and acting and to contribute to the earnest efforts we make in order to become more aware of divine friendship? When speaking of meditation on the psalms, St. Augustine said, "Your prayer is a conversation with God. When you read, it is God who speaks; when you pray, it is you who speak with God."[5] But this parallel reading demands that we keep in mind the historical context of the work and ministry of Jeremiah, a prophet for a time of crisis and conversion.

"Take a Scroll and Write"

The Book of Jeremiah is an obviously composite work: the attempt to connect scattered elements with a tenuous thread does nothing at all to remedy the disconnected character of the documentation and reported events. Disjointed chronological indications, frequency of doublets, alternation of oracles and biographical or autobiographical passages, differences in the length and order of the Hebrew text and the Greek version—the Septuagint: all this cannot fail to give us the impression that the work is incongruous and unfinished. We must remember that, at that time, "books that are not simple inscriptions were rarely written at one sitting and retain the trace of successive rewritings."[6]

A tragic incident recorded in chapter 36 sheds some light on the formation of the book. After a more or less lengthy period, when Jeremiah only preached, he seems to have realized a written version was needed. *Verba volant, scripta manent* ("Words fly away while writings endure"). Faced with uncomprehending contemporaries, he had recourse to the services of a professional scribe, who transcribed, under his dictation, a collection of oracles whose substance, perhaps, are intact in chapters 1 to 18. This scroll recorded threats and invectives uttered by Jeremiah during the first twenty years of his preaching "against Israel, Judah, and all the nations" (36:2), that is, from 628 to 605 B.C. This scroll was read in the presence of King Jehoiakim, who wasted no time in cutting and burning this text, considered too damning. Hence, the necessity of a new dictation, which bears the mark of the irreparable disappointment felt by Jeremiah, realizing the failure of his preaching.

Other short books of oracles would be added later to the collection of 605, according to circumstances. Probably Baruch, Jeremiah's scribe, or some other disciple, kept a sort of journal of the painful events in Jeremiah's life. A certain number of biographical passages written in the third person make this supposition plausible.[7] To these same disciples, before or after their master's death, we are indebted for the addition of several passages, very personal in style, that make of Jeremiah "a kind of Hebrew St. Augustine."[8] In his "Confessions," the prophet relates the persecutions that he endured and the inner conflicts that were his lot because of the impossible mission to which God called him.[9]

In all likelihood, it was in Egypt, to where his master was dragged off, that Baruch completed his work (Jer 43:8). But it was in Babylon, in the circles of exiles who revered the prophet's memory and whose message was life to them, that the book received its final form. It was augmented by additions: the letter of Jeremiah to the exiles (27–30), the booklets against kings, as well as false prophets (23:9-40). The events surrounding Jeremiah's arrest and deportation to Egypt were narrated (37–45). The oracles of happiness in the "Book of Consolation of Jeremiah" were reworked and amplified.

All this presupposes the work of successive generations, both in the circles of Deuteronomists, so close to Jeremiah in their approach, and at the synagogue readings that took the place of the sacrificial worship at Jerusalem during the Exile in Chaldea. Jeremiah did not have followers as Isaiah did. But he inspired Ezekiel's thoughts by his words on the new covenant[10] and the thoughts of Isaiah's disciple speaking of the sufferings of the mysterious Servant of the Lord.[11] His message of hope would be remembered after the return from exile (Isa 56–66). And we must add so many psalmists who were imbued with his prayer.[12] Many poor and unfortunate people have identified with his trial of faith; like him, they have foreseen other dawns, despite the dark and seemingly endless nights of despair. A legendary figure, Jeremiah ended his work with an unfinished page that others, inspired by him, continued to write until the advent of Christ.[13]

From the Days of Josiah to the Exile

Jeremiah's ministry extended over a period of some forty years. From 628 to about 580 B.C., the prophet "covered" the great political upheavals in the Middle East. After the destruction of the northern kingdom by Assyria in 721, Jerusalem was no longer anything but a precarious refuge in a field of ruins. Provisionally spared, it became, in fact, a political and cultural vassal (see 2 Kgs 35-37; Isa 37:36-38). From that time on, those with a strong faith foresaw that Jerusalem would be battered by a succession of great powers: Assyria, in a slow decline; Egypt, not content to play second fiddle; Chaldea, ready to seize the first place. Isaiah exhorted the kings to trust God alone, to refuse to enter into ephemeral alliances. But they too often engaged in opportunistic politics and played with fire. More serious still, the gods of the pact nations or the conquerors of the day crossed the border with their masters. Under impious kings like Manasseh and Amon, the worship of the Lord was paganized; the God of the covenant was integrated into the pantheon of the Baals and the Astartes.

From 624 on, events accelerated. Assyria tottered under Babylonian attacks and revolutions by smaller states. In 622, Josiah, king of Judah, regained the northern provinces and for a time assuaged the nostalgia for a "united Israel" that existed under David and Solomon. In 620, the political conquest was followed by a religious reform, thanks to the "discovery" in the Temple of a forgotten book, attributed to Moses. Deuteronomy proposes a whole program: to make of Israel again a people of brothers and sisters gathered around a unique place of worship, Jerusalem.[14] Although we cannot affirm that Jeremiah was directly part of this movement, we may think that he was influenced by its spirit, since the many connections he had with the promoters of this reform and many themes of his preaching make this supposition plausible.

But alas, in 609, the good king Josiah was killed in the battle of Megiddo in an attempt to defeat Egypt, an ally of the moribund Assyrian power (see 2 Kgs 23:29). This proved that it served no purpose to oppose the irresistible ascendancy of new masters, Medes and Chaldeans. It was not in military confrontations that Israel would find salvation, but in conversion and surrender to the Lord.

Jehoiakim, Josiah's successor and puppet of Pharaoh, reigned in turn under Egyptian influence and, when the wind changed, under Babylonian sway. Idolatrous practices flourished anew, and Jeremiah could only announce imminent catastrophes. For him, henceforth, the future seemed completely hopeless and he entered into a period of disenchantment and disillusionment.

Here began a new period and a new style. This extremely shy man now used actions as well as words (see Jer 13:1-11; 19:1-11). He cried "Deathtrap." But he also gave voice to the torments he endured on account of a people with whom he was more involved than ever and of God himself, who forced him into a "job" for which he was not made. It was probably at this time that he wrote the "Confessions of Jeremiah," those cries of a heart finding life hard to bear in the crisis of vocation he was undergoing. Heart-rending revelations that continue to move us, complaints of a man disappointed to the core, without illusions, even about God, who is "a treacherous brook / whose waters do not abide" (15:18).[15]

In 602, Jehoiakim played his worst card by revolting against his Babylonian overlord (see 2 Kgs 23:36–24:4). Only death during the siege saved the king from captivity, but his son Jehoiachin was taken prisoner along with some three thousand Judeans, while the exiled king's uncle Zedekiah pledged fidelity to the Chaldean sovereign, Nebuchadnezzar (see 2 Kgs 24:8-17). From this time on, Jeremiah would campaign for submission to the conqueror. For years, he multiplied warnings against those who would not submit to the Babylonian yoke (see Jer 27–28). It was impossible, he said, to rely upon the unsteady Zedekiah or the exiled king, whose prompt return could not be expected (see 29:16; 22:24-30). For Jeremiah, sacred history's center of gravity had already been moved from Jerusalem to Chaldea, where the first exiles, shepherded by Ezekiel, prepared the new Israel of the future (see 24 and 29).

Meanwhile, in Jerusalem itself, an extremist and vengeful party constantly pushed King Zedekiah to join an anti-Chaldean coalition, strongly encouraged by Egypt. The climate of hostility to Jeremiah continued to worsen: he was about to know his Gethsemane (see 27:2-7). Chapters 37 to 42 of his book are among the most vivid in the Bible. These archival documents, which we owe to one of his disciples, record in exact detail the vicissitudes of his eventful life from 588, when the second siege began. Accused of defeatism and treason, imprisoned in a cistern where he nearly perished, he was delivered in extremis by a servant of the king. Scarcely out of prison, this shy man, unwillingly thrust into the political limelight, obstinately and vehemently declared that the king must capitulate (see 38:14-28). But it was too late to stop the course of events set in motion by a too human—and also incoherent—political decision. When we read certain passages of the Bible, we realize what a terrible trauma the second siege of Jerusalem left in the collective memory (see Jer 39 and 52; Lam 2 and 4; Ps 74). The strangulation of the city would last from January 588 to July 587. A second exile would be the consequence of the fall of Jerusalem (see 2 Kgs 24:18—25:7; Jer 52:29).

Then suddenly, when everything seemed lost, Jeremiah accomplished the second part of his prophetic task. Now that the "hammer" of the Lord had struck (see 23:29; 50:53; 51:20), after the collapse of all pretenses of faith, it was time "to build and to plant" (1:10). "Days will surely come. . . (16:14).[16] Jeremiah was certain of it: God would build anew, for he watches over his word to fulfill it; he would open a future to his rebellious people after they had atoned for their sin. And Jeremiah himself, wounded, victimized, defeated on all scores, and soon to be exiled to this Egypt he never stopped battling against (see 43:6), received the order to do a last act, astonishingly hopeful. While the specter of the disaster prowled about the city, he bought his uncle's field in Anathoth. "For thus says the LORD of hosts, the God of Israel: Houses and fields and vineyards shall again be bought in this land" (32:15).

Jeremiah did not see the accomplishment of his prediction. He had only a glimpse of it as in a dream—"but my sleep was sweet to me" (31:26)— of the religion of the future and the return of the chosen people to the land of the patriarchs. For him, as for them,[17] the kingdom remained a promise. And it must be so for "a long time" (32:14). The one concern of those who were entitled to dwell in it was to testify to their profound hope for the benefit of generations to come.

I Place My Words in Your Mouth

If it is true that prophets are persons who, out of their creative faithfulness to God's plan, preach the word in season and out of season and thus build the religion of the future simply by living the present in a more authentic way, then Jeremiah is the perfect prophet, as well as a surprising forerunner of Christianity. Among his many teachings, the implacable criticism of spurious expressions of the religion of his time is well suited to prepare us during Lent to welcome the risen Christ, only mediator of the new covenant, as presented to us by the Letter to the Hebrews. Besides, Jeremiah teaches us to live in nearness to the God of Exodus, who draws all human beings after him beyond themselves, into the adventure of faith.

"Put not your trust in deceitful words" (Jer 7:4). This is a radical censure of the traditional religion that Jeremiah begins during the reign of King Jehoiakim (609–598). At the time, in spite of threats weighing on the Kingdom of Judah, confidence remains strong in the promises of the covenant and the signs that express it: the Temple and the worship that take place in it, the prophetic institution, circumcision, the theocratic state are as many divine gifts upon which the people rest assured, seeing only dimly the demands that are implied in these gifts. Deepening the spirit of the Deuteronomic reform, Jeremiah ends by pitilessly condemning the false securities of religion. For him, the most sacred institutions and the most time-honored structures of the chosen people count for nothing if they do not express attachment to a God to whom all have to wholeheartedly come back.[18]

"Stand at the gate of the house of the LORD" (Jer 7:2). Unlike Isaiah (see Isa 6:1), Jeremiah was not called by God in his Temple, but outside any liturgy, any manifestation of divine grandeur. Perhaps in the peace of some garden, on a spring morning (see 1:11)? But his ministry takes place almost completely in the shadow of the Temple. There is nothing surprising in this: although belonging to a priestly family evicted and cast far away from its natural environment,[19] Jeremiah is convinced of the holiness of God's place of residence.

Since the failed siege of Jerusalem in Isaiah's time, around 702, his fellow citizens are more than ever certain of the inviolability of God's abode (see Isa 37:36). Jeremiah vigorously reacts against this false assurance: no, God is not necessarily with us because his people have built a Temple of stone to him. This building offers no protection if it is not a place of authentic worship.

> Put not your trust in the deceitful words: "This is the temple of the LORD! The temple of the LORD! The temple of the LORD!" Only if you thoroughly reform your ways and your deeds; if each of you deals justly with his neighbor; if you no longer oppress the resident alien, the orphan, and the widow; if you no longer shed innocent blood in this place, or follow strange gods to your own harm, will I remain with you in this place, in the land which I gave your fathers long ago and forever.
>
> But here you are, putting your trust in deceitful words to your own loss! Are you to steal and murder, commit adultery and perjury, burn incense to Baal, go after strange gods that you know not, and yet come to stand before me in this house which bears my name, and say: "We are safe; we can commit all these abominations again"? Has this house which bears my name become in your eyes a den of thieves? I too see what is being done, says the LORD. You may go to Shiloh, which I made the dwelling place of

my name in the beginning. See what I did to it because of the wickedness of my people Israel.
(Jer 7:4:12)[20]

This diatribe of the prophet can only turn everyone against him (see 26:1-19). He will be saved only by the intervention of influential friends who will make the point that already in the time of King Hezekiah the prophet Micah had announced the destruction of the Temple. In this case, they say, is it not better to listen to the call to conversion rather than put to death the person who exhorts people to it?

Besides condemning reliance on the Temple, Jeremiah also condemns the spiritless liturgy carried on in it. He recalls with nostalgia the simple and stark worship celebrated by Israel during the journey through the wilderness:

Thus says the LORD of hosts, the God of Israel: Heap your holocausts upon your sacrifices; eat up the flesh! In speaking to your fathers on the day I brought them out of the land of Egypt, I gave them no command concerning holocaust or sacrifice. This rather is what I commanded them: Listen to my voice; then I will be your God and you shall be my people.
(Jer 7:21-23)

Like Jeremiah, other prophets will censure the worship without soul that does not lead one ''to know God''[21] and will also suffer for it. When the evangelists narrate the trial of Jesus, they will remember his will to purify the Temple from all commerce (see Mark 11:17), his prediction concerning the replacement of the old Temple with another ''not made with hands'' (Mark 14:58). Stephen, the deacon and first Christian martyr, will speak in the same vein (see Acts 6:13-14). As for Paul the Apostle, people will accuse him of preaching to everyone everywhere ''against the people and the law and this place'' (Acts 21:28).

''*Through the blood of Jesus we have confidence of entrance into the sanctuary*'' (Heb 10:19). The Book of Acts clearly mentions many converts among Jews, ''all zealous observers of the law'' (21:20), and ''even a large group of priests . . . becoming obedient to the faith'' (6:7). We can well imagine the dilemma faced by this latter group. On the one hand, Jesus has come, the unique high priest of the good things to come, and he has accomplished everything by his unique sacrifice. On the other hand, the old worship continues in the Temple, and priests still offer ''gifts according to the law'' (Heb 8:4).

The author of the Letter to the Hebrews applies himself to resolve this dilemma by looking up to the heavenly sanctuary now accessible, thanks to the sacrifice of Christ. From the idea of ''house''—with its twofold meaning of "family" and "building"—he imperceptibly passes to that of a heavenly sanctuary toward which the pilgrims of faith in Christ Jesus are journeying. Superior in this to Moses, Jesus has been placed at the head of his "house" in his quality of son and we belong to this house. "We are his house if [only] we hold fast to our confidence and pride in our hope" (3:6). Hence, the certainty of this hope "we have as an anchor of the soul, sure and firm, that reaches into the interior behind the veil, where Jesus has entered in our behalf as forerunner, becoming high priest forever according to the order of Melchizedek" (6:19-20; cf. 7:28; 9:9).

The comparison refers to the Temple of Jerusalem. Once a year, on the great day of the Day of Atonement, the high priest enters alone, beyond the veil, into the holy of holies, in order to offer for himself and the people the sin-offering (see Lev 16). As for Jesus, he has entered once for all into the sanctuary, giving us free access to the throne of divine grace, in his quality of "minister of the sanctuary and of the true tabernacle that the Lord, not man, set up" (Heb 8:1-2). Farther along, the author explains in more detail:

> But when Christ came as high priest of the good things that have come to be, passing through the greater and more perfect tabernacle not made by hands, that is, not belonging to this creation, he entered once for all into the sanctuary, not with the blood of goats and calves but with his own blood, thus obtaining eternal redemption.
> (Heb 9:11-12)

The true temple where we find rest is, first of all, the heavenly sanctuary into which Jesus entered at the moment of his death, when the veil of the Temple was rent from top to bottom. But it is also the body of Christ opened by the spear, this body henceforth glorious, whose blood, poured out, washes us from all sin. As early as in Paul's writings, it is the assembly of believers, gathered into the Church, that is the Body of the risen Christ.[22] The author of Hebrews concludes with an exhortation that brings us back to the theme of the "house-family," the home of baptized persons:

> Since through the blood of Jesus we have confidence of entrance into the sanctuary by the new and living way he opened for us through the veil, that is, his flesh, and since we have "a great priest over the house of God," let us approach with a sincere heart and in absolute trust, with our hearts sprinkled clean from an evil conscience and our bodies washed in pure water.
> (Heb 10:19-22)

Although the author uses the categories of the conventional priestly theology, he speaks of the Temple of Jerusalem, made of stone, only to distance himself from it. Like Jeremiah before him, he has nostalgia for the
tabernacle of Exodus, of the tent in the wilderness, moveable sanctuary
from which God was guiding his people on their march to the Promised
Land. For him, Christ's disciples are also of the lineage of these great
ancestors in the faith, such as the patriarchs, who "acknowledged themselves to be strangers and aliens on earth . . . seeking a homeland"
(11:13-14).

"I will make a new covenant" (Jer 31:31). In the account of the calling
of Jeremiah, in addition to the verbs "to root up and to tear down / to
destroy and to demolish," there are also "to build and to plant" (1:10).
If he pulls down a shaky house, it is only to outline the building of a
new one. There is no absolute pessimism in the Bible. When everything
totters—Jerusalem, the royal dynasty, the theocratic state, the Temple and
its worship—when everything seems threatened in the besieged city, Jeremiah pronounces words of hope that point to a religion of the future.

> The days are coming, says the LORD, when I will make a new covenant with
> the house of Israel and the house of Judah. It will not be like the covenant
> I made with their fathers the day I took them by the hand to lead them
> forth from the land of Egypt; for they broke my covenant and I had to show
> myself their master, says the LORD. But this is the covenant which I will
> make with the house of Israel after those days, says the LORD. I will place
> my law within them, and write it upon their hearts; I will be their God,
> and they shall be my people. No longer will they have need to teach their
> friends and kinsmen how to know the LORD. All, from least to greatest,
> shall know me, says the LORD, for I will forgive their evildoing and remem-
> ber their sin no more.
> (Jer 31:31-34)

This oracle is the only one of its kind. Before Jeremiah, no one in Israel
would have dared to consider the possibility of a dissolution of the Mosaic covenant, which is a divine reality whose stability rests on the very
faithfulness of God to his word. The covenant is "a permanent order,
not outside of history, but an expression of history as God would want
it, because the characteristic of the Covenant is faithfulness. The Covenant is the Jewish category corresponding to the Greek notion of nature
as the permanent law of things established by God."[23]

But if it is true that God does not go back on his word, it is also necessary to take into account God's partners with their repeated infidelities
to their promises. Hence, the diagnosis of an incurable moral disease,

to which Jeremiah came little by little, and his denunciation of the radical state of sin in which the people live.[24] One century earlier, Hosea—often called the Jeremiah of the North—was already God's spokesperson when he reproached the people with the feebleness of their repentance.

> What can I do with you, Ephraim?
>   What can I do with you, Judah?
> Your piety is like a morning cloud,
>   like the dew that early passes away.
> For this reason I smote them through the prophets,
>   I slew them by the words of my mouth;
> For it is love that I desire, not sacrifice,
>   and knowledge of God rather than holocausts.
> (Hos 6:4-6)

Very soon after the reform undertaken by Josiah in 620, Jeremiah foresees that a mere restoration of the broken covenant will be insufficient. God alone can disentangle his people from their sinful state by setting up an entirely new relationship without common measure with the former one. They fool themselves by their quasi-magical confidence in circumcision as a sign of the covenant.[25] More is necessary: a renewal of the heart in order to set free within it its capacity to coincide with God's will. This, only God can achieve.

> One heart and one way I will give them, that they may fear me always, to their own good and that of their children after them. I will make with them an eternal covenant, never to cease doing good to them; into their hearts I will put the fear of me, that they may never depart from me. (Jer 32:39-40)[26]

It matters little that this text and some others are rewritings of Jeremiah by his disciples. The insistence on the creative intervention of God comes from the conviction that he alone can bring about Israel's conversion, "If you allow me, I will return / for you are the LORD, my God" (31:18). The religion of the future cannot not be born except by God's direct intervention in the recesses of the human heart, in this core of personhood where spirit and will, freedom and faithfulness are equally involved. It is there, in this center of action and of communion between persons, that the Lord will act. First, in order to forgive and radically change human beings. Then, in order to set in them an interior inspiration and motivation, no longer regulated by a charter or an exterior law, but by the very will of God, who wants only the good of his creation. In a constant dialogue with humans, God then will be known, served, and loved in an immediate and personal way.

Even before Jeremiah stops preaching, another voice begins to be heard: that of Ezekiel, the priest, who was part of one of the first convoys of deportees after 598. He speaks of the failure of the old covenant and of the new covenant that God will establish by his Spirit, interpersonal communion awakened by him in the depths of hearts.[27] The priest Ezekiel is close to the prophet Jeremiah on all the points that will characterize tomorrow's religion. We shall therefore not be surprised to find the same traits again in the Letter to the Hebrews, a piece intent on dissipating the nostalgia of certain believers remaining attached to the Temple and the Mosaic priesthood and worship.

Jesus "is mediator of a better covenant" (Heb 8:6). Jeremiah willingly compares the force of God's word to that of a hammer pounding on rock, an image that for him expresses the violent hold God has on his prophet's life.[28] The Letter to the Hebrews uses another image to describe the penetrating action of the divine word into the innermost parts of hearts:

> Indeed, the word of God is living and effective, sharper than any two-edged sword, penetrating even between soul and spirit, joints and marrow, and able to discern reflections and thoughts of the heart.
> (Heb 4:12)

The author reproaches those of his readers he deems too strongly attached to the past with having remained at the first stage of faith and with having failed to reach the intimate knowledge of God that characterizes the new covenant. He will have to catechize them all over again from the beginning:

> Although you should be teachers by this time, you need to have someone teach you again the basic elements of the utterances of God. You need milk, [and] not solid food.
> (Heb 5:12)[29]

He recalls the radical newness of which Jesus is the guarantor. Not only is he the high priest of a new law, better than the former one, but he leads us by his sacrifice into a state vastly superior to that of the past (see 7:11-27). Comparing the worship, sanctuaries, and sacrifices of the old alliance and the new, he underscores the provisional character of the former and its disappearance for the benefit of another, better and definitive, announced by Jeremiah:

> Now he has obtained so much more excellent a ministry as he is mediator of a better covenant, enacted on better promises. For if that first covenant

had been faultless, no place would have been sought for a second one. But he finds fault with them and says:

"Behold, the days are coming, says the Lord,
when I will conclude a new covenant with the house of Israel
and the house of Judah. . . ."

When he speaks of a "new" covenant, he declares the first one obsolete. And what has become obsolete and has grown old is close to disappearing.
(Heb 8:6-8, 13)[30]

The imperfection of the old covenant is due to the fact that it promised imperfect goods: it did not definitively remit sin; it did not fundamentally change human beings (see Heb 10:12).

Farther on, the author compares Christ's sacrifice with old sacrifices. What insures its efficaciousness is the perfect obedience of Jesus to his Father (see 10:5-6; Ps 40:7-9) and also the uniqueness of this sacrifice that is sufficient to render perfect forever those it sanctifies.

He takes away the first to establish the second. By this "will," we have been consecrated through the offering of the body of Jesus Christ once for all.

Every priest stands daily at his ministry, offering frequently those same sacrifices that can never take away sins. But this one offered one sacrifice for sins, and took his seat forever at the right hand of God; now he waits until his enemies are made his footstool. For by one offering he has made perfect forever those who are being consecrated. The holy Spirit also testifies to us, for after saying:

"This is the covenant I will establish
with them after those days, says the Lord:
'I will put my laws in their hearts, and I
will write them upon their minds,' "

he also says:

"Their sins and their evildoing
I will remember no more."

Where there is forgiveness of these, there is no longer offering for sin.
(Heb 10:9-18)

The new covenant sealed by the blood of Jesus is the very same one Jeremiah announced. He dreamed of an eternal covenant that would be realized "in those days."[31] The author of Hebrews declares it fulfilled "in these last days" (Heb 1:2) because God has sent his Son to purify us from sin.

This fulfillment, realized once for all, is celebrated and made present in the day-to-day liturgical action, at least if we, in our turn, listen to the Lord's voice (see Heb 3:7ff.) and if we ratify by our conversion, day in day out, the new covenant he has come to conclude with each of us.

"They shall know that my name is LORD" (Jer 16:21). Jeremiah is not only the prophet God chose to topple false religious securities and announce the religion of the future. He is also an extraordinary witness of God because he himself was overwhelmed by the divine grip on his life and by the blazing words that were torn from him. When we read him, we think of what Georges Bernanos has the pastor of Torcy say, "I simply am convinced that when, by chance, the Lord draws from me a word useful to souls, I know it by the pain it causes me."[32]

Throughout Jeremiah's life and trials, there appears progressively a new definition of prophetism: the very person is message, sign. By the celibacy imposed on him as a sad omen (see 16:1), by the solitude and desolation to which his mission drove him, Jeremiah suggests the destiny the people will know, as well as the bereavement of God first rejected by Israel. Thus Jeremiah becomes for his time, as he is for ours, the revealer of a God at once "too close and too far."[33] Too close, because he invades the prophet's entire life and violently imposes upon him words and actions which he cannot refuse (see 20:9) and which plunge him into anguish (see 15:18). Too far, because this God often seems to abandon him to his fate, in the night of doubt and dereliction.

More than any other person in his time, Jeremiah lived the paradox of a distant God constantly transcending humans. God above everything created. God of the Exodus, who calls us to continually go beyond the representations we have of him. God distant and yet absolutely close, involved with humanity and attaching himself to it by the covenant. God of Abraham, Isaac, and Jacob. God revealing himself.

God is difficult to live with—O how difficult! Religious persons always dream of a God on a human scale, of a reachable God whom they can manage by sanctuaries, rites, and sacrifices. They want a God who, thanks to a political or religious power, can be identified with those who bear the responsibilities and are, as it were, the embodiment of divine kindness. For Jeremiah, this is the blasphemous approach par excellence; his censure of false religious certainties, as well as of a covenant lowered to the level of a contract—"I give so that you give"—clearly shows this. For him, God is at once close and far away: this is the negative face of the message of this smasher of idols who wants to give back to God his true place, beyond the convenient intermediary regions that people would like to assign to him.

It is not without a fight with himself that the prophet succeeds in this undertaking. And it is only at the end of a strenuous battle, in contrast to Job who could but fall silent in the face of the divine mystery (see Job 40:4; 42:8), that Jeremiah receives the revelation of the infinite nearness of a God whom he, however, experiences as distant.

When you were "following me in the desert" (Jer 2:2). At the center of Israel's history, the remembrance of the God of Exodus remains the object of faith and hope. It was a fortunate time when, although they could not look on God without dying, the people walked behind him, seeing him from the back. In the tradition of the prophets of the northern kingdom, and especially his inspiration Hosea, Jeremiah sees in the events of the Exodus a manifestation of the proximity and intimate presence of Yahweh in the midst of a people who, then, fully responded to him:

> This word of the LORD . . .
>   I remember the devotion of your youth,
>   how you loved me as a bride,
>   Following me in the desert,
>   in a land unsown.''
> (Jer 2:2)[34]

It was the time of simple and loyal love, beyond the rites that, today, express for Jeremiah only the hypocrisy of those who observe them. Following Amos and Hosea, he goes so far as to assert that when God took Israel out of Egypt, he did not command anything concerning sacrifices and holocausts: let Israel hear his voice and he will be their God.[35] It is the moral law flowing from the covenant that has to condition the behavior of the chosen people:

> Cursed be the man who does not observe the terms of this covenant, which I enjoined upon your fathers the day I brought them up out of the land of Egypt, that iron foundry, saying: Listen to my voice and do all that I command you. Then you shall be my people, and I will be your God. Thus I will fulfill the oath which I swore to your fathers, to give them a land flowing with milk and honey: the one you have today.
> (Jer 11:3-5)

But the people do not listen to the voice of their God. As a consequence, God begins to send against them all the curses resulting from a scorned covenant. He will no longer listen to their prayers, not even those made by the most devout persons in Israel; they will plead a cause lost in advance (11:11; 15:1). The punishment will be purely and simply the return to the conditions of slavery they suffered before the Exodus. More serious still. What counts is not only the guarantee of a land to inhabit but the indwelling of God among his own, rather than a passing visit from time to time. Unless the people repent, it is possible that God might absent himself, distance himself, abandon the people to their sad fate.

> O Hope of Israel, O LORD,
>   our savior in time of need!
> Why should you be a stranger in this land,
>   like a traveler who has stopped but for a night?
> Why are you like a man dumbfounded,
>   a champion who cannot save?
> You are in our midst, O LORD,
>   your name we bear:
>   do not forsake us!
>   . . . remember your covenant with us,
>   and break it not.
> (Jer 14:8-9, 21)

Sin, this "vagrancy" of the people of the covenant (see 4:1), can only cause them to become again an errant people, a homeless people, a people without God, since he threatens to withdraw from them, to leave his heritage behind. Sin is actually leading them to the roads of exile, at least if Israel does not turn back.

"*If you repent . . .*" (Jer 15:19). From the beginning of his preaching career, Jeremiah has repeated the exhortations to conversion uttered by his predecessors. During the reign of Jehoiakim, Baruch, Jeremiah's secretary, sums up the message of his master:

> These three and twenty years—the word of the LORD has come to me and I spoke to you untiringly. . . . This message [was]: Turn back, each of you, from your evil way and from your evil deeds; then you shall remain in the land which the LORD gave you and your fathers, from of old and forever. (Jer 25:3, 5)

Jeremiah addresses this call to conversion to his contemporaries with the eloquence of a man who senses within the depths of his consciousness the calamities that are going to befall them all. The whole earth seems to him to revert to chaos (see 4:19-23; see also Gen 1:2). Like Hosea before him, he compares his people to a prodigal son, to an unfaithful wife (see 3:19-20). Let Israel have no illusions about their fate: God is going to take them to court (see 2:35).

Commentators have often pointed out Jeremiah's originality in his use of the verbal root that in Hebrew expresses the act of conversion. In many passages *shub* emphasizes the break caused by conversion, by a turn of phrase unknown before Jeremiah, using the preposition *min*. What is meant is "to turn away from."[36] It is the heart that must be converted.[37]

In Jeremiah, the frequency of the expression "the hardness of their evil hearts" shows at what depth conversion must occur.[38]

In order to suggest the radical nature of authentic conversion, Jeremiah transposes onto the moral plane the rite of circumcision, which incorporates every Israelite male into the covenant. Bodily circumcision is nothing if it is not accompanied by a total conformity to God's will:

> For the sake of the LORD, be circumcised,
>   remove the foreskins of your hearts,
>   O men of Judah and citizens of Jerusalem:
> Lest my anger break out like fire,
>   and burn till none can quench it,
>   because of your evil deeds.
> (Jer 4:4)[39]

In an oracle probably directed first against the northern kingdom punished by exile, then later on rewritten and amplified to fit the southern kingdom, Jeremiah inveighs against the pride of the Judeans who are sure God's anger will spare them. Woe to them if they do not acknowledge their sins!

> The LORD said to me in the days of king Josiah: See now what rebellious Israel has done! She has gone up every high mountain, and under every green tree she has played the harlot. And I thought, after she has done all this she will return to me. But she did not return. Then, even though her traitor sister Judah saw that for all the adulteries rebellious Israel had committed, I put her away and gave her a bill of divorce, nevertheless her traitor sister Judah was not frightened; she too went off and played the harlot. Eager to sin, she polluted the land, committing adultery with stone and wood. With all this, the traitor sister Judah did not return to me wholeheartedly, but insincerely, says the LORD.
>
> Then the LORD said to me: Rebel Israel is inwardly more just than traitorous Judah. Go, proclaim these words toward the north, and say:
> Return, rebel Israel, says the LORD,
>   I will not remain angry with you;
> For I am merciful, says the LORD,
>   I will not continue my wrath forever.
> Only know your guilt. . .
> (Jer 3:6-13)

And despite everything, Jeremiah imagines what the response of the people could be.

> Return, rebellious children,
>   and I will cure you of your rebelling.

"Here we are, we now come to you
   because you are the LORD, our God."
(Jer 3:22)

During the Exile in Babylon, the best among the exiled will finally understand that the return from captivity can happen only by a change of heart, a conversion of the people that only God can effect.[40] Hope will spring up again: yes, God will create new things; he will bring about the return of the unfaithful wife to her husband.

> Thus says the LORD:
> Cease your cries of mourning,
>   wipe the tears from your eyes.
> The sorrow you have shown shall have its reward,
>   says the LORD,
>   they shall return from the enemy's land.
> There is hope for your future, says the LORD;
>   your sons shall return to their own borders.
> I hear, I hear Ephraim pleading:
>   You chastised me, and I am chastened;
>   I was an untamed calf.
> If you allow me, I will return,
>   for you are the LORD, my God.
> I turn in repentance;
>   I have come to myself, I strike my breast;
> I blush with shame,
>   I bear the disgrace of my youth.
> Turn back, O virgin Israel,
>   turn back to these your cities.
> How long will you continue to stray,
>   rebellious daughter?
> The LORD has created a new thing upon the earth:
>   the woman must encompass the man with devotion.
> (Jer 31:16-19, 21-22)

It is with the evocation of this idyllic future that Jeremiah's message ends.[41] The prophet himself, a sign and harbinger for his people in his very person and destiny, passes through the crucible of suffering, of exile.[42] He even had to endure the trial of doubting this exacting God who forced him to change all the representations he entertained about him.

"The LORD appears to him from afar" (Jer 31:3). We may guess something of the torments all those sent by God suffer when their mission transforms them into unrelenting messengers of divine wrath. Such suffering is perfectly normal. For in full solidarity with the people they are addressing, prophets are also in full sympathy with what one may dare to call

"divine feelings": the tenderness of the God of the covenant, his wrath and indignation at seeing his love scorned, his own repentance at the sight of repenting sinners. The God of the prophets is a God who feels, who is moved by vehement passions, which his witnesses often experience in their own lives.

Jeremiah, better than anyone else, gives us a glimpse of the interior drama and intimate reactions that are his under God's powerful hand. In his book, we have more than isolated indications to substantiate our conjectures. He hides nothing from us, neither his resistance—indeed, his revolts—nor his suffering, which appears, unvarnished, throughout his writing. Is not his first movement, in the face of the divine call, one of retreat and terror?

> "Ah, Lord God!" I said,
> "I know not how to speak; I am too young."
> (Jer 1:6)

There is nothing of a superman or an athlete of God in Jeremiah. He has no natural inclination to go up to Jerusalem to do battle for the cause of God's interests. He is a shy man, made for the ordinary joys of family life, a country youth close to nature. But God chooses whom he wants, according to criteria that are not ours, and his choices are final. He does not grow irritated by the resistance that Jeremiah, aware of his natural limits, offers him; but neither does he take back any of the demands made by his call. He assures the prophet of the one essential thing: his divine support. "If God is for us, who can be against us?" Paul will later exclaim (Rom 8:31).

> But the Lord answered me,
> Say not, "I am too young."
> To whomever I send you, you shall go;
> whatever I command you, you shall speak.
> Have no fear before them,
> because I am with you to deliver you, says the Lord.
> (Jer 1:7-8)

"I am with you": this is an assurance that should forever strengthen human faintheartedness. But prophetic inspiration and even divine help do not change the nature of the conscious and free instruments God uses. The great mystics whom he one day approaches go through the "nights of faith" during which their humanity, faced with the mystery, loses its footing, is bewildered, like a disturbed compass needle searching for the pole. "Nights of faith" during which the soul is refined, purified as gold in a crucible, and little by little discovers God's presence in the very core of his absence.

The "Confessions of Jeremiah," which evoke those of St. Augustine,[43] preserve for us a direct echo of the inner drama lived by the prophet. Assured as he is of God's protection, he obeys and delivers his message. Nonetheless, he is disconcerted by the hostility he meets with. This divine word, in which he delights, brings him nothing but hatred and contempt.

> When I found your words, I devoured them;
>   they became my joy and the happiness of my heart,
> Because I bore your name,
>   O LORD, God of hosts.
> (Jer 15:16)

However, everybody curses him.

> All the day I am an object of laughter;
>   everyone mocks me. . . .
> The word of the LORD has brought me
>   derision and reproach all the day.
> (Jer 20:7-8; see 15:10)

Soon, people will not stop at contesting his preaching. They will go so far as to plot against him: first his neighbors in Anathoth who plan to assassinate him (see 11:18), then other opponents, probably in Jerusalem.

> "Come," they said, "let us contrive a plot against Jeremiah. It will not mean the loss of instruction from the priests, nor of counsel from the wise, nor of messages from the prophets. And so, let us destroy him by his own tongue; let us carefully note his every word" (18:18).

The priest, the sage, the prophet: by his threats, Jeremiah has alienated these official representatives of the people. Sure that he is in the right, he then appeals to this God who has promised to be with him:

> Must good be repaid with evil
>   that they should dig a pit to take my life?
> Remember that I stood before you
>   to speak in their behalf,
>   to turn away your wrath from them.
> (Jer 20:20)

It is a disheartened prophet who here gives voice to his bewilderment. A believer, certainly, since he calls on the remembrance of God. But also a being of flesh and blood who, in the silence and anguish of midnight, ends by wondering whether God is the one who told him, "I shall be with you."

> You have indeed become for me a treacherous brook,
>   whose waters do not abide!
> (Jer 15:18)

Dizziness seizes him: Is the God to whom he wholly gave himself really God? Revolt brushes against this timid man who feels he has been deceived by a Seducer who now is dropping him.

> You duped me, O LORD, and I let myself be duped;
>   you were too strong for me, and you triumphed. . . .
> I say to myself, I will not mention him,
>   I will speak in his name no more.
> But then it becomes like fire burning in my heart,
>   imprisoned in my bones;
> I grow weary holding it in,
>   I cannot endure it.
> (Jer 20:7, 9)

The crisis of faith is of necessity accompanied by a crisis of his identity as a prophet: Is Jeremiah himself, the accuser of false prophets who speak "visions of their own fancy" (23:16), a genuine prophet of God? Is he still able to separate the true from the false, to avoid self-deception concerning the efficacy of his words?

> Heal me, LORD, that I may be healed;
>   save me, that I may be saved,
>   for it is you whom I praise.
> See how they say to me,
>   "Where is the word of the LORD?
>   Let it come to pass!"
> Yet I did not press you to send calamity;
>   the day without remedy I have not desired.
> You know what passed my lips;
>   it is present before you.
> Do not be my ruin,
>   you, my refuge in the day of misfortune.
> (Jer 17:14-17)

Such an entreaty expresses well the darkness in which Jeremiah walks. It is a prelude to the anguished prayer of Jesus in the garden of Gethsemane; it announces his cry of distress on the cross, a cry into which he willed to assume all our cries.[44]

The long complaint of chapter 20 expresses in an exemplary manner Jeremiah's alternation between despair and revolt on the one side and faith on the other. It is futile to pretend to find any logical order in this cry of pain in which, despite everything, faith expresses itself in its two-fold dimension of doubt and certainty, of insecurity and peace, of night and light.[45] In the last analysis, faith is often doubt overcome. In the admirable development that the Letter to the Hebrews devotes to the faith of great believers, the author specifies that "faith is the realization of what is hoped for and evidence of things not seen" (11:1). In this respect, the case of Jeremiah is exceptional: the questions he asked himself tormented him to the end. He got nothing of what he hoped for; he did not grasp what he could not see. All he did was cling with all his soul to the promises inherent in his struggles. By living his questions to the end, he advanced toward the answer, but always in the dark.

> But the Lord is with me, like a mighty champion:
>   my persecutors will stumble, they will not triumph.
> In their failure they will be put to utter shame,
>   to lasting, unforgettable confusion.
> O Lord of hosts, you who test the just,
>   who probe mind and heart,
> Let me witness the vengeance you take on them,
>   for to you I have entrusted my cause.
> Sing to the Lord,
>   praise the Lord,
> For he has rescued the life of the poor
>   from the power of the wicked!
> (Jer 20:11-13)

The Obedience of Faith

The long career of Jeremiah is a good illustration of what Paul calls the "obedience of faith" (Rom 1:5).

Dramatic was his obedience to the command received at the time of his call: "to destroy and to demolish / to build and to plant" (1:10). The prophet exhausted himself to root up and tear down sin by attacking the paganizing tendencies remaining in Judah, the narrow-minded nationalism of the chosen people, the spiritless ritualism of Temple worship. He also built and planted, especially when he announced the new covenant and the religion of the future, when Christ, the mediator of the definitive covenant, would open to everyone by his blood the temple where God is present.

Dramatic was his obedience to God himself. Jeremiah was not the witness of tranquil faith. What he makes us discover in his own journey is faith as experience of unending exodus. He also makes us discover that God himself is a God of exodus, an unending mystery that initiates in us a search for the fullness of faith that is always before us. Adherence to God, which at the outset is a fight against oneself, continues to rule over us as long as we live, always to be begun again, never possessed. Here below, all we can ever do is "to seek God" by purifying the notions we have of him. "To follow God wherever he leads is to see God."[46] Here below, all we can ever hope for is to see his back. But for those who, like Jeremiah, painfully learn the obedience of faith, little by little the distance of God becomes infinite closeness. As a light in the darkest hour of night, the assurance that God is seeking us even before we seek him breaks forth. This divine presence in the distance is not like a mirage that vanishes as soon as we try to seize it; it invites us to start walking behind a God who never ceases to reveal to us that he fills heaven and earth (see Jer 23:23-24).

Because of his obedience to his vocation and his obedience to a God who unveils himself, Jeremiah, a prophet for a time of crisis and conversion, offers us in his book a reading doubly appropriate for our time, especially during Lent.

Passion Sunday (Palm Sunday)

On the next day, that is, the Lord's Day, which begins the Paschal week, and which they call here the Great Week, when all the customary services from cockcrow until morning have taken place in the Anastasis and at the Cross, they proceed on the morning of the Lord's Day according to custom to the greater church, which is called the martyrium. It is called the martyrium because it is in Golgotha behind the Cross, where the Lord suffered. When all that is customary has been observed in the great church, and before the dismissal is made, the archdeacon lifts his voice and says first: "Throughout the whole week, beginning from tomorrow, let us all assemble in the martyrium, that is, in the great church, at the ninth hour." Then he lifts his voice again, saying: "Let us all be ready today in Eleona at the seventh hour" . . . . After the dismissal from the martyrium, every one hastens home to eat, that all may be ready at the beginning of the seventh hour in the church in Eleona, on the Mount of Olives, where is the cave in which the Lord was wont to teach.

Accordingly at the seventh hour all the people go up to the Mount of Olives, that is, to Eleona, and the bishop with them, to the church, where hymns and antiphons suitable to the day and to the place are said, and lessons in like manner. And when the ninth hour approaches they go up with hymns to the Imbomon, that is, to the place whence the Lord ascended into heaven, and there they sit down. . . . And as the eleventh hour approaches, the passage from the Gospel is read, where the children, carrying branches and palms, met the Lord, saying: *Blessed is He that cometh in the name of the Lord*, and the bishop immediately rises, and all the people with him, and they all go on foot from the top of the Mount of Olives, all the people going before him with hymns and antiphons, answering one to another: *Blessed is He that cometh in the Name of the Lord*. And all the children in the neighbourhood, even those who are too young to walk, are carried by their parents on their shoulders, all of them bearing branches, some of palms and some of olives, and thus the bishop is escorted in the same manner as the Lord was of old. . . . For all . . . accompany the bishop all the way on foot in this manner, making these responses, from the top of the mount to the city, and thence through the whole city to the Anastasis, going very slowly lest the people should be wearied; and thus they arrive at the Anastasis at a late hour. And on arriving, although it is late, *lucernare* takes place, with prayer at the Cross; after which the people are dismissed.[1]

That is how the liturgy of Palm Sunday was carried out in Jerusalem in the fourth century, on the eve of the "Great Week." A Sunday Eucharist inaugurated Passion Week. It was followed by a procession in honor of Christ the King. During this procession, hymns and antiphons, punctuated by the refrain ''Blessed is he who comes in the name of the Lord,'' were sung, the Gospel of Jesus' entry into the holy city was proclaimed. This long liturgy slowly unfolded in the midst of a large assembly.[2]

Etheria's description thus proves to us that the Jerusalem liturgy in the fourth century already contained the essential elements of today's liturgy. Beyond the vicissitudes of this rite in the West, beyond the modifications or heavy additions and enlargements of certain of its elements,[3] the emphasis has remained the same: while the doors of his city are opened for the King, the Church already celebrates his triumph, being assured of the victory he will gain by his glorious cross.

The Procession with Palm Branches

The Gates of the City Open for the King

All during Lent, the assembly of believers walk behind Christ as he goes up to Jerusalem. In this "favorable time" of forty days, the Church intensifies its efforts unceasingly to this dynamic journey from earth to heaven, toward him who "is the head . . . the firstborn from the dead" (Col 1:18). This march of the Church militant is like a procession ascending, until the end of time, toward our mother, Jerusalem on high. The entrance of Jesus, the Messiah-King, into the holy city prophetically anticipates his paschal triumph and his entry into heavenly glory, into which the multitude of his disciples follow him. It also suggests what weapons he will employ to conquer the enemy: soon, the humble Savior will walk carrying his cross on the other side of the hill.

This is what the liturgy of Passion Sunday commemorates by taking up, in the procession that opens the celebration, the homage of an entire people, young and old, a few days before Passover. The welcome given to the Lord, ephemeral though it was, was already addressed to "the Son of David . . . he who comes in the name of the Lord." While singing this verse from Psalm 118 (opening antiphon of the procession), the Church acclaims him who once again comes to save his people by the sacrament of paschal celebration. Yes, he is the one sent by the Father. He comes to fulfill what has been said of him in the Law, the Psalms, and the Prophets. Even prior to reenacting the diverse steps of his Pasch during the Easter Triduum, the Church, in advance, acclaims the triumph of Christ and asks God to follow him into the everlasting Jerusalem (prayer for blessing the branches).

The procession with branches must not be mistaken for any kind of folkloric reconstruction of an event, memorable certainly, but definitively belonging to the past. What could this contribute to our faith? The processional liturgy of Passion Sunday is a celebration of the mystery of salvation in which we already share and from which, year in year out, the feast of Easter allows us to benefit more fully. As the procession starts

us walking to meet Christ, King and Savior, we join the immense cortege of God's people throughout the centuries—an assembly that is not
immobile or still, but is carried by an ascending motion up to God's
throne.[4] This is a solemn procession in which he is both present and always to come. This is a presence symbolized by the cross, the Gospel
book, the icon of Christ, or even by the presider.[5] This is a presence within
absence, since people walk to meet Christ by going toward the altar in
the middle of the church where the sacramental memorial of his passover
is about to be celebrated. This is a glorious cortege, no doubt, but also
a prelude to Passion Week. There is great gladness, but the fullness of
joy is reserved for Easter and its renewal. How could the Church forget
that it is about to live anew, day after day, in the one who is its high
priest, the phases of his glorious passion? And this, not through an un-
wholesome interest in the sufferings of its master, but because his wounds
heal us. The Church knows that by choosing for himself this way
"through the cross to the light"—*per crucem ad lucem*—the Savior has also
traced for the multitude of his disciples the way of salvation.

> See, the gates of the city open for the king:
> Hosanna! Blessed are you, Lord!
> Why will you close over me the tombstone
> in the garden?
>
> *God Savior, forget our sin,*
> *but remember your love*
> *when you come into your kingdom!*
>
> I am coming, riding a donkey colt, as the sign
> of my glory:
> Hosanna! Blessed are you, Lord!
> Why will you lead me out among evildoers
> and accursed ones?
>
> Your streets are strewn with cloaks thrown on my way:
> Hosanna! Blessed are you, Lord!
> Why will you defile my body with purple and spittle,
> my body delivered for you?
>
> Your hands lift branches at the hour of triumph:
> Hosanna! Blessed are you, Lord!
> Why will you bruise my forehead with thorns and reeds
> while mocking me?[6]

The Gospel on the Road

Before the procession begins, the proclamation of the Gospel also expresses the encounter between the Church and the one it acclaims as king.
In order that this encounter might happen, it is not enough that the word
be pronounced and heard; it is necessary that it be welcomed with joy.
It is quite natural that the entrance into Jerusalem, a few days before the
Passover,[7] be evoked in one of the four versions: Matthew (Year A), Mark
or John (Year B), and Luke (Year C). Despite basic data that refer to one
and the same event, each of them has its particular perspective because
of biblical, liturgical, or cultural preoccupations.[8]

The Places

The places mentioned by the evangelists are not insignificant for listening hearts. Readers familiar with Scripture know well what the Mount
of Olives, from which Jesus departs with his own, suggests. Is it not from
there that the Messiah will come at the end of time? "That day his feet
shall rest upon the Mount of Olives, which is opposite Jerusalem to the
east. The Mount of Olives shall be cleft in two from east to west by a
very deep valley" (Zech 14:4).

Is not Bethany, where Jesus comes from and where he will return to
after crossing Jerusalem, "the house of the poor" in Hebrew? Humble
and peaceful, the Lord does not linger in this Jerusalem that kills prophets
and stones those sent to it.

As to Bethphage, "the house of figs" in Aramaic, Jesus will soon curse
the barren fig tree, as if wanting to warn Jerusalem one last time that it
has not borne the fruit God expected of it.

The Cortege

The cortege recalls several royal enthronements narrated in the Old Testament. At the time of Elisha (ninth century), in the northern kingdom,
the supporters of Jehu spread their cloaks under his feet as a sign of royal
enthronement (see 2 Kgs 9:13; Matt 21:7). When, toward the end of his
reign, David designated his successor to the throne, he gave this command to his officers, "Mount my son Solomon upon my own mule" (1
Kgs 1:33; Luke 19:35). Moreover, all accounts mention the little donkey
borrowed by Jesus to make his entrance. According to several oracles,
the Messiah will use this peaceful mount when he comes among his
people (see Gen 49:11; Zech 9:9). Mark and Luke insist on the quasi-

consecrated character of the animal: no one has ever sat on it (see Mark 11:2; Luke 19:30), as if the one to ride it is himself a person consecrated to sacrifice.[9]

The Fourth Gospel underlines in its own way the royal aspect of the episode: it is an advent that borrows from the ceremonial of the "joyous entrances" (*parousias*) of sovereigns into Hellenistic cities. For Christians of Greek culture, the crowd that goes to meet Jesus, upon learning of his nearing Jerusalem, prefigures what will happen at the last coming (*parousia*) of the Lord. His triumphal entrance into Jerusalem thus acquires a coloration suggestive of his manifestation at the end time (*eschaton*).

A Liturgy

Finally, let us take note of the liturgical dimension of the episode. Jesus is welcomed by a crowd carrying palms (see John 12:13) and singing a few verses from Psalm 118 (mentioned in all four accounts). As signs of victory, adornment of royal triumph, and symbol of power in Israel, palm branches were used, at least since the second century B.C., during the feast of Booths. After the Maccabean revolt against the Greek occupation and the purification of the Temple that followed the victory, this liturgical feast reinforced the messianic hope and collective expectation of the last times, still strongly attested by Revelation (see Rev 7:9; see also 2 Macc 10:6-7).[10] The crowd acclaims in Jesus "the one who comes," an expression that certainly designates the Messiah and has become current in Christian usage.[11]

Four Gospels on the Road

The four accounts of Jesus' entrance into Jerusalem take on their full significance once we have noted the traits just mentioned.

The Liturgical March of the Son of David

In Year A, we read Matthew's Gospel (21:1-11). This narrative must be placed within the context of the liturgical march that forms its framework (Matt 20:29–21:16). It unfolds in three stages, each being punctuated by the acclamation "Son of David."

First of all, in Jericho, two blind men implore Jesus to cure them, in spite of the "great crowd" that wants to silence them, "[Lord], Son of

David, have pity on us!'' (Matt 20:29-30). At the time of the entrance into Jerusalem, "the crowds preceding him and those following" repeat this title as an acclamation, "Hosanna to the Son of David." Unknowingly, they thus fulfill the praise the Psalmist addressed to God and is now applied to Jesus, "O LORD, our Lord, / how glorious is your name over all the earth!" (Ps 8:2).[12] But how can Jesus be "Lord"? Matthew suggests it: by his lowliness and humility, highlighted by the textual quotation from part of the oracle of the prophet Zechariah (see Zech 9:9). Jesus is the "Son of David" because he is the humble king announced in Scripture, also the model of this people, "meek" and "humble," to which Matthew likes to refer (see 5:5; 11:29). Well known to the Jews, Zechariah's oracle becomes Christianized, not without Matthew's softening the aspect of joy that it had. How, on this day, could the daughter of Zion "shout for joy," while its inhabitants, despite a fleeting enthusiasm, prepare to reject and crucify the "Son of David" (see Matt 27:37)?

If, for the first sentence of Zechariah's oracle, we should substitute the beginning of Isaiah's, "Say to daughter Zion . . ." (62:11), we have the vision of the definitively restored Jerusalem that Matthew wants to evoke (see Isa 60:1–62:12). When Jesus will have suffered his passion, the liturgical march will come to a stop before a Son of David, "a just savior [and] meek" (Zech 9:9).

The Paschal Course of the Lord

In Year B, we read Mark's Gospel (11:1-10). In the context of the Second Gospel, there is a profound similarity between the entrance into Jerusalem and the Last Supper, which is prelude to the passion (see 11:1-10; 14:12-16). In both cases, Jesus gives precise instructions concerning the unfolding of events: he wants to order everything according to his intention. At the Last Supper, it is the "Master" who speaks; here, it is the "Lord" who commands. This latter expression is the more remarkable in that it is unique in Mark's Gospel, and the Savior is about to receive his first royal ovation. Still, we must understand it correctly.

By acclaiming in Jesus "the kingdom of our father David that is to come," the crowd expresses its hope in a political messianism. The Old Testament oracle could probably transform the crowd's so earthly conception of the Davidic royalty (see Zech 9:9). However, for that to happen, the crowd would have to accept to belong to the race of the humble and peaceful ones: only then could it see how vast the distance is between the prophecy and its realization.

Having come from Bethany, "the house of the lowly," Jesus, in order to correct it, challenges the acclamation of a people slow to understand. The Son of David will become the Lord only by suffering his passion—very much the contrary of what the crowd hopes for! Bethphage, "the house of the fig tree," is, alas, close also to the Mount of Olives. But who among the multitude will understand this and comprehend the curse addressed to the sterile fig tree?

The Joyous Entrance of the King of the Universe

In Year B, we may also choose to read John's Gospel (12:12-19). As it is related in the Fourth Gospel, the "joyous entrance" of Jesus into Jerusalem must be understood in the perspective of his approaching paschal glorification. Once more, the context of the narrative is important. Differing from Mark and Matthew, who place the anointment in Bethany at the beginning of the passion account, John tells the story immediately before the entrance of "the King of Israel" into his city.[13] Thus, by the anointment he has just received and by his triumph over death at the raising of Lazarus, Jesus establishes his claim to be enthroned as king.[14]

It is in his quality of "King of Israel" that the crowd, which "went out to meet him," greets him. In the manner of the populace of any Hellenistic city, palms in hand, it acclaims the joyous coming of its ruler. The acclamation is political, strongly smacking of nationalism: this is not the first time the crowd expresses its misunderstanding of Jesus (see John 1:49; 6:14). He cannot let this demonstration pass without setting things straight. He does this by a prophecy in action: taking a donkey's colt, he mounts it, thus fulfilling the Scriptures—"as it is written." Here we have a reference to Zechariah's oracle (9:9) cited also by the Synoptics. But another oracle pronounced by Zephaniah sheds as much light on his behavior.

> Shout for joy, O daughter Zion!
>   sing joyfully, O Israel!
> Be glad and exult with all your heart,
>   O daughter Jerusalem!
> The LORD has removed . . .
>   . . . your enemies;
> The King of Israel, the LORD, is in your midst,
>   you have no further misfortune to fear.
> On that day, it shall be said to Jerusalem:
>   Fear not, O Zion, be not discouraged!
> He will rejoice over you with gladness,
>   and renew you in his love,

He will sing joyfully because of you. . . .
(Zeph 14-17)

In this oracle, the (divine) image of the king who is the Lord is entirely stripped of any nationalistic color.[15] Jesus sets himself in front of a parade of peoples whose lips he will "change and purify . . . that they all may call upon the name of the Lord" (Zeph 3:9). He is no longer only the "King of Israel" acclaimed by a crowd mistaken on his account. As the Pharisees bitterly recognize, Jesus is the universal king: "Look, the whole world has gone after him." In any case, the Fourth Gospel has just recalled the universal mission that Jesus will realize on his glorious cross: he came "to gather into one the dispersed children of God" (John 11:52).

Immediately after his joyous entrance into Jerusalem, some Greeks will express the desire to see him, to meet him through Philip as an intermediary; they are the first-fruits of all those who go to meet him who came to save them, him who is the king of the universe (see 12:20-23).

The Non-Entrance of Jesus into Jerusalem

In Year C, we read Luke's Gospel (19:28-40). The narrative joins Jesus in his ascent to Jerusalem; he approaches it, but it is the Temple that he will enter (see 19:45). This is one of the original and well-known traits of Luke's Gospel, which begins and ends in the Temple (1:9; 24:53).

Another significant feature is that here Jerusalem is called by its Greek name, *Hierosolyma*, different from the Hebrew form, *Hierousalem*, which Luke habitually uses to speak of the holy city.[16] At the moment when he who comes in the name of the Lord is going to be crucified, the secular name of the city is seen as more fitting than its sacred name.

Other redactional details allow us to perceive even better the meaning of the episode. It is "the whole multitude of his disciples" that blesses its king, he who comes in the name of the Lord. This praise corresponds exactly to what Jesus was announcing at the end of his lament over Jerusalem, "I tell you, you will not see me until [the time comes when] you say, 'Blessed is he who comes in the name of the Lord' " (13:35). In Luke's mind, the "multitude of his disciples" is composed of the community of the faithful, whose life and missionary activity he describes in the Acts of the Apostles. This new people of God lives in the hope of the definitive return of him who already has entered into the heavenly temple.

The praise the disciples utter confirms our impression that Luke addresses himself to a Church that occupies in some way "the middle time."

"Peace in Heaven / and glory in the highest." This acclamation on Passion Sunday corresponds to that of the "multitude of the heavenly host" at Christmas: "Glory to God in the highest / and on earth peace to those on whom his favor rests" (2:13). Disciples and angels are together the actors of a liturgy in which the acclamation "Peace in heaven" corresponds, from now on, to the praise "Peace on earth."

The exaltation of the King at Easter is in stark contrast to the lowliness of the child at Christmas. Without opposition between heaven and earth—or the group of angels and that of the disciples—it is one single and unanimous praise that from now on is directed toward Jesus, our king, who came in the name of the Lord.

At the end of the exodus that Jesus has accomplished in Jerusalem (see 9:31) the end of all things is in some way woven into the story of humankind. The parable of the ten gold coins is a good illustration of this meantime, where the eschatological end already weaves the fabric of history: "A nobleman went off to a distant country to obtain the kingship for himself and then to return" (19:12). The non-entrance of Jesus into Jerusalem prophetically represents the exaltation of Christ already realized, and yet still expected in its full manifestation by the multitude of believers.

> Humble Savior
> for what glory
> do you enter the city?
> "Hosanna! Hosanna!"
> The crowd cries its joy.
> But you are already approaching the hill,
> on the other side of the city,
> carrying the cross . . .
>
> *Son of David,*
> *open our eyes,*
> *and we shall see your glory!*
>
> Jerusalem, Jerusalem,
> how often I wanted to gather your children,
> and you did not want it!
>
> Jerusalem, Jerusalem,
> if you had understood my message of peace . . .
> but it remained hidden from your eyes!
>
> Jerusalem, Jerusalem,
> you who kill and stone the prophets,
> you have not known the time of my visit.[17]

Mass of the Passion

We Recall Your Death, Lord Jesus

Whereas the procession with branches celebrates, in its multiple aspects, the triumph of Christ the King, the Mass of Passion Sunday chiefly evokes the harsh conditions of his victory: the persecutions he endured (Isa 50:4-7, First Reading), his humility and obedience until death (Phil 2:6-11, Second Reading), his harrowing Passion According to Matthew (Year A), Mark (Year B), and Luke (Year C). But hope never dies: the Suffering Servant trusts in his God and God exalts him to the point of conferring on him the name that is above all names. Even in the passion narratives, tension slackens with the last breath of the Son and his entombment.

The prayers accompanying the readings of the scriptural texts are in harmony with Paul's exhortation in the introduction of his Christological hymn, "Have among yourselves the same attitude that is also yours in Christ Jesus. . ." (Phil 2:5). How could we conceive of a more beautiful model of life and death? The contemplation of the suffering Christ invites us to pray to him who has mysteriously willed the humbling of his Son.

> Help us to bear witness to you
> by following his example of suffering
> and make us worthy to share in his resurrection.
> (Opening Prayer)

In order to obtain forgiveness, we do not count on our merits, but we pray to God, saying,

> Alone we can do nothing
> but may this perfect sacrifice
> win us your mercy and love.
> (Prayer over the Gifts)

Moreover, in our participation in the sacramental memorial of his passion, we dare to ask,

> May his resurrection give us perseverance
> and lead us to salvation.
> (Prayer after Communion)

"I Gave My Back to Those Who Beat Me"

The Liturgy of the Word opens each year with the proclamation of that text from Isaiah which is called the third song of the Suffering Servant (Isa 50:4-7).[18]

This text exalts the Servant's perseverance and constancy: he faithfully dispenses a teaching that shocks the hearers to whom he is sent. This faithfulness is certainly meritorious, even though the Servant cannot evade it, because the teaching he imparts is not his own. The Lord himself instructs him; the constant contact with the Lord's word keeps him watchful and goads him so that he cannot not speak. The daily nearness of the Servant to his Master explains his courage, his ability to comfort others who are worn out. Whence his strength of soul, his nonviolence. He does not defend himself. He puts his trust in God, since it is because of his word that he is reduced to such dire straits.

But who is he? A wise master who, while fulfilling his mandate, knows how to keep the serenity that befits his mission? More than that: a prophet who, without being as tormented a figure as Jeremiah, reminds us of so many spokespersons of a God they instinctively know will not abandon them. Although forewarned of the obstinacy and hostility of the listeners they will have to challenge, they do not flinch when contradiction arises.

> The Lord GOD is my help,
>   therefore I am not disgraced;
> I have set my face like flint,
> knowing that I shall not be put to shame.

This is a monologue that we find in Jeremiah and Ezekiel (see Jer 1:18; Ezek 3:8-9), figures of the old covenant that Jesus came to fulfill. He, too, has courageously taken the road to Jerusalem.[19] He did not protest against the blows he received (see Mark 14:65). By presenting Jesus as this Servant of God, the Church wants to show that far from holding the divine plan in check, the outrages inflicted on him were rather its profound realization. Such is the logic of the cross: to die by the hatred of others in order that they may live again by Christ's love. Only God can give all of us the proofs of his love and render us capable, through the example of his Servant, of hoping against all hope in the victory of love stronger than death.

> *My God, my God, why have you abandoned me?*
>
> All who see me scoff at me;
>   they mock me with parted lips, they wag their heads:

"He relied on the LORD; let him deliver him,
    let him rescue him, if he loves him."
Indeed, many dogs surround me,
    a pack of evildoers closes in upon me;
They have pierced my hands and my feet;
    I can count all my bones.
    . . . they divide my garments among them,
    and for my vesture they cast lots.
But you, O LORD, be not far from me;
    O my help, hasten to aid me.
I will proclaim your name to my brethren;
    in the midst of the assembly I will praise you;
"You who fear the LORD, praise him;
    all you descendants of Jacob, give glory to him. . . ."
(Ps 22:8-9, 17-18a, 19-20, 23-24b)

He Humbled Himself; God Raised Him Up

On this Passion Sunday, the Christological hymn from the Letter to the Philippians invites us to contemplate the whole paschal itinerary of Christ. Is it not also ours, the very object of our faith in a salvation that reaches all human beings and the totality of each human being? We must meditate on this hymn together with the songs of the Suffering Servant in the second part of Isaiah's book. Reminiscences are many, even though the liturgical translation at times sacrifices precision for the sake of rendering the text easier to understand, always a risky proposition (Phil 2:6-11).[20]

In the first stanza (vv. 6-7a), the hymn reminds us that the Son of Man "did not regard equality with God / something to be grasped"; this cannot but bring the fourth song of the Suffering Servant to mind.[21] In contrast to Adam and Eve, and their pretense to "be like gods" (see Gen 3:4), Christ chose to assume "the form of a slave" and to "humble himself."[22] This refers also to the Suffering Servant who "surrendered himself to death" (Isa 53:12). Assuredly, the Son did not cease to be God when he became a human being, but he renounced all divine privileges— honor, power, glory—in order to become the obedient servant of his Father's plans.

Furthermore, as the second stanza states (vv. 7b-8), he took on our sinful nature by accepting to suffer in this nature, he the Innocent One, in the place of the guilty ones who had deserved death (see Isa 53:11). The author's conviction is clear: if the Son of God put on true human nature, and not just an appearance of humanity and vulnerability, it was in order to justify us, to make us righteous, and thus to obtain for us the forgiveness of our faults (see Mark 10:45; Heb 5:7).

"Coming in human likeness and found human in appearance," Jesus had, in his contemporaries' eyes, the exterior appearance of a true human being; but this appearance does not belong to an ordinary human. When Pilate presented him to the mob, crowned with thorns and bearing the marks of the scourging, the expression "Here is the man" (John 19:5) summed up all the frailty and precariousness by which, from manger to cross, Jesus' life presaged his death.

The insistence on Jesus' humiliation and radical obedience, brings to memory several reminiscences from the songs of the Suffering Servant. Did God not grant him an ear to hear, that is, to obey (see Isa 50:4; Heb 10:5-10)? Did he not resolve, in his mysterious designs, "to crush him in infirmity" (Isa 53:10)? And, in fact, Jesus, Son of God, humbled himself, emptied himself in death (see Isa 53:7-12); he made his Father's will his food.

"Because of this . . ." The third stanza (vv. 9-11) describes the reversal of the situation: the glorification that comes to reward the voluntary obedience of the Son to his Father (see Isa 53:12). Whereas the beginning of the hymn recalls the condition of servant, assumed by Jesus, here he receives "the name / that is above every name," the name of "Lord," a title that expresses his divine dignity, his transcendent messiahship.[23] He exercises his power "in heaven and on earth and under the earth," that is to say, the whole creation. By its prostration and confession of faith, creation recognizes in him the one whom the second song of the Suffering Servant already announced.

> When kings see you, they shall stand up,
>   and princes shall prostrate themselves
> Because of the LORD who is faithful,
>   the Holy One of Israel who has chosen you.
> (Isa 49:7; see 52:15)

Did Jesus conceive of his ministry little by little according to the tragic progression of the songs of the Suffering Servant? Beginning with the mysterious experience he knew at his baptism in the Jordan (see Mark 1:10-11; Isa 42:1), the Gospels show him to us in turn toiling in vain (see Isa 49:4), experiencing bitter persecutions (see Isa 50:5-6), and finally meeting an ignominious death (see Isa 52:13–53:12). Thus, progressively assuming his role, he truly became, at the end of his life, the perfect Servant of God, the Lamb who takes away the sin of the world, according to John's formula (see 1:29-36).

The hymn in Philippians goes farther. True to the liturgical mode, it immediately places us at the center of the divine mystery, and therefore of the human mystery. When faced with the great question of the redemptive incarnation, it addresses the believer's "Why?" Why did the divine Word come into the world, and why did his own not receive him and end by crucifying him?

> But why such insistence? Because human existence was designed to rest not only on divine creation and bountiful all-inclusive activity, but also upon human decision—precisely *because* God's omnipotence is crowned in the freedom of the individual to accept or reject him.
>
> There are two kinds of freedom: a first and a second. The second consists of being free to act in truth and goodness: I recognize so clearly, so overwhelmingly who God is, that I have no choice but to accept him. This is the true freedom, but it presupposes the other, the primary freedom, which consists of my ability to accept God or to reject him. Fearful possibility, yet the gravity and dignity of human existence depends on it. God could not spare us the burden of this freedom. In order that it might exist, his own power had to be curtailed, for had he come to earth as the Omnipotent One, it would have been impossible to reject him.
> (2 Cor 8:9; Phil 2:7)[24]

From beginning to end, the earthly life of Christ was a "Yes" to God so that all divine promises had their fulfillment in him. Mirror image of sinful Adam, Jesus is the new Adam who reorients the whole of humankind toward its end. "Therefore, the Amen from us also goes through him to God for glory" (2 Cor 1:20).

Mystery of Calvary, Scandal of the Cross

We read the Gospel accounts of the passion successively: Matthew's (Year A), Mark's (Year B), and Luke's (Year C). Each version tells the story with a distinctive literary and didactic accent. But all of them present as one indivisible account the story of one event in several episodes. Unlike what we read in other parts of the Gospels, we do not have a series of distinct and independent episodes grouped in a continuous narration.

If we except the introduction treating of the plot against Jesus, the anointing in Bethany,[25] and the betrayal by Judas, the narrative centers on one day: from Thursday evening to Friday evening. In the course of this unique day take place the Eucharistic supper, the agony in Gethsemane, the arrest of Jesus, the appearances before the Sanhedrin and Pilate, the sentence of death, the carrying of the cross, the crucifixion, and, finally, the burial.

The narrative is unified and develops, from one evening to the next, its irresistible progression. It must be read from beginning to end, without any commentary. It must be received as a grace allowing us to discover, beyond the personal testimony of each writer and the originality of his composition, the density of one single message of faith: Christ died for our sins, according to the Scriptures.[26] We have here one Gospel.

The Gospel of the Passion According to Matthew

Matthew addresses himself to a gathering of believers. In a doctrinal and quasi-liturgical style, he offers Christ's disciples some keys to understanding the passion. He wants to introduce his readers to the Christian understanding of the disconcerting events that led their Master and Lord to die on the cross. Thus, they will be able, by sharing in the faith of the Church, to situate the cross within the coherent whole of the divine salvific plan (Matt 26:14–27:66).

The text is punctuated, in a rather solemn way, by words that highlight contrasts by repeatedly having recourse to the testimony of Scripture, especially the psalms and prophets. What is striking from this ensemble is the responsibility of the leaders of the people in Jesus' death, as well as the end of the old covenant and the birth of Christ's Church. But, even more, the emphasis is placed on the profound and filial submission of Jesus to his Father's plan, on his perfect obedience expressed by the necessary fulfillment of the Scriptures, and on his power and authority as Son of God.

Matthew very closely follows Mark's text. To this somewhat amplified edition of his model, he nevertheless adds certain episodes that come to him from other traditions. He is the only one to report Judas' remorse and suicide. He mentions the behavior of Pilate, who, ignoring his wife's warning to spare Jesus, washes his hands of any responsibility and lets others act as they please. Matthew also notes the miraculous happenings that marked the death of the Son of God.[27]

As is his wont, Matthew develops the scriptural argument more fully than the other Gospel writers. The fulfillment of the Scriptures is a divine necessity: it expresses God's plan as it was gradually revealed to prophets like Isaiah, Daniel, Zechariah; to psalmists taken from among the humble people of the "poor of the Lord." The evangelist has so thoroughly assimilated biblical language that we pass without transition from what he says to what was written in the Scriptures. Sometimes, Matthew is content to state "it is written" or else "to fulfill what the Lord had said through the prophet. . ." (1:22), "this was to fulfill what had been spoken through Isaiah the prophet" (12:17). No, all that has happened is not due to blind chance. We must enter with faith into the painful passion of Jesus, because it inaugurates the new world where God wants his Son's disciples to live.

This Christological perspective eminently characterizes Matthew's narrative. We cannot fail to be struck by the frequent occurrence of the name of Jesus, as well as by the fact that before the high priest Jesus solemnly declares that he is "seated at the right hand of the Power" (26:64). He is not overwhelmed by his destiny, he remains its master. He knows that his time is near and he knows who will betray him. In Gethsemane, he could call upon his Father to place twelve legions of angels at his disposal (see 26:53). He is the one to tell Judas to do what he has come for (see 26:50). False witnesses testify that he said "I can destroy the temple of God and within three days rebuild it" (26:61). His crown of thorns, his scarlet cloak, the reed derisively placed in his hands, do not make of him a king of comedy: they adorn him with emblems of his majesty. The earth that trembles at the moment of his death, the tombs that open, the saints who rise and appear to many—all these are as many supernatural phenomena attesting Jesus' victory over the reign of death and the inauguration of a new era. All these events derive their meaning from faith in Jesus, Son of God (see 26:63; 27:40, 43, 54).

Last of all, Matthew's Passion crowns the Gospel he presents to us. It is within the faith of the Church that the evangelist shows Jesus as the stone rejected by the builders becoming the cornerstone of the Church. More than any other writer of his time, Matthew seems to have measured the chasm opening between the Synagogue and the community of the Lord Jesus' disciples. Had not his Master promised that a new people would produce the fruits of the vine planted by God (see 21:43)? But the Church too must nonetheless remain watchful; it, too, could one day forget its Lord by becoming unfaithful to his Gospel . . . .

> You were clad with purple,
> you put on the scarlet cloak
> as a sign of shame, in the thoughts
> of Pontius Pilate's soldiers.
>
> Take from me the haircloth of sin,
> the red-purple, the color of blood,

and clothe me with the joyous garment
you once put on the first humans.[28]

The Gospel of the Passion According to Mark

The Passion According to Mark is the shortest of all (Mark 14:1–15:47). It aims at being a recitation of the objective reality of facts to such an extent that some have seen in Mark a direct witness of what he relates (see 14:51-52). It is a paradoxical narrative that makes complete the "gospel of Jesus Christ [the Son of God]" (1:1). Of course, the cross is a scandal, but it nevertheless reveals what has been called the "messianic secret" in the Second Gospel.[29] The shock of such an event must foster the submission of faith in the mystery of a Messiah who is the Son of God.

The announcement of the plot against Jesus immediately puts the reader at the heart of a drama Jesus knows in advance. After the sacramental passion of Jesus—the institution of the Eucharist—we have here his secret passion in the Garden of Olives, his solitary anguish, his intimate prayer to his Father (*Abba*), his progressive abandonment by all those who had surrounded him and pledged faithfulness to him.

The physical passion of Jesus begins with his appearance before the high priest and the Sanhedrin. For the first time in Mark, Jesus, before the Jewish religious power, unequivocally declares that he is the Messiah—"I am." Thereby he signs his death warrant. He confirms his declaration before the Roman procurator by stating that he is a king, and that in him, it is the king of the Jews who is delivered to torture. The Roman trial is orchestrated by the chief priests who arouse the crowd. An insurrectionist is acquitted, not Jesus. Imposed by the soldiers, the cruel "king's game" appears as the reverse side of the condemned man's claims.

Finally, here is the so-called King of the Jews enthroned on the cross, flanked by two thieves. Naked, humiliated to the extreme, forsaken by his people and, in his humanity, apparently by God himself, Jesus dies with a loud cry in a paroxysm of abandonment. But in the depths of this obscure cloud in which God chose to dwell (see 1 Kgs 8:12; 2 Chr 6:1), light suddenly bursts forth from darkness.

Mark is the only one who brings together two events that express the triumph of faith, two facts that show the significance of the death on the cross for the work and person of Jesus. The veil of the Temple is rent asunder: the Temple is made useless and obsolete by the sacrifice of the Son of God (see Heb 6:19-20; 10:19-20). A temple "not made with hands" begins to replace the Temple of stone (see 14:28; 15:29, 38). At the same time, a pagan centurion recognizes in Jesus "the Son of God" who sits on the right side of the throne (see 14:62; 15:39). This confession of faith is the more significant as Mark reserves this appellation—Son of God— either for theophanies (see 1:11; 9:7) or for exclamations of expelled demons (see 3:11; 5:7). Mark's account of the passion ends with a solemn act of faith to which the Church of imperfect believers is invited to adhere little by little with all its soul.

Jesus speaks only three times after his arrest. His silence is impressive in view of the questions urged upon him. He declares before the high priest that he is the Messiah and the Son of Man. Before Pilate, he acknowledges he is King of the Jews. On the cross, he cries the lament of the Suffering Servant. The veil covering our eyes can be torn in two only by accepting, in the company of the Roman centurion, the paradox of his mysterious existence. Then the confession of faith can burst forth upon our lips—"Truly this man was the Son of God!"

> With the tearing of the veil
> on account of Adam's debts,
> tear my ingrained meanness,
> destroy the bond of my life's sins.
>
> I believe with all my soul
> and adore you, O only Son,
> forgive me the faults I committed;
> may my past sins not be remembered![30]

The Gospel of the Passion According to Luke

The narrator of Luke's Passion is not an impartial and coldly objective writer. He proposes a teaching for the faithful disciples as he himself conceives them. The combat Jesus wages against darkness and the drama of his scorned innocence convey an appeal: Will we have enough courage, faith, and perseverance to walk behind Jesus, carrying our crosses, both his and ours? The presence of numerous persons mentioned in the course of the story invites readers to side with one of the categories described: disciples, crowd, soldiers, Jewish leaders, thieves, and so forth (Luke 22:14–23:56).

Everything develops according to the same pattern as in Matthew and Mark, with some important differences. The anointing in Bethany is missing and the Sanhedrin session is abridged; whereas, the description of the Last Supper, of the interview with Pilate, and of what happens at the foot of the cross are more detailed because of the pedagogical content of the facts.

Luke's account of the institution of the Eucharist shows the ardent desire Jesus has to consummate his passover with his disciples. They will have to celebrate the Supper in memory of his sacrifice during the whole time of the Church's mission in the expectation of the inauguration of the banquet in the kingdom. The discourse of Jesus to his disciples evokes that which the Fourth Gospel records after the washing of the feet (see John 12:31–17:26). Its content concerns the behavior of the apostles after Jesus' departure: it is directed to the leaders of the Church. The sharing in the Eucharist will assume a serious character, will entail a duty of mutual service, will lead everyone to be united to the one they commemorate. Far from "lord[ing] it over" others (22:25), like the powerful of this world, they will act as servants, as he was among them. Recalling the trials they shared with him will manifest their connection with their Master. They will have to pray, to resist temptation, having the assurance they will reign with him in his kingdom. But, today, Jesus is going to remain alone. He leaves his disciples to go and pray; and Luke, always so delicate—he will abridge for his readers the scene of outrages inflicted on Jesus—does not hesitate to describe in utmost detail the anguish of the Savior's soul: drops of blood fall to the ground.

When "the time for the power of darkness" (22:53) begins, Jesus is left alone, more than ever. He who used to lead the unfolding of events now allows himself to be led. Clearsightedness, refusal of all violence, generosity toward his attackers: such are the characteristics that Luke loves to stress. He notes Jesus' look at Peter after his denial, his knowledge of people's hearts, and his authority before the high priest. He underscores Jesus' silence before Herod, "that fox" (13:32), and the clear affirmation of his innocence stated several times by Pilate. He tones down the culpability of Roman power, but without denying the cowardice of its representative.

Luke relates three words of Jesus on the cross: a plea for his Father's forgiveness of his tormentors, the promise of shared salvation to the second thief, the entrusting of his spirit into the Father's hands. Thus Jesus shows his total confidence in God and his assurance of having his filial prayer heard. Throughout his passion, and to the end, Jesus does not cease to do good. What an admirable model for the disciples of such a Master!

Luke invites his readers to participate in their Savior's passion with the proper sentiments. For Jesus is really "the Savior" (see 23:35-39). Let those who want to follow him keep themselves from betraying him like Judas, from denying him like Peter. Let them eschew the irreverent curiosity of Herod and not resemble the easily led crowd, now accusing, now intrigued, even at times showing sympathy or repentance. It is difficult to side with Jesus when the hour of darkness comes.

Let the disciples rather be inspired by these other persons who appear on the way to Calvary or who stand at the very spot of the crucifixion: a man coming back from the country who helps Jesus carry his cross, a thief who begs for salvation, a Roman centurion who glorifies God for this just man he sees die, a pious Jew who dares to show his attachment to the crucified innocent and his trustful expectation of the coming of the kingdom, holy women who accompany the Master throughout his way of the cross and lament his suffering.

Around the cross, are we spectators from a distance, indecisive or fearful? Or vigilant disciples who confess their faith in Jesus' victory over darkness and show their trust in the salvation he offers to everyone? Are we ready to help him carry his cross, to wait for the resurrection of the dead? In which camp do we truly place ourselves?

> To the thief on your right
> you opened the door of the Garden of Eden;
> remember me also when you come back
> with the royal power of your Father.

> May I too hear what causes us to exult,
> the answer pronounced by you:
> "Today you will be with me in Paradise,
> in your primordial homeland."[31]

It is by a great and long liturgy that on Passion Sunday the Church enters Holy Week, which culminates with the celebration of the Easter Triduum.[32]

Pedagogically, and in order that the events of this "Hour" be celebrated and lived in their true perspective, the liturgy begins with the End: the glorious entrance of Jesus, Son of David, into Jerusalem. During his earthly life, the event did precede his passion; but he has prefigured and announced his entrance into the heavenly Jerusalem by going through the door of his passover. The celebration of the holy mysteries, therefore, does not take us backwards; but, on the contrary, it affords us a glimpse of the future toward which the Church is walking. And this ultimate step of accomplished salvation must be present—in faith—within the minds of those who celebrate the Lord's passion.

This passion is gospel, it announces the good news of the salvation won for everyone by Jesus, who, handing over his life, has manifested God's infinite love for humankind and who, by "becoming obedient to death / even death on a cross," has been exalted above everything.

It is the Lord's passion that we celebrate, and we proclaim "the name / that is above every name" by falling to our knees to adore him and to give thanks to the Father.

> Father, all-powerful and ever-living God,
> we do well always and everywhere to give you thanks
> through Jesus Christ our Lord.
> Though he was sinless, he suffered willingly for sinners.
> Though innocent, he accepted death to save the guilty.
> By his dying he has destroyed our sins.
> By his rising he has raised us up to holiness of life.
> We praise you, Lord, with all the angels
> in their song of joy
> [Preface of Passion Sunday]:
>
> Holy, holy, holy Lord, God of power and might,
> heaven and earth are full of your glory.
>   Hosanna in the highest.
> Blessed is he who comes in the name of the Lord.
>   Hosanna in the highest.

Lent and Sacramental Reconciliation

When the pilgrim, when the guest, when the traveler
Have long wandered in the mud of the roads,
They carefully wipe their feet before crossing the threshold of the church,
Before entering,
Because they are attentive to cleanliness
And the mud of the roads must not soil the church floor.
But this being done, once they have wiped
    their feet before entering,
Once they have entered, they do not continue
    to think of their feet,
They do not constantly check whether their
    feet are well wiped.
Their hearts, their eyes, their voices are
    entirely turned
To the altar where Jesus' body
And the memory and the expectation of Jesus' body
Shine into eternity.[1]

Lent is a time given to Christian communities and to every believer to readjust their lives, to be converted. Conversion is at the center of the whole liturgy of this period of the year, of the biblical readings, and of the prayers. Conversion is the motive and the goal of the traditional Lenten practices. But we know full well that we cannot return to God unless he himself makes us return, unless he grants us the grace of the forgiveness of our faults by saying to us: "Your sins are forgiven you. Go in peace." We hear these efficacious words when, at the end of sacramental confession, the priest says to us, "In the name of the Father and of the Son and of the Holy Spirit, I absolve you from all your sins."

To receive the sacrament of reconciliation during Lent is traditional in the Church[2] and continues to be an obligation. But Lent is, in itself,[3] an initiation to the sacrament and its various steps as they are found in the *Rite of Penance* promulgated by Vatican II.[4] Lent is also the ideal time to discover its meaning anew and to recapture the sound practice Christian life cannot do without.[5] We can say that Lent by its very nature tends toward this genuine repentance. It implies participation in the sacrament of reconciliation. Besides, by its liturgical, ecclesial, and spiritual dynamics, it is the best time in the liturgical year to celebrate this sacrament—in all its truth—with the greatest profit.

Objections and Deviations Seen by the Light of Lent

What was for a long time called "confession" has for several decades experienced a crisis so grave that it is becoming obsolete in large segments of the Church. "One does not go to confession any more!" This often-heard remark expresses for certain persons—especially priests—a painful statement of fact, accompanied by a feeling of powerlessness: they do not see how to reverse the trend. Others, on the contrary—especially among the faithful—experience the discontinuance of confession as a liberation with, at times, the regret of having lost something they do not know how to replace.

In fact, the causes of such disaffection are multiple and complex. We cannot make an exhaustive inventory of them; an enumeration would be inadequate and would even produce an erroneous picture of the ins and outs of the crisis, because each one has his or her reasons that are not deemed of equal value and are inextricably entangled with each other. The argument advanced to answer an objection only raises other objections; the solution given successively to all objections leaves the problem untouched, or almost untouched. Indeed, the objections are of a psychological nature, drawn from unfortunate or disappointing experiences, or they are—less often—of a theological nature. It has always been painful to confess one's sins to a priest.[6] The emphasis is then placed especially, if not exclusively,[7] on the confession of sins and, by the same token, on the person of the penitent.

Of course God is not forgotten. It is to him or before him that we confess: "I confess to God Almighty." It is from him that we implore forgiveness, to him that we express our regret of having offended him "who [is] all good and deserving of all [our] love," from him finally that we receive absolution "in the name of the Father and of the Son and of the Holy Spirit."

And yet the practice—and the sermonizing—gave the impression that, in fact, everything depended on the penitents' attitude: the sincerity of their sentiments of contrition, the integral nature of the confession. For many, such a concentration on oneself entailed risks that ranged from scrupulosity to formalism. Nevertheless, we must not minimize the spiritual fruits and even the holiness that a great number of Christians derived from regular, even frequent, confession, practiced as a true sacrament, as an encounter with God, Father of mercies, who forgives. Their preparation was much more than a scanning of a list of sins in order to discover which to confess.

Whatever we think of this recent past—and with it the marks it left on minds and imaginations—today, we no longer speak of "confession" but of the "sacrament of reconciliation," which is no mere change of title. The confession of sins retains its place in the sacramental process—but its rightful place. It is integrated into a ritual ensemble no step of which can be judged negligible or optional.[8] Fortunately, the new rite has put back in place the components of the sacramental action in their proper perspectives. Lent offers the opportunity to walk through the diverse steps of the sacrament of reconciliation.

"Together, as a Church, Before God"

Every sacrament is a common, ecclesial celebration. It is not enough to know and affirm this; it is necessary to make this visible so that all may effectively share this perspective. The way a sacrament is celebrated has, therefore, a determining importance—an absolutely self-evident fact. Indeed, a sacrament is constituted by an ensemble of gestures, movements, words, and certain verities, all of which must have their own consistency and immediate significance. Without these, the sacramental sign would lack a foundation and its indispensable human dimension. Moreover, sacraments are made for human beings and through them. From this point of view, there are rhythms to respect, especially for a progressive entrance into the heart of the celebration. This requirement is now well satisfied in the liturgy of the Mass. The entrance rite, with the presider's greeting, a few words of introduction, and a song, are conducive to experiencing a sense of community for the participants gathered to celebrate. Thus, they place themselves together, as Church, before God.

The entrance into Lent is exemplary in this aspect. We take the time to gather into one before undertaking the itinerary that is going to last five weeks. We linger under the "porch" of the first four of the forty days.[9] Also, the distribution of ashes expresses the meaning of the journey in which each one is personally engaged, but as a Church, with all others. The biblical readings explain with utmost clarity that it is God who calls us together to march toward Easter. At the same time, they proclaim loud and clear in what spirit and manner we must undertake and pursue the Lenten itinerary.

It is important that we make a similar entrance into the sacrament of reconciliation, even if it does not take the form of a community celebration. This is why the new rite appropriately insists on the importance of a time of mutual welcome that allows priest and penitent "to place themselves together, as a church, before God."[10]

A meeting lacks the most elementary humanity if the participants do not first greet one another and state the purpose of their coming together. This lack of preliminaries often proves to be a source of misunderstanding and ambiguities and can even gravely compromise the normal unfolding and result of the interview.[11] This would be particularly harmful in the case of the sacrament of reconciliation, and the risk is the greater because, in its most common form, it is celebrated by one priest and one penitent. It is therefore necessary to explain with simplicity that we are "about to celebrate a sacrament which manifests God's action in his Church."[12] "A prayer or a formula is useful," according to the rite, which proposes several examples.[13] When the sacrament is celebrated during Lent, there is no need to resort to a stereotyped formula to express the sacramental character of the action in which God's initiative and power are manifested in his Church. It is enough to refer to any reading proclaimed during the liturgy or to any number of themes in God's word with which the sacrament accords well.

From God's Word to the Sacrament

Vatican Council II has mandated the proclamation of God's word in connection with the celebration of all sacraments. For it is God himself who invites us to the sources of salvation; to approach the sacraments is to answer his call. His word authoritatively proclaims the meaning of the efficacious signs of salvation and the demands they make. The word carries grace and creates in well-disposed hearts the feelings without which sacraments cannot produce their effects. Consequently, before coming to a sacramental rite, we must listen to God's word. This is particularly important when it comes to the sacrament of reconciliation. "Through the word of God the Christian receives light to recognize his sins and is called to conversion and to confidence in God's mercy . . . The genuineness of penance depends on . . . heartfelt contrition."[14] This, of course, has always been the case. Whatever was or may be the form of its celebration, the sacrament of reconciliation has always kept, in principle, a close connection with God's word. But we can never say often enough how important it is for this connection to be made explicit in one way or another in the course of the celebration.

We do not have here the mere reminder of a fundamental principle. Listening to the word helps the penitents place themselves on the plane where everything takes place. Listening to the word projects light on obstacles that are to be avoided by dissipating the possible misunderstandings and faulty conceptions that may give rise to attitudes and behavior contrary to the truth of the sacrament and regrettable for the persons involved.

The awareness of having committed sins is apt to produce a depressing and even morbid feeling of guilt that has nothing to do with the contrition urged by the word. When we realize our own weaknesses and the difficulties we have to mend our ways, we may fall prey to a paralyzing discouragement; whereas, God's word invites us to pick ourselves up and assures us that conversion is possible with God's grace. Self-absorption due to repeated examinations of conscience that foster an introspection which soon becomes addictive does not endure when faced with the revelation of a God who denounces sin but does not overwhelm the sinners to whom he opens his arms. Finally, the word incites us to trust God and his grace instead of remaining on the level of psychotherapy, with which we must not confuse the sacrament of reconciliation.[15] If, indeed, sacramental confession frees the conscience, it is not because one dares to reveal one's sins, but because one presents them for the pardon God grants. The ensuing peace is that which God gives, not that which one gives to oneself.

All of Scripture describes the true dimensions of the confession of sin and the renewal of human beings who, sinners, turn to their Father. We can acknowledge and feel guilt when we observe ourselves and become conscious of our moral misery. We recognize our sinfulness only when we hear God denounce sin. God's word presses us to lift up our heads and look, in faith and hope that do not deceive, to the cross on which Christ died to deliver humankind and the world from sin.

This good news is unceasingly heard throughout Lent. "Repent, for the kingdom of heaven is at hand" (Matt 4:17).

> So whoever is in Christ is a new creation: the old things have passed away; behold, new things have come. And all this is from God, who has reconciled us to himself through Christ and given us the ministry of reconciliation, namely, God was reconciling the world to himself in Christ, not counting their trespasses against them and entrusting to us the message

of reconciliation. So we are ambassadors for Christ, as if God were appealing through us. We implore you on behalf of Christ, be reconciled to God. For our sake he made him to be sin who did not know sin, so that we might become the righteousness of God in him.
(2 Cor 5:17-21)[16]

Awake, O sleeper,
  and arise from the dead,
and Christ will give you light.
(Eph 5:14)[17]

Conversion and penance, inspired by the discovery and certitude of the love which God has shown us through Christ and which the Spirit infuses into our hearts, lead to fullness of life. The sacrament of reconciliation thus appears in its true light as a paschal sacrament.

Confessing God's Love and Our Sin

Rightly set in this context and in these perspectives, the confession of sins loses the character of painful humiliation that it would often have when taken in isolation and seen as the only element in the penitent's role in the reception of the sacrament. It can no longer be felt and experienced as the condition imposed by a judge to obtain remission of sins. It is not the recitation of a list of sins we establish exactly, minutely, even scrupulously, or on the contrary with calculations to lessen our culpability. It is an expression of confidence in a merciful God to whom sins are entrusted in order to receive purity from him; it is a confession of his love.

The priest—no one seeks to forget or hide it—remains a human being among other human beings, a sinner among sinners, in short, a brother who confesses, along with all others, God's mercy at the same time he confesses his own sins. But through Christ, God entrusts to him "the ministry of reconciliation" (2 Cor 5:18) in order that forgiveness of sins gained by Christ may effectively reach all humans for whom the Lord gave his life. Therefore, there is no need to indulge in theological or spiritual acrobatics—as unconvincing as inaccurate—to surmount one's difficulties by behaving "as if" the priest were Christ. He is not! He is his servant—"He must increase; I must decrease" (John 3:30). The sacred nature of the priestly ministry appears in all its truth in this self-effacement before Christ. This is why we can, with trust born of faith, confess to another human being God's love at the same time as our sin.

A Sign of Conversion and Penance

Participation in the sacrament of reconciliation is part of the dynamics of a movement of conversion that certainly can be suddenly triggered, but most often entails a period of gradual progress. Gradually, we become conscious of the necessity to concretize this conversion by acts, and to give ourselves a sign that expresses it by recalling it.

Not long ago, after the confession of sins and before the absolution, the priest "imposed" what was called a "penance" or a "satisfaction," usually a prayer to recite before the penitent left the church.[18] This way of proceeding could be construed as a price owed—according to a very low tariff[19]—to receive absolution.[20]

The new rite expresses well the meaning of "a sign of conversion and penance" by saying, "If one chooses to suggest a prayer, let it be one that expresses a progress of openness to God and others. For instance, the priest can invite penitents to pray for persons in difficult circumstances, for persons who have participated in the same celebration, for the needs of the Church and the world. One can also suggest a prayer of thanksgiving or praise."[21] But in a more general manner, Scripture exhorts us, with a particular insistence during Lent, to produce worthy fruits of penance.[22] If we have attentively listened to and meditated on this word of God proclaimed at the time the sacrament is celebrated, we shall not have to search far or elsewhere for "a sign of conversion and penance."

The Sacramental Word of Forgiveness of Sins

At the end of the sacramental process, after a prayer said by the priest and penitent together or by the latter alone,[23] comes the simple, yet solemn, sacramental word of absolution.

> God, the Father of mercies,
> through the death and resurrection of his Son
> has reconciled the world to himself
> and sent the Holy Spirit among us
> for the forgiveness of sins;
> through the ministry of the Church
> may God give you pardon and peace,
> and I absolve you from your sins
> in the name of the Father, and of the Son, ✝
> and of the Holy Spirit.[24]

Today, we hear this word in our own language and we welcome it by saying, "Amen."

In itself, the word of sacramental absolution is pregnant with meaning. The Lenten liturgy still adds to it, if it is possible, because all one hears, under diverse forms, is the pardon offered and given by God, his tenderness, and his mercy. For their part, the psalms sung after the first reading on Sundays and weekdays prepare us to receive this marvelous answer of God to the entreaties, the sentiments of conversion untiringly expressed with an ever increasing confidence.

In the Joy of Forgiveness and Thanksgiving

In the parable, the merciful father organized a great feast to celebrate the return of his prodigal son whom he had embraced and pardoned. He then invited everyone to take part in the festivities by sharing in his joy (see Luke 15:11-32).[25] Although the parable says nothing about it, we may think that the prodigal son, surprised at first by this completely unexpected welcome on his father's part, quickly joined in the songs and dances with overflowing joy.

When, at the end of a journey of conversion and the end of the sacrament of reconciliation, we hear the word of forgiveness, we might be moved to add—even in Lent—an Alleluia to the Amen prescribed by the rite. In any case, we will not fail to express our joy and thanksgiving to God by adopting some canticle of praise—the *Magnificat*, for instance— or by giving free rein to the gladness of our hearts. In this, too, the Lenten liturgy shows us the way. The most pressing calls to penance and conversion flow into the great liturgical thanksgiving.

> Father, all-powerful and ever-living God,
> we do well always and everywhere to give you thanks
> through Jesus Christ our Lord.
>
> Each year you give us this joyful season
> when we prepare to celebrate the paschal mystery
> with mind and heart renewed.
> You give us a spirit of loving reverence for you, our Father,
> and of willing service to our neighbor.
>
> As we recall the great events that gave us new life in Christ,
> you bring the image of your Son to perfection within us.[26]

But do not all the Lenten readings—prophetic oracles, apostolic texts, gospels—point to praise of God and thanksgiving? This period of the liturgical year is truly the favorable time to discover or rediscover the Eucharistic dimension of the sacrament of reconciliation and to celebrate it in this spirit and from this perspective.[27]

Unfolding of the Sacrament Over Time

One of the difficulties of the sacrament of reconciliation is due to the fact that its celebration is, of necessity, compressed into a very brief time. As a consequence, the different steps and procedures so well described in the rite become more or less a mere formality. Moreover, the ecclesial dimension of the sacrament is not really obvious. We have, it is true, the possibility of participating in what is called a "reconciliation of several penitents with confession and absolution."[28] This liturgical form has the great advantage of precisely being communal. Each step of the celebration is given its rightful place. The general climate of these liturgies during which people sing and pray together is of the best as a rule: it is the feast of forgiveness, of reconciliation celebrated as a church. But we sometimes experience a feeling of frustration and a certain malaise. Frustration, because the time given to the dialogue with the priest for confession and absolution is extremely short. Malaise, because, by reason of the very rapidity with which one meets the priest, these individual confessions and absolutions seem a formality from which one might as well dispense oneself. Lent, however, allows us to unfold the sacrament over time.

Ash Wednesday is the liturgical entrance into the yearly itinerary of penance and conversion. All through the Sunday and weekday liturgies God's word is proclaimed, pressing us to be converted and to return to God with all our hearts. As we listen to God's word, we become conscious that we must be converted and must take the necessary steps and means to be reconciled with God, others, and oneself.

We have five weeks at our disposal—which is not too long—to undertake what the Church suggests: moves toward reconciliation; conversion on the personal and communal levels; recourse to the help, the counsel, the encouragement, the lights of a priest, a brother, a sister. The one thing remaining is to go to a priest for the celebration of the sacrament itself. The several ritual steps recapitulate, in one liturgy, all the personal actions done in community during the preceding weeks.

A Paschal Sacrament

In the early Church, the reconciliation of penitents took place at the end of Lent. "Perhaps, at the beginning, it even took place during the Paschal Vigil itself. In any event, we soon see it placed on Holy Thursday in Rome and Milan, on Good Friday in Spain, so as to enable sinners to take part in the Easter Eucharist."[29]

At any time, the sacrament of reconciliation has a definite paschal dimension. But how much more visible and explicitly is it lived when it is celebrated in order to participate in the passover of Christ, in whom we are "dead to sin and living for God in Christ Jesus" (Rom 6:11).[30]

At the end of this itinerary begun on Ash Wednesday this sacramental reconciliation would find its perfectly appropriate day on Holy Thursday before the liturgy of the Last Supper.

> *Change your hearts,*
> *believe in the Good News!*
> *Change your lives,*
> *believe that God loves you!*

> I do not come "to condemn the world":
> I come "that the world might be saved."
> (John 3:17)

> I do not come for those who are well or for the righteous:
> I come for the sick, the sinners.
> (see Mark 2:17)

> I do not come to judge anyone:
> I come to give them the Life of God.
> (see John 8:15; 10:10)

> "I am the Good Shepherd," says Jesus:
> I look for the stray sheep.
> (John 10:14; see Luke 15:1-7)

> "I am the gate," says Jesus:
> "Whoever enters through me will be saved."
> (John 10:9)

> "Whoever believes [in me] has eternal life":
> Believe in my words and you will live.
> (John 6:47; see 6:63)[31]

Lent, a Parable
of Christian Life

Taking up an expression of St. Benedict and extending its scope, we may say that the lives of individual Christians and of the Church as a whole "ought to be a continuous Lent."[1] This assertion might appear to be a pious exaggeration and, in addition, a hardly realistic one, to those who see Lent as a period essentially defined by ascetical practices, penances, self-imposed deprivations, attempts at self-imposed deprivations—in a word, as a defined and limited time of painful spiritual exercises accepted as such. But, with further reflection, and especially with the experience of having attentively followed the Lenten celebrations, we come to recognize how pertinent is the view of Lent exemplified by St. Benedict. It is an all-important time of the liturgical year aiming at redressing Christian life. The works of Lent—prayer, almsgiving, fasting—do not have their value in themselves, as the Scriptures proclaimed on Ash Wednesday, and the following Thursday and Friday clearly recall. If the Church exhorts us to a greater emphasis on private prayer and the liturgy, it is in order that they may recapture during Lent their rightful place in Christian life at all times.

Almsgiving and sharing practiced during Lent is a movement of conversion as regards the use of goods. Far from jealously and selfishly keeping them for themselves, Christians possess them as though not possessing them: they manage them as good stewards, with constant concern for their poorer brothers and sisters. This is not an occasional practice either. The ideal continues to be relevant and remains, at any time, that of Christian communities in which there are no poor persons, thanks to the sharing of riches (see Acts 2:44-45; 4:32; 5:12).

Finally, whatever ascetical value a seasonal, or even a habitual, fasting may have, fasting is essentially an attack on uncontrolled appetite for earthly foods of all kinds, an appetite to which people yield, especially in countries where over-consumption is blatant. Such a search for carnal and material satisfactions—in the broadest sense of the terms—is pagan. Christians must rectify their behavior in order to go back to an everyday lifestyle in harmony with their faith and hope. This is what is spoken of here: ''If the dead are not raised:

'Let us eat and drink,

for tomorrow we die. . . .'

But now Christ has been raised from the dead, the first-fruits of those who have fallen asleep'' (1 Cor 15:32, 20).[2] All the works—even the most ascetical—have a theological motive and aim.

The texts from Scripture proclaimed during this liturgical time help us raise our eyes to God and his plan of salvation, to Christ and his mystery that bring this plan to realization, to its fulfillment in the ''now'' of the Church and the world. Of course, this can be said about all times of the liturgical year. What characterizes Lenten liturgies are the density, the wealth, and the strength of the texts, especially those of the great Gospel readings of Christian initiation, the selected apostolic catecheses, the remembrance of the most significant steps of salvation history. Lent thus proves to be catechumenal not only for those who are preparing for baptism but also for those who are already living the life of baptized persons. Lent repeats to Christians, with a particular insistence, the call that the Church never ceases to address to them: ''Become what you are.''[3]

Finally, Lent is a paschal itinerary, since it leads to and prepares us for the Easter celebrations. In this sense, it has a fixed place in the liturgical calendar: it begins on Ash Wednesday and ends on Holy Thursday before the evening Mass. But Christian and ecclesial life is wholly paschal: it is an exodus toward the eternal Easter. Thus, especially from this point of view, Lent is a parable—paradigm—of the lives of Christians and of the Church. What is intensely experienced for forty days every year must give a new and enduring dynamism to our lives in the succession of the Days of the Lord.

The Church and Christians are called to live at all times in the joy of the Holy Spirit and the spiritual longing for a holy Easter.[4]

> Come into the day!
> Christ is preparing his return!
> Christ is preparing the nuptial era!
> Let times pass away! Let flesh pass away!
> The Spirit of God blows in the desert,
> announcing the paschal dawn!
>
> Strip yourselves!
> When you die, you lose everything!
> Make your exodus in advance!
> Let death fall! Let evening fall!

Do not wait until it is too late
for God to give you birth.

Do not fear
to undo yourselves, he will create again
what you let go;
close your eyes! Bow your heads!
Come and beg for his creation
in the depths of human darkness.

Do not slide any longer
on your uncertain slope,
for here another age begins;
turn around! Learn God!
He has promised his kingdom to those
who will walk along his ways!

The day will come
when the desert will bloom again
and the shadow will give back the light!
Go through them! Already now,
go and look in the testament
for what is not born of earth![5]

NOTES

Forty Holy Days—Pages 1–12

1. It is not until that time that the Roman Pontifical incorporated the liturgical distribution of ashes, instituted in Rhenish countries in the tenth century and adopted in Italy in the eleventh and twelfth centuries. As for the rest, Lent properly so-called and three preparatory weeks (Septuagesima, Sexagesima, and Quinquagesima), one could place the end of this first period in the eighth century.

2. There were some alterations, but they were all minor, i.e., in the discipline of fasting and abstinence since 1939–40 because of the war in Europe.

The most important reforms of the years before Vatican II concerned the Easter Triduum. They will be mentioned in due course.

3. See, A.G. Martimort, *The Church at Prayer: The Liturgy and Time*, vol. IV (Collegeville, Minn.: The Liturgical Press, 1986) 65–76, with a bibliography; A. Nocent, *Célébrer Jésus Christ: L'année liturgique III: Carême* (Paris: Delarge, 1976) 89–100.

4. Celebrated every Sunday of the year.

5. The liturgical year, divided into weeks, begins on Saturday night before the First Sunday of Advent and ends on the Saturday following the Thirty-fourth Sunday in Ordinary Time, unlike our reckoning for the calendar year, which is counted in days (365 or 366) from January 1 to the December 31.

6. *Calendarium romanum* 1969, No. 18. See also, Vatican Council II, The Constitution on the Sacred Liturgy (*Sacrosanctum Concilium*), *The Conciliar and Post Conciliar Documents*, ed. Austin Flannery, O.P. (Collegeville, Minn.: The Liturgical Press, 1975), nos. 5 and 106.

7. Given these two dates, we can indeed establish the calendar of any given liturgical year.

8. This celebration "begins today with the Mass of the Lord's Supper; it has its center at the Easter Vigil; and it ends with the Vespers of Easter Sunday" (*Calendarium romanum*, No. 19).

9. Constitution on the Sacred Liturgy, no. 5.

10. See, for example, *Vocabulaire de théologie biblique* (Paris: Cerf, 1970) cols. 885–89.

11. These three Gospels—Third, Fourth, and Fifth Sundays of Lent—may be repeated every year.

12. "To believers also the Church must ever preach faith and penance; she must prepare them for the sacraments, teach them to observe all that Christ has commanded and encourage them to engage in all works of charity, piety and the apostolate" (Constitution on the Sacred Liturgy, No. 9).

13. It is here that the precept of paschal communion finds its theological foundation and its full meaning. Not to participate in the Eucharist comes down to excommunicating oneself until the day when, having done penance, one participates again in the sacrament that is the very being of the Church.

14. See, R. Reckinger, "A propos de la célébration étalée du sacrement de pénitence," *Communautés et liturgies* 58 (1976) 509–14.

15. St. Benedict (ca. 480–547), *The Rule of St. Benedict*, ed. Timothy Fry, O.S.B., et al. (Collegeville, Minn.: The Liturgical Press, 1981) ch. 49.

16. This text is read at the Mass for Friday after Ash Wednesday. The prophet is speaking of fasting, but his words apply to the whole of Lent, of which fasting is an expression.

17. The practice of this form of reading is monastic in origin. It is part of the daily schedule of monks, who must devote themselves to it for longer periods and with more concentration during Lent (St. Benedict, *Rule*, chs. 48 and 49). But for a long time this reading

has been part of general spiritual tradition. See, E. Bianch, *Prier la Parole: Une introduction à la "lectio divina,"* Vie monastique 15 (Abbaye de Bellefontaine, 1983).

18. See below, "Jeremiah—Prophet in a Time of Crisis and Conversion," p. 187.

19. A simple guide: N. Berthet—R. Gantoy, *Chaque jour ta Parole: Le Lectionnaire de semaine, Notes de lecture, Textes pour la prière,* vol. 2, *Temps du Carême* (Paris: Cerf—Publications de Saint-André, 1980).

20. In spite of their desire to live Lent intensely, many Christians cannot attend Mass during the week. Reading and meditation of the daily biblical texts are a way of sharing in the Mass.

21. As noted above, Exodus and Jeremiah are read in Lent as Isaiah is in Advent and the Acts of the Apostles and the First Letter of John are in paschal time.

22. This is said without forgetting that the reading of Scripture is done—must always be done—in an ecclesial context, even when done in private. Anyhow, "pious practices," whatever part of personal initiative they entail, must be in conformity with the laws and norms of the Church and be in harmony, as much as possible, with the liturgy, be imbued with its spirit (Constitution on the Sacred Liturgy, no. 13; see also, nos. 17 and 105).

23. At that time, people spoke of the "station" being held at Santa Sabina all'Aventino, at Santa Maria Maggiore, and so forth. Formerly, missals mentioned these stational churches. Until recently, the celebration that took place at the stational church drew a large number of Romans, at least on certain days: thus on Ash Wednesday at Santa Sabina or, on certain other days, at the great basilicas.

24. It is at this time that a proper formulary was assigned to every day of Lent. The number of stational churches was increased so that every day had its own station. Among those stational churches, some that were once well-frequented places of worship have ceased to be regularly used and in a few cases only on the day of the "station."

25. Thus, *Le petit Robert,* 1973 edition, "Lent. A period of forty-six days of abstinence and deprivation between Shrove Tuesday and Easter during which, except for Sundays, certain Christians fast. . . . Fasting, abstinence practiced during Lent."

26. In Jewish communities, the great fast still remains that of Yom Kippur (Day of Atonement).

27. *La doctrine des douze apôtres,* 2-3, in Sources chrétiennes 248 (Paris: Cerf, 1978) 143, 145. See also, ibid., 8,1, p. 173.

28. This discipline is described in detail in the Rule of St. Benedict in ch. 41. The fast from September 13 to the beginning of Lent is a monastic practice. We note that this fasting regulation must be kept with discretion since in summer, heavy work in hot weather is a consideration.

29. It is true that some Desert Fathers, on learning of the rigorous fast kept by another monk, hastened to go one better. But we must know how to read this sort of memorable story (apothegm). More than the desire to set records, such an anecdote shows the holy emulation among those ancient monks.

30. The partial or total deprivation of food imposed as a sanction for a fault has nothing to do with religious fasting, even when it is prescribed as a penance in religious rules. Thus, see chs. 23-25 in the Rule of St. Benedict.

31. The eyes of all look hopefully to you,
    and you give them their food in due season;
You open your hand
    and satisfy the desire of every living thing
(Ps 145:15-16).

32. "Beware that your hearts do not become drowsy from carousing and drunkenness and the anxieties of daily life" (Luke 21:34). This admonition is set in the framework of the watchfulness that we must observe while expecting the Lord's return.

33. Again, St. Benedict is a model of moderation, discretion, and humanity. Other than what he says concerning fasting (see n. 29), we read, "It is . . . with some uneasiness that we specify the amount of food and drink for others" (Rule, ch. 40); "Should it happen that the work is heavier than usual, the abbot may decide—and he will have the authority—to grant something additional, provided it is appropriate" (ch. 39); "The superior may break his fast for the sake of a guest, unless it is a day of special fast which cannot be broken" (ch. 35); the old and young will "not be required to follow the strictness of the rule with regard to food" (ch. 37); "To regain their strength, the sick who are very weak may eat meat" (ch. 36).

34. Today, there is no lack of persons—groups, schools, sects also—who commend the practices of fasting, in particular abstinence from meat, not only by reason of their conception of alimentary hygiene and dietetics, but also for "spiritual" reasons. This adjective does not have the fullness of sense we are giving it here. It can express many things—psychic and mental balance, and so forth—that are not always—and often are far from being connected with faith or with what we may call a "Christian anthropology." It would be more exact to speak of a spiritualistic perspective. It even happens sometimes that the attachment to these dietetic options verges on a certain sectarianism, that it becomes, as one says, a religion. This is very far from the Christian spiritual tradition and the position of its spiritual masters.

35. The relationship between fasting and prayer is not very explicit in the Old Testament. But fasting, as it is prescribed and practiced in certain circumstances, is manifestly a way of entreating God: 1 Kgs 21:9, 12; 2 Chr 20:3; Esth 4:3, 16; Jer 36:9; Jonah 3:1-5; etc. However, we read in the Book of Tobit: "Prayer and fasting are good, but better than either is almsgiving accompanied by righteousness. A little with righteousness is better than abundance with wickedness" (12:8).

36. See, A. Guillaume, *Jeûne et charité dans l'Eglise latine, des origines au XIIᵉ siècle, en particulier chez saint Léon le Grand* (Paris: Editions S.O.S.[=Secours catholique] 1954).

37. *Apology of Aristides*, 15:7, probably addressed to the emperor Hadrian (74-138).

38. *Didaskalia Apostolorum*, 1:5. This work dates back to the first half of the third century.

39. See, A. Guillaume, *Jeûne et charité dans l'Eglise latine*.

40. St. Peter Chrysologus (ca. 380-450), "Sermon 43," Patrologia Latina 52, ed. J.-P. Migne, in *The Liturgy of the Hours*, vol. 2 (New York: Catholic Book Publishing Co., 1976) Office of Readings, Tuesday in the Third Week of Lent, pp. 231-32.

41. St. Basil, Bishop of Caesarea, (ca. 329-379), *Homélie 6 contre la richesse (Lc 12,7)*, quoted in J.-B. Franzoni, *La terre appartient à Dieu* (Paris: Centurion, 1973) 1962. A. Hamman, tr., *Riches et pauvres dans l'Eglise*, in Lettres chrétiennes 6 (Paris: 1962) 76.

42. Ibid.

43. St. Ambrose, bishop of Milan (339-97), *Sur le psaume 118, 8,22*. Quoted in J.-B. Franzoni, *La terre appartient à Dieu*, p. 83.

44. St. Ambrose, ibid.

45. See, A. Guillaume, *Jeûne et charité dans l'Eglise latine*.

46. St. Augustine, bishop of Hippo, (354-430), *Traité sur le psaume 42*.

47. Commission Francophone Cistercienne, *Prières au fil des Heures*, Vivante liturgie 99 (Paris: Publications de Saint-André—Centurion, 1982) 71.

48. In spite of this, the first Sunday has kept the name *caput Quadragesimae* (beginning of Lent), a vestige of the former structure of Lent.

49. Practically, they are the Chair of St. Peter (February 22) and the solemnities of St. Joseph (March 19) and the Annunciation (March 25). However, if these last two occur during Holy Week, their celebration is transferred to Easter time.

50. In the Rule of St. Benedict, Chapter 49, "The Observance of Lent," contains this beautiful expression: "[to] look forward to holy Easter with joy and spiritual longing."

51. This is a custom of the Western Church, not shared by the Eastern Church.

52. J. Martin (Fiche de chant G 128).

The Porch of Lent
Ash Wednesday—Pages 13–21

1. Josh 7:6; 2 Sam 13:19; Ezek 27:30; Job 2:12, 42; Jonah 3:6; Esth 4:3; Jdt 9:1; Isa 58:5-7; Dan 9:3; Joel 2:12-13.

2. We see here a vestige of its nonliturgical origin.

3. The Hebrew noun *hesed* means "loyalty" between two persons united by a variety of bonds; the adjective *hasid* means "pious." The Septuagint translation uses the words *eleos*, meaning "mercy" and *eleemon*, meaning "merciful." Such loyalty implies faithfulness, *hemet* in Hebrew.

Rehem ("womb") or, in the plural *rahamin* ("entrails"), designates an instinctive, visceral attachment, "tenderness." The person who has this feeling is said to be *rahum* ("compassionate," "moved to the core"). The Septuagint most often renders this word by *oiktirmoi*, *oiktirmon*.

Finally, the word *hen*, meaning "favor," "grace," is sometimes joined to the first two; the *hannum* is the person who forgives.

4. The *Bible de Jérusalem*, editio major (Paris: Cerf, rev. 1973), and the *Traduction oecuménique de la Bible*, édition intégrale (Paris: Brepols, 1987), translate more literally, "so that in him we might become the goodness of God."

5. Thus, at the conclusion of an inquiry, Pliny the Younger, the governor of Bithynia, writes around 111-13 in a report to the Emperor Trajan that Christians "are wont to gather on a fixed day before daybreak and to sing together a song to Christ as to a god." This text, along with some others of Christian origin, are quoted by A.G. Martimort, "Dimanche, assemblée et paroisse," *La Maison-Dieu* 57 (1959) 58–59. See also, A.G. Martimort, *The Church at Prayer: Principles of the Liturgy*, vol. I (Collegeville, Minn.: The Liturgical Press, 1987) 91, n. 10.

6. In fact, there is a choice of two. They are directly inspired by two prayers of the old formulary, but are written in a simpler style. Only the second alludes to the return to the earth signified by ashes.

7. Only the second prayer speaks of blessing the ashes. The first one asks God to bestow his blessing on "those who receive these ashes." In any case, the rite is no longer in two parts as formerly: blessing of the ashes and giving of the ashes. Finally, the sprinkling of the ashes with holy water is optional and, if performed, is done "in silence." In the past, there was a threefold sprinkling, with the antiphon *Asperges me*, followed by incensing.

8. Prayer I.

9. Prayer II.

10. This does not mean that private giving of the ashes is meaningless: it was in use before the introduction of the rite into the liturgy.

11. Memorial Acclamation C from the Eucharistic Prayer, in the course of which the expectation of Christ's return is proclaimed several times.

12. J. Akepsimas and M. Scouranec, *Des mots et des notes pour célébrer*, Vivante liturgie 98 (Paris: Centurion—Publications de Saint-André, 1982) 93–94. (Fiche de chant G 212).

Thursday after Ash Wednesday—Pages 21–24

1. Opening prayer.
2. St. Bernard (1090–1153), *Traité de l'amour de Dieu*, 1,1; 6,16, in *Oeuvres mystiaues*, preface and tr. A. Béguin (Paris: Seuil, 1953) 29, 50.
3. In the Bible, "I AM" is the divine name revealed to Moses (Exod 3:1⁴   )hn's Gospel, all the great texts that begin thus are solemn affirmations in which Je   :lares himself as God in history.
4. St. Ambrose, *Commentaire sur le psaume 36*, in J.-M. Migne, ed., Patrolo¡   ₁e 14, col. 985.
5. St. Gregory Nazianzen (329–89), *Discours*, VII, 23, in J.-M. Migne, ed   )logie grecque 35.

Friday after Ash Wednesday—Pages 24–29

1. Opening prayer.
2. "Indeed someone might say, 'You have faith and I have works.' Dem<   your faith to me without works, and I will demonstrate my faith to you from my work   2:18).
3. Jas 2:14, 17.
4. Vl. Soloviev, *Les fondements spirituels de la vie* (Paris, 1948) 88–89. Quote<   Guil- laume, "Jeûne, prière, aumône dans le monde moderne," *Assemblées du Sei¡   st se- ries, No. 25 (Bruges: Publications de Saint-André, 1966) 75–76.
5. St. Maximus, bishop of Turin (5th c.), *Homélie 90 sur les habitants de N*   uoted by A. Guillaume, ibid., 74.
6. There are still societies called "primitive" (!) that realize this ideal as   ₁ they are not reached by "civilization" (!).
A certain number of Old Testament prescriptions aim at an equitable red   ion of riches that have accumulated with the passage of time. Thus, in particular, tl   :ution of the year of jubilee, in which all returned to their own familial property   :13).
7. See, "Jeûne" in *Vocabulaire de théologie biblique*, 2nd ed. (Paris: Cerf, 1970)   )8–10.
8. This is why the discipline of fasting has legitimately varied in the cour₁   ₂ ages and according to the traditions proper to diverse Christian Churches.
9. Matt 22:1-14; Luke 12:35-39.

Saturday after Ash Wednesday—Pages 29–34

1. Opening prayer.
2. Matt 12:9-14 (the man with a withered hand); Mark 3:1-6 (the man wi   :hered hand); Luke 13:10-17 (the crippled woman); John 5:1-18 (the sick man at the   Gate); 9:1-14 (the man born blind).
3. N. Berthet and R. Gantoy, *Chaque jour ta Parole*, vol. 2, *Temps du Ca₁*   13.
4. P. de La Tour du Pin (Fiche de chant T 9).

The Three Paths of Lent—Pages 35–38

1. See, A. Aubry, "Points de repère pour une explication génétique du Car   nain," *Assemblées du Seigneur*, 1st series, No. 21 (Bruges: Publications de Saint-André   12–13.

2. The readings assigned to Year A may be repeated every year, especially in communities where there are catechumens.

3. This is what is called "semi-continuous reading."

4. The Gospel readings of the Samaritan woman (John 4:5-42), of the man born blind (John 9:1-41), and of Lazarus (John 1:1-45) in Year A; the Passion Gospel on Passion Sunday.

5. During Advent (and the time of Christmas-Epiphany) and Easter time, as well as during Lent, the principle of the semi-continuous or continuous reading of an apostolic writing (second reading) or a Gospel is abandoned.

6. Constitution on the Liturgy, no. 5.

7. Matt 6:1-6, 16-18; Isa 58:1-14: Ash Wednesday and the following Friday.

8. What St. Benedict said of monks, because he wrote his Rule for them, is true of all Christians, whatever their status: "The life of a [Christian] ought to be a continuous Lent."

The First Two Weeks—Page 39

1. See, A. Chavasse, "La structure du Carême et les lectures des messes quadragésimales dans la liturgie romaine," *La Maison-Dieu* 31 (1952) 76–119; A. Aubry, "Points de repère pour une explication génétique du Carême romain," 7–22; A.-G. Martimort, *The Church at Prayer: The Liturgy and Time*, vol. IV, 67–69.

2. Matthew devotes twelve verses to the temptation; Mark, four; Luke, fifteen. On the other hand, the three devote nine verses each to the transfiguration.

First Sunday, Year A—Pages 40-47

3. This is the reason why, even today, we may use these texts every year.

4. See, A. Chavasse, "La structure du Carême . . . ," and A. Aubry, "Points du repère . . ."

5. The first two Sundays constitute what has been called "Matthew's penitential Lent," as distinct from "John's catechumenal Lent" of the Third, Fourth, and Fifth Sundays.

6. "For a long time, our knowledge having progressed thanks to modern science, we believed that such progress invalidated the answers of the Bible. Thus, the question was to choose between the answers of a naive time or the progress of knowledge. But it is dangerous to believe too firmly in the naiveté of ancient peoples; this becomes another sort of naiveté that is not even redeemed by freshness. We now know that the category of "primitive" is an ethnocentric projection of the consciousness that Western people have of their own culture. No one single time is more competent than any other to decipher the spiritual history of humankind. If we were to read the riddles of the Bible as a textbook listing of the positive descriptions of human origins, this would not be a progress over ancient peoples, but a regression." P. Beauchamp, "Comment le péché entra dans le monde," *Assemblées du Seigneur*, 2nd series, no 14 (Paris: Publications de Saint-André—Cerf, 1972) 7-8.

7. Ten verses out of forty-five: Gen 2:4b-3:24.

8. Whatever is implied by certain sources of this text, the sin of the first couple was not a sexual one. For immediately afterwards we read, "The man had relations with his wife Eve, and she conceived and bore Cain, saying, 'I have produced a man with the help of the LORD.' Next, she bore his brother Abel" (Gen 4:1-2).

The fecundity of the human couple, as the Bible incessantly affirms, is a blessing of God. Paul will go so far as to see in the bond between man and woman, in their union, a great mystery "in reference to Christ and the church" (Eph 5:31-32).

9. We should however avoid taking the text as an excuse for any sort of elaboration. F. Smyth-Florentin, "Jésus, le Fils du Père, vainqueur de Satan (Mt 4, 1-11; Mc 1, 12-15; Lc 4, 1-13)," *Assemblées du Seigneur*, 2nd series, No. 14 (Paris: Publications de Saint-André—Cerf, 1973) 72–73, writes, "Last year, we heard a famous Anglican preacher transpose into modern events all he could find in various interpretations. He roughly followed Matthew's plan—which can, if worst comes to worst, be used as a harmonizing reading—and then, on this basis, launched into polemics against the three great temptations of the modern world: that of Soviet Russia, which seeks to feed humankind without bothering about the means; that of the United States, ready to go to extremes through love of prestige (the moon landing, and so forth); and that of Mao, who claims to inaugurate the kingdom at the price of radical servitude! . . . No exegetical principle absolutely excludes any other, and preachers feel free to rely on their intuitions. Therefore, it seems wise finally to go back to the main lines of an analysis that requires homilists to let the text question them, rather than use it to bolster ever new discourses more or less allegorical."

10. However, between the two narratives, Luke inserts his genealogy of Jesus, whereas Matthew places his at the beginning of his Gospel (Matt 1:1-18). As for Mark, he has no such document.

11. The reading of Luke shows the second and third temptations in reverse order.

12. This aspect is explicitly developed in Christian spiritual tradition, in particular that of those monks called the Desert Fathers. See, L. Derousseaux, "L'épreuve et la tentation," *Assemblées du Seigneur*, 1st series, No. 26 (Bruges: Publications de Saint-André, 1977) 62–78; L. Bouyer, *La vie de saint Antoine. Essai sur la spiritualité du monachisme primitif*, Spiritualité orientale 11 (Abbaye de Bellefontaine, 1977) 69–98 ("La lutte contre le démon"); *Lumen vitae* 5 (1961), special issue on temptation; "Désert" in *Vocabulaire de théologie biblique*, cols. 261–66.

13. We all experience the need to immerse ourselves in solitude to see clearly into our inner selves and to make the great decisions of our lives, the reluctance to go to the desert where—we feel it—the Spirit drives us, the trial and the struggles of the retreat, the profound peace that follows the storm of the spiritual combat.

14. This putting God to the test has remained burned into biblical memory as the epitome of doubting the word of God by asking him for additional proofs: Num 20:13-14, 24; Ps 81:8; 106:32.

15. We notice that at this moment Jesus calls Satan by his name. This identification, first in the Gospels, then in tradition, signals the end of all exorcism: the devil is unmasked.

16. The fundamentalist reading of a text consists in taking it in its literal sense without regard for the context.

17. R. Jacob, "La nouvelle solidarité humaine (Rm 5, 12-19)," *Assemblées du Seigneur*, 2nd series, No. 14 (Paris: Publications de Saint-André—Cerf, 1973) 38.

18. Commission Francophone Cistercienne, *Prières au fil des Heures*, 65.

First Sunday, Year B—Pages 48–55

19. This expression is that of R. Jacob, "La nouvelle solidarité humaine," 15.

20. The expression "flesh with its lifeblood still in it" may be surprising. But it reflects everyday experience: flesh empty of blood is dead.

21. According to the ancient conceptions, the justice of the heads of families overflows on all their kin.

22. See, R. Didier, "L'intériorisation de l'Alliane dans l'Esprit," *Assemblées du Seigneur*, 1st series, No. 51 (Bruges: Publication de Saint-André, 1963), 88–109.

23. "His lightnings illumine the world; / the earth sees and trembles" (Ps 97:4); "He raises storm clouds from the end of the earth; / with the lightning he makes the rain" (Ps 135:7); "Flash forth lightning, and put them to flight, / shoot your arrows, and rout them" (Ps 144:6); and so forth.

24. Nothing is sadder and, in the last analysis, falser, than the reduction of living things and nature itself to a collection of material mechanisms. An example of this is to say that a human body is nothing other than an ensemble of physical and chemical aggregates: Can we still call this a living body?

25. In texts predating the account of Genesis by a thousand years, we find a "tradition of the flood." In these epic poems, the gods decide to destroy humankind. But a man—named Utnapishtim—escapes the catastrophe with the seeds of all life. He then becomes a god. This interpretation of the Flood is quite different from that of the Bible. See, "Déluge" and "Gilgamesh" in the *Dictionnaire encyclopédique de la Bible* (Paris: Brepols, 1987); more succinctly, "Déluge" and "Noé" in *Vocabulaire de théologie biblique*. The passages of the Bible on the Flood (Gen 6:5–9:13) are read almost in their entirety from Tuesday to Thursday of the Sixth Week in Ordinary Time, odd years.

26. This letter contains only 105 verses. Of these, 39 (that is, 40.5%) are given in the Sunday Lectionary and 54 (that is, 51%) in the Weekday Lectionary.

27. Here are the other two: "'[You realize] that you were ransomed from your futile conduct, handed on by your ancestors, not with perishable things like silver or gold but with the precious blood of Christ as of a spotless unblemished lamb. He was known before the foundation of the world but revealed in the final time for you, who through him believe in God who raised him from the dead and gave him glory, so that your faith and hope are in God" (1 Pet 1:18-21—Third Sunday of Easter, Year A). "If you are patient when you suffer for doing what is good, this a grace before God. For to this you have been called, because Christ also suffered for you, leaving you an example that you should follow in his footsteps.

'He committed no sin,
and no deceit was found in his mouth.'

"When he was insulted, he returned no insult; when he suffered, he did not threaten; instead, he handed himself over to the one who judges justly. He himself bore our sins in his body upon the cross, so that, free from sin, we might live for righteousness. By his wounds you have been healed. For you had gone astray like sheep, but you have now returned to the shepherd and guardian of your souls" (1 Pet 2:20-25—Fourth Sunday of Easter, Year A).

28. The title "Apostles' Creed" does not mean that our traditional wording of it dates back to the apostles, but that we find equivalent formulas in apostolic writings, for instance, the one we read this Sunday.

29. This is a literal translation. See, the *Bible de Jérusalem* and the *Traduction oecuménique de la Bible*.

30. See, *Dictionnaire encyclopédique de la Bible*, 99–100.

31. Especially Jude 14-15: "Enoch . . . prophesied also about them. . . ." See also, 2 Pet 2:4-9; Jude 6-7.

32. We must not be troubled because inspired texts make reference to legends. The whole Bible is inspired, but all is not a revelation, far from it. There is nothing shocking about an inspired author having recourse to a legend—here the Book of Enoch—in order to express a truth—here, the redeeming, peerless power of the risen Christ.

33. This is the term we find in the original text. See, the *Bible de Jérusalem* and the *Traduction oecuménique de la Bible*.

34. P. Beauchamp, "Aux jours de Noé, la nouvelle alliance," *Assemblées du Seigneur*, 2nd series, No. 14 (Paris: Publications de Saint-André—Cerf, 1973) 17.

35. D. Rimaud, *Les arbres dans la mer* (Paris: Desclée, 1975), 117; (Fiche de chant G 184) in *Liturgie des Heures,* vol. 2 (Paris, 1980), 5.

First Sunday, Year C—Pages 56–62

36. This profession of faith is not the only one in the Bible. It is found in the Passover ritual: "Later on, when your son asks you what these ordinances, statutes and decrees mean which the LORD, our God, has enjoined on you, you shall say to your son, 'We were once slaves of Pharaoh in Egypt, but the LORD brought us out of Egypt with his strong hand. . . .'" (Deut 6:20-21). The Book of Joshua repeats the same story with more details (Josh 24:10-24, Thursday and Friday of the Nineteenth Week in Ordinary Time, even years). Similarly, the Book of Nehemiah has a long prayer pronounced during a liturgy of atonement (Neh 9:7-25).

37. This formula is from the Ordinary of the Mass, at the preparation of the gifts. At the beginning of the Easter Vigil, the priest may cut a cross into the paschal candle while saying, "Christ yesterday and today, the beginning and the end."

38. Prayer after the offering of bread and wine.

39. Here, too, Paul evokes what Scripture says. For instance, we may recall a text from Isaiah:

> See, I am laying a stone in Zion,
> a stone that has been tested,
> A precious cornerstone as a sure foundation;
> he who puts his faith in it shall not be shaken (Isa 28:16).

We do not have here a textual quote, but a reference to a prophetic text understood in a Christological sense by the New Testament writers (see, Matt 16:18; 21:42; Eph 2:20; 1 Pet 2:6).

40. The whole of the Letter to the Romans deals with salvation, to which one has access through faith and not through the Law.

41. The prophet was speaking of all those in Israel who would call upon the name of the Lord and contrasting them with those belonging to the "nations."

42. This emphasis on the Holy Spirit is characteristic of Luke. He very often speaks of the Spirit in his second book, the Acts of the Apostles. See, the *Bible de Jérusalem,* 1571, n. *f* on Acts 1:8.

43. St. Irenaeus (bishop of Lyon ca. 135-202), *Contre les hérésies,* livre III, 22,3; 23,1, in Sources chrétiennes 211 (Paris: Cerf, 1974) 439, 445.

44. *The Jerusalem Bible* (London: Darton, Longman & Todd, 1966).

45. J. Akepsimas and M. Scouarnec, *Des mots et des notes pour célébrer,* 99 (Fiche de chant G 213).

The First Week—Pages 63–64

46. Text of J. Servel (Fiche de chant G 221).

From Monday through Saturday—Pages 64–72

47. These are different from many modern compositions. They catch the attention when first read. But many rapidly pale, by reason of their very precision and originality.

48. Verses 13, 15, 18, 23, 27: at least once in every one of the twenty-two sections of this psalm.

49. Prayer after Communion, Friday.

50. We might want to reread Racine's rendition of this prayer in his tragedy *Esther*, Act 1, Scene 4.

O, my Sovereign King!
Here am I, trembling and alone before Thee.
My father often told me in my childhood
that with us you swore a holy covenant. . . .

51. *Jerusalem Bible*, (Matt 6:12).

52. See, Ph. Rouillard, "La lecture de l'Ecriture dans la tradition juive et les traditions occidentales," *Paroisse et Liturgie* 51 (1969), 483–487 (la liturgie juive).

53. Constitution on the Sacred Liturgy, no. 90.

54. Thus we successively read Exod 1:1-22; 2:1-22; 3:1-20; 5:1–6:1; 6:2-13; 6:29–7:25; 10:21–11:10; 12:1-20; 12:21-36; 12:37-49 and 13:11-16; 13:17–14:9; 14:10-31; 16:1-18, 35; 17:1-16; 18:13-27; 19:1-19 and 20:18-21; 20:1-17; 22:20–23:9; 24:1-18; 32:1-20; 33:7-11, 18-23 and 34:5-9, 29-35; 34:10-28; 35:30–36:1 and 37:1-9; 40:16b-38. Those who do not have the Liturgy of the Hours can read these texts in their Bibles.

55. St. Augustine often gave the homily on the psalm of the Mass. See, I. Rigolot, "Les psaumes graduels dans la prédication de saint Augustin," *Liturgie* 64 (March 1, 1988) 28–60 (review of the C.F.C., Abbaye de Campénéac, 56800 Ploërmel).

56. St. Augustine, *Commentary* on Ps. 60 (61):2-3 (CCL 39, 766), *Liturgy of the Hours*, 2:87–88.

57. St. Gregory Nazianzen, *Oratio 14*, De pauperum amore, 23–25 (PG 35, 887-890), *Liturgy of the Hours*, 2:96–97.

58. St. Cyprian, *Treatise on the Lord's Prayer*, Cap. 1-3 (CSEL 3, 267-268), *Liturgy of the Hours*, 2:104–106.

59. St. Aphraates, *Demonstration 11*, "On Circumcision," 11–12 (PS 1, 498-503), *Liturgy of the Hours*, 2:113–115.

60. St. Asterius, *Homily 13* (PG 40, 355-358, 362), *Liturgy of the Hours*, 2:122-124.

61. St. Aelred, *The Mirror of Love*, 3, 5 (PL 195, 582), *Liturgy of the Hours*, 2:131-132.

62. The Church in the Modern World, nos. 9-10, *Liturgy of the Hours*, 2:139-140.

Second Sunday, Year A—Pages 73-81

1. Gen 12:1-25:11. Abraham is placed among the descendants of Shem, one of the three sons of Noah (Gen 10:1; 11:10-26); and through Shem, Abraham belongs to Adam's posterity (Gen 5). On the literary function of biblical genealogies, their origin, their meaning, see, "Généalogie" in *Dictionnaire encyclopédique de la Bible*, 521-22; "Génération" in *Vocabulaire de théologie biblique*, cols. 501-02.

2. The same goes for the other patriarchs and, more generally, for what is called sacred history. Its true topic is God, who acts and saves. This is why this history is called sacred, whereas it is not always—far from it—edifying. For the same reason, it is not disqualified by the fact that sometimes in their work the hagiographers make use of the legends, the various traditions of other peoples. Neither is it disqualified by well-known discrepancies, for instance, the genealogies of the patriarchs . . . and of Jesus.

3. "Because you have done this, you shall be banned from all the animals and from all the wild creatures," God said to the serpent (Gen 3:14). Then, "Cursed be the ground" (Gen 3:17). Then God said to Cain, "You shall be banned from the soil" (Gen 4:11). Finally, "Cursed be Canaan!" (Gen 9:25).

4. See, "Bénédiction" and "Malédiction" in *Vocabulaire de théologie biblique*, cols. 120-28, 703-07.

5. "All the communities of the earth / shall find blessing in you," says the Lectionary. The Bible of Jerusalem says "by you," which corresponds better to the Hebrew and is more consonant with what is said afterwards: Gen 18:18; 22:18; 26:4; 28:14.

6. Rom 3:28; 4:2-5; Eph 2:8-9.

7. "We speak God's wisdom, mysterious, hidden, which God predetermined before the ages for our glory. . . .

'What eye has not seen, and ear has not heard,
and what has not entered the human heart,
what God has prepared for those who love him' " (1 Cor 2:7-9).

"The mystery hidden from ages past in God. . . . the eternal purpose that he accomplished in Christ Jesus our Lord" (Eph 3:9-11). "The mystery hidden from ages and from generations past . . . now manifested to [God's] holy ones" (Col 1:26). See also, Eph 1:4, 9, 10.

8. This distinction is found, more or less explicitly, in several New Testament writings, in particular in Peter's First Letter (1:20; 3:18b, 22b; 4:6a). There probably are vestiges of a first century hymn in these texts. See, M.-E. Boismard, *Quatre hymnes baptismales dans la Première épître de Pierre*, Lectio divina 30 (Paris: Cerf, 1961) 60–102.

9. Besides the numerous texts in which God affirms it, the story of the creation attests to it. See, "Parole de Dieu" in *Vocabulaire de théologie biblique*, cols. 906–08.

10. It is noteworthy that this word has been transmitted to us by Mark, who insists that the secrets of the kingdom must not be prematurely and indiscriminately revealed. The phrase "messianic secret" has been used in this regard. See, J. Rouquette, "Le 'caché' et le 'manifesté' dans le Nouveau Testament," *Concilium* 69 (1971) 37–52, in particular, 46–52.

11. Immediately after having written these words, Paul speaks of "the mystery hidden from ages and from generations past but now . . . manifested to his holy ones" (Col 1:26).

12.

	Matt	Mark	Luke
Peter's confession in Caesarea	16:13-20	8:27-30	9:18-21
Prediction of the passion	21–23	31–33	22
Conditions of discipleship	24–27	34–38	23–26
Announcement of return	28	9:1	27
Transfiguration	17:1-9	2-10	28-36

The Preface of this Sunday evokes this context: "On your holy mountain he revealed himself in glory in the presence of his disciples. / He had already prepared them for his approaching death."

We must note, however, that Luke places the transfiguration a little after Jesus "resolutely determined to journey to Jerusalem" (9:51). Thus, it is set in the perspective of the "exodus" of Jesus, which is to take place in Jerusalem and which is the topic of the conversation with Moses and Elijah.

13. To be more precise, we should say: within the context of a Sunday in Lent (the montage of its Liturgy of the Word), itself placed in the broader context of Lent itself.

14. X. Léon-Dufour, "La Transfiguration de Jésus (Mt 17, 1-9)," *Assemblées du Seigneur*, 1st series, No 28 (Bruges: Publications de Saint-André, 1962) 27.

15. The case of the transfiguration is especially striking, but the Liturgy of the Word is always an integral part of the celebration of the mystery. It is worth observing that in the context of the feast of the Transfiguration of the Lord (August 6), the same Gospel (Matt, Year A; Mark, Year B; Luke, Year C) is integrated into another montage (Dan 7:9-10, 13-14 and 2 Pet 1:16-19) that expresses another aspect of the mystery, as the Preface of that day makes clear.

He revealed his glory to the disciples
to strengthen them for the scandal of the cross.
His glory shone from a body like our own,
to show that the Church,

which is the body of Christ,
would one day share his glory.

16. Isa 2:2-3; Dan 9:16; etc.

17. This text (Dan 12:1b-3) is in the Lectionary for the burial of an adult.

18. Whiteness "as light" is the color of the heavenly realities of the last times: Dan 7:9; Mark 16:5; John 20:21; Rev 1:13-14; 4:4; 14:14; 19:11; 20:11.

19. See, J. De Fraine, "La 'gloire' dans l'Ancien Testament," *Assemblées du Seigneur*, 1st series, No 28 (Bruges: Publications de Saint-André, 1962) 45-63.

20. Thus Matt 17, n. *c*, in the Jerusalem Bible.

21. Note *v*, p. 90, *Traduction oecuménique de la Bible*, denies this interpretation.

22. These verses from Matthew are read on Saturday of the Second Week of Advent.

23. It may appear surprising that John—one of the three witnesses—does not report the transfiguration. The same is true for Jesus' baptism, for the institution of the Eucharist, for the agony in Gethsemane. But we must not conclude that John ignores what he alludes to in another way. " 'I am troubled now. Yet what should I say? "Father, save me from this hour"? But it was for this purpose that I came to this hour. Father, glorify your name.' Then a voice came from heaven, 'I have glorified it and will glorify it again' " (John 12:27-28).

John sees Jesus' glory—that according to the Synoptics is manifested by a flash of lightning on the mountain—illuminating all the words and acts of Jesus. "The fourth Gospel is an unceasing theophany in which the scene of the transfiguration, described by the Synoptics, could not find its place since it had no raison d'être and is, by its very concept, much inferior to the glory that shines in all the discourses and all the acts of the Incarnate Word." A. Loisy, *Le quatrième évangile* (Paris: Picard, 1903) 104-05.

24. Peter's proposal—"If you wish, I will make three tents here"—is not due to a reflex of hospitality. The tents designate the "eternal dwellings" of Luke 16:9.

25. See, "Nuée" in *Vocabulaire de théologie biblique*, col. 845. Thus on Sinai (Exod 40:34-35), at the time of the dedication of the Temple by Solomon (1 Kgs 8:10-12), and at the end of time (Ezek 10:3-4). Similarly, at the ascension, Jesus disappears in "a cloud" (Acts 1:9). The cloud is present in Old Testament theophanies (Exod 13:22; see, n. *f* in the Jerusalem Bible). And it characterizes the last manifestation of the Son of Man (Matt 24:30; 1 Thess 4:17; Rev 1:7; 14:14-16).

26. St. John of the Cross, *Ascent of Mount Carmel*, trans. and ed. E. Allison Peers (Garden City, N.Y.: Image Books, 1958) 288-89.

27. See, J. Dupont, "L'évangile de saint Matthieu: quelques clés de lecture," *Communautés et liturgies* 57 (1975) 10-12. Besides the case of the transfiguration, "Matthew mentions ten instances of these prostrations before Jesus: the episodes of the Magi (three times, 2:2, 8, 11) and after the resurrection (two times, 28:9, 17); the cured leper (8:2), the synagogue official (8:18), and the Canaanite woman (15:25), all of whom beg for a healing; the mother of the sons of Zebedee, asking Jesus for the first places for her sons (20:20); finally, the episode of the calming of the sea, when the disciples 'did [Jesus] homage, saying, "Truly, you are the Son of God" ' (14:33). According to Matthew, *Kyrie* is said eight times by the disciples addressing Jesus (8:21, 25; 14:28, 30; 16:22; 17:4; 18:21; 26:22) eleven times by people begging for a cure (8:2, 6, 8; 9:28; 15:22, 25, 27; 17:15; 20:30, 31, 33)."

28. Matt 7:21-22; 25:11, 37, 44.

29. D. Rimaud, *Les arbres dans la mer*. (Fiche de chant G 184).

Second Sunday, Year B—Pages 82–87

30. In Jerusalem, on the former esplanade of the Temple, the famous and magnificent mosque called the "Dome of the Rock"—and sometimes, improperly, the "Mosque of Omar"—preserves the memory of Abraham and his son. This rock is believed to be the

place where Abraham went to sacrifice his son (Ishmael, in the Moslem tradition). This building was erected between 687 and 691 by the caliph Abd-el-Malek.

31. There is a vast difference between this narrative and those of Jephthah's sacrifice of his daughter (Judg 11:34-40) or David's lamentations after the death of his son Absalom (2 Sam 19:1-9). True, the situations are different. Jephthah had made an atrocious vow that should he be victorious over the Ammonites, he would kill the first person who came out to meet him. God—and this is the lesson of the sacrifice of Abraham—does not want human sacrifice. As for David, he uncontrollably wails over the death of a son killed in combat.

32. In the Bible, this story contains nineteen verses (Gen 22:1-19). The liturgical reading omits eight of them, which does not change the concise character of this passage.

33. We do not have here a cruel trial imposed on a father to see how far he will go. Such a demand would smack of sadism in the person who makes it, even if he or she intends to intervene before the fatal blow falls. On the other hand, to submit to such a demand would not leave a person unscathed. There is bound to be bitterness against the one who required such an extreme action, anger and even contempt for oneself. In a word, to push anyone this far is odious; to accept the challenge is immoral.

34. Rom 4:1-25; Gal 3:6-14; Jas 2:21; Heb 11:17.

35. This is the case, in particular, of those who, after Origen (ca. 185–253), have written commentaries or delivered homilies on that passage of the Book of Genesis, for example, St. John Chrysostom (ca. 350–407), St. Augustine (354–430), and St. Cyril of Alexandria (ca. 380–444), as well as Maximus of Turin (5th c.), Paulinus of Nola (353–431), Isidore of Seville (ca. 554–636), Rabanus Maurus (780–856).

36. See, F. Cabrol and H. Leclercq, *Dictionnaire d'archéologie chrétienne et de liturgie*, vol. 1/1 (Paris: Levouzey, 1924) cols. 111–19. The sacrifice of Isaac on stained glass windows as it was often represented in the Middle Ages.

37. *In figuris praesignatur, / cum Isaac immolatur. . . . .*: Truth the ancient types fulfilling, / Isaac bound, a victim willing. . . .

38. Mark frequently emphasizes the disciples' lack of comprehension: Mark 4:13 (parable of the sower); 40:40-41 (the calming of the storm at sea); 6:50-52 (the multiplication of the loaves); 8:17-21 (the leaven of the Pharisees); 9:32 (the second prediction of the passion); 10:24 (the danger of riches); 10:32 (the third prediction of the passion); 10:38 (the ambition of James and John).

39. Exegetes generally agree that the conclusion of Mark's Gospel (Mark 16:9-20, appearances of the risen Christ) was added afterward by another writer. This does not detract from its value (inspiration and canonicity). See the notes in the *Bible de Jérusalem*, 1479, and in the *Traduction oecuménique de la Bible*, 179–80.

40. B. Standaert, *L'Evangile selon saint Marc. Composition et genre littéraire* (Bruges: Abbaye Saint-André, 1978), has defended his dissertation on the subject of Mark's Gospel, seen as explicitly composed for the paschal liturgy, during which baptism was administered.

41. J. Servel (text) and M.-A. Rétif (music), *Chants notés*, vol. 4, coédition (Paris, 1984) 289–90.

Second Sunday, Year C—Pages 88–94

42. He is named 186 times in the Old Testament and 75 times in the New.

43. Gen 12:1-4a.

44. Gen 22:1-19.

45. The Lectionary omits verses 1-4 and 13-16.

> Some time after these events, this word of the LORD came to Abram in a vision:
> "Fear not, Abram!
> I am your shield;

I will make your reward very great.''
But Abram said, ''O Lord GOD, what good will your gifts be, if I keep on being childless and have as my heir the steward of my house, Eliezer?'' Abram
continued, ''See, you have given me no offspring, and so one of my servants
will be my heir.'' Then the word of the LORD came to him: ''No, that one shall
not be your heir; your own issue shall be your heir'' (Gen:15:1-4—Wednesday
of the Twelfth Week in Ordinary Time, odd years).

Then the LORD said to Abram: ''Know for certain that your descendants shall
be aliens in a land not their own, where they shall be enslaved and oppressed
for four hundred years. But I will bring judgment on the nation they must
serve, and in the end they will depart with great wealth. You, however, shall
join your forefathers in peace; you shall be buried at a contented old age. In
the fourth time-span the others shall come back here; the wickedness of the
Amorites will not have reached its full measure until then'' (15:13-16).

46. These are the events enumerated by a commentator of vv. 13-16.

47. This rite, with this meaning, is attested to in the Book of Jeremiah (34:17-21). But the
oath, taken with the stipulation that one would submit to a terrible punishment if one did
not keep it, was a current practice in Middle Eastern cultures.

If I forget you, Jerusalem,
    may my right hand be forgotten!
May my tongue cleave to my palate
    if I remember you not,
If I place not Jerusalem
    ahead of my joy (Ps 137:5-6).

''Let people do anything they want to me; I give my hand to cut; I swear to you on the
head of my mother, the heads of my children,'' and so forth. In court, we also swear to
tell the truth and accept the penalty ordained by the law in case of perjury.

48. D. Rimaud, ''En quel pays de solitude,'' *Les arbres dans la mer*, 117 (Fiche de chant G 184):
    Follow Jesus transfigured:
    tomorrow he will be crucified
    to ratify the Covenant.

49. The *Bible de Jérusalem* reads ''rubbish''; the *Traduction oecuménique de la Bible*, ''refuse.''

50. This ultimatum, to choose between two paths, is found in the Old Testament: Deut
11:26-28; 30:15-20; Prov 8:32-36; and so forth.

51. Mark, seven; Matthew, eight; Luke, nine.

52. ''Since many have undertaken to compile a narrative of the events that have been
fulfilled among us, just as those who were eyewitnesses from the beginning and ministers
of the word have handed them down to us, I too have decided, after investigating everything accurately anew, to write it down in an orderly sequence for you, most excellent The-
ophilus, so that you may realize the certainty of the teachings you have received'' (Luke
1:1-4).

53. This prayer is always connected with an important phase or circumstance of Jesus'
mission: before choosing the Twelve (6:12); before asking for a ''vote of confidence,'' which
will give Peter the opportunity to profess his faith (9:18-21); when he confronts a temptation to deviate from his mission, as when the crowds show their ambiguous enthusiasm
(5:15-16); when, on the contrary, he sees his mission in the process of being fulfilled (10:21-22,
often called ''the hymn of jubilation'' upon the return of the seventy-two disciples); at the
time of the dire trial in Gethsemane (22:39-46); on the cross (23:34, 46); finally, at the time
of the ascension when he leaves his disciples with a prayer of blessing (24:5-51).

Jesus instructs his disciples in prayer (11:1-13) and urges them to pray in prevision of
the great trial which they, too, will know (21:36; 22:31-32). We find the same insistence,

the same viewpoints in Acts: Matthias' election, Pentecost, Ananias' vision, Peter's deliverance and his visions in Joppa, the sending forth of Paul and Barnabas on their mission, and so forth.

54. Lazare de Selve (18th c.), *Regards sur Jésus Christ*, French texts assembled by Ph. Sellier (Paris: Cerf, 1964) 55.

55. Commission Francophone Cistercienne, *La nuit le jour* (Paris: Desclée—Cerf, 1973) 110–11. (Fiche de chant G 293-1).

56. D. Rimaud, *Les arbres dans la mer*, 117.

Second Week, from Monday through Saturday—Pages 95–104

57. Monday, opening prayer.

58. Monday, prayer over the gifts.

59. Monday, prayer after Communion.

60. Thursday, opening prayer.

61. The relationship between the first reading and the Gospel is often quite loose.

62. This parable is found four more times in the Lectionary: Fourth Sunday of Lent, Year C; Mass of Reconciliation; Mass for the Remission of Sins; and Luke 15:4-10 is but one selection for votive Masses of the Sacred Heart of Jesus.

63. Exod 13:17—14:9 (Sunday); 14:10-31 (Monday); 16:1-18, 35 (Tuesday); 17:1-16 (Wednesday); 18:13-27 (Thursday); 19:1-19; 20:18-21 (Friday); 20:1-17 (Saturday). The Liturgy of the Hours is limited to excerpts in order to keep the usual length of texts for this reading in common. But, in private, we may easily prolong the time of this reading. In total, this occupies only nine pages of the Jerusalem Bible, i.e., 184 verses.

64. In choral celebration, the responsory, to be correctly placed, comes only after a time of silence following the reading; this aims at giving each participant the opportunity of interiorizing the reading—or receiving it—without external pressure.

65. St. Leo, Sermon 51, 3-4. 8 (PL 54, 310–11, 313), *Liturgy of the Hours*, 2:149–51.

66. St. John Chrysostom, Catecheses, 3, 24–27 (SC 50, 165–67), *Liturgy of the Hours*, 2:160–61.

67. St. Irenaeus, *Against Heresies*, Lib. 4, 14, 2-3; 15, 1 (SC 100, 542. 548), *Liturgy of the Hours*, 2:177–78.

68. Ibid., Lib. 4, 16, 2-5 (SC 100, 542-48), *Liturgy of the Hours*, 2:195–96.

69. St. Hilary, *Treatise* on Ps 127, 1-3 (CSEL 24, 628-30), *Liturgy of the Hours*, 2:185–87.

70. St. Augustine, *Commentary* on Ps 140, 4-6 (CCL 40, 2028-29), *Liturgy of the Hours*, 2:168–70.

71. St. Ambrose, *Treatise on Flight from the World*, Cap. 6, 36; 7, 44; 8, 45; 9, 52 (CSEL 32, 192. 198–99). 204), *Liturgy of the Hours*, 2:203–04.

72. Responsory (Matt 22:37; Deut 10:12) following second reading, Office of Readings, Saturday, Second Week of Lent, *Liturgy of the Hours*, 2:202–03.

From the Third to the Fifth Week of Lent—Pages 105–106

1. The readings of Year A can be repeated in Years B and C, especially in communities that accompany catechumens on their journey. Besides, in Years B and C, it is possible to read during the week the Gospels of Year A that have not been read on Sunday.

2. Year A: Rom 5:1-2, 5-8; Eph 5:8-14; Rom 8:8-11. Year B: 1 Cor 1:22-25; Eph 2:4-10; Heb 5:7-9. Year C: 1 Cor 10:1-6, 10-12; 2 Cor 5:17-21; Phil 3:8.14.

3. Year A: water from the rock (Exod 17:3-7); the election and anointing of David (1 Sam 16:1b, 6-7, 10-13a); the prediction of the return from exile (Ezek 37:12-14). Year B: the giv-

ing of the Law (Exod 20:1-17); the edict of Cyrus allowing the exiles to return (2 Chr 36: 14-17, 19-23), and the announcement of the new covenant (Jer 31:31-34). Year C: the burning bush (Exod 3:1-8a, 13-15), the entrance into the Promised Land and the celebration of the Passover at Gilgal (Josh 5:9a, 10-12), and the prediction of a new exodus of liberation (Isa 43:16-21).

Third Sunday, Year A—Pages 107-118

4. Numerous biblical texts call this to mind: Exod 14:11; 15:24; 16:3; 32; Num 11:1-4; 12:1; 14:1-4; 16:3-14; 20:2-5; 21:5; Ps 78:15-17; etc.

5. "Well" translates the Hebrew *beer*. This word is part of many place names: Beer (Num 21:16), Beeroth (Josh 9:17), Beer-sheba (Gen 21:14).

6. See, A. Jaubert, "Les images d'eau vive dans le Judaïsme contemporain du IVᵉ évangile," *Approches de l'Evangile de Jean* (Paris: Seuil, 1976) 140-47. Also, D. Mollat, "Le puits de Jacob (Jn 4, 1-42)," *Bible et vie chrétienne*, 6 (1956) 83-91; I. de La Potterie, "Jésus et les Samaritains," *Assemblées du Seigneur*, 2nd series, No 16 (Paris: Publications de Saint-André— Cerf, 1971) 34-49.

7. In fact, many ways of reading, many approaches are possible, and none can pretend to exclude others or to be the definitive synthesis. On the other hand, we can and must demand that a reading, a meditation of such a text, remain open to further reading and meditation.

8. On the two following Sundays, the readings were those of the man born blind (John 9:1-41) and Lazarus (John 11:1-45). When the forty-day Lent was established, these Gospels were read on the Third, Fourth, and Fifth Sundays of Lent. See, A. Aubry, "Points de repère pour une explication génétique du Carême romain," 7-22.

9. In fact, to shorten the celebration, the Lectionary proposes a "short form" (4:5-15, 19b-26, 39a, 40-42) in which the dialogue with the disciples is omitted.

10. The parallelism is striking. The Samaritan woman wonders that Jesus should speak to her; the disciples are surprised to see him talking with a woman. Jesus asks for a drink from this stranger; the disciples bring food to the Master and urge him to eat. To the woman Jesus says that he possesses a marvelous living water; to the disciples he answers that he has a food that they do not know. The Samaritan woman thinks he is speaking of well water; the disciples think of food of the same kind as what they bring. In both cases, the clear revelation follows these manifestations of misunderstanding. We have here something akin to the method of the parables (see John 16:25).

11. The words he has said are those of the Father (John 3:34; 7:16; 8:26, 38, 40; 14:10, 24; 17:8, 14). Similarly, the works he has accomplished are those of the Father (John 5:17, 19-20, 30, 36; 8:28; 10:25-37; 14:10; 17:4). He has never done anything but the Father's will (John 5:30; 6:38).

12. Origen (ca. 185-254), *Commentaire sur saint Jean*, livre XIII, 36, 235, Sources chrétiennes 222 (Paris, Cerf, 1975) 159.

13. To be truthful, we must recognize that verses 35-38 are obscure in several places. However, it seems that "In four months the harvest will be here" records a remark actually made by the disciples and showing their lack of understanding. See, I. de La Potterie, "Jésus et les Samaritains," 46-49.

14. Origen, "Homélie sur les puits d'Isaac," *Douzième homélie sur les Nombres*, Sources chrétiennes 29 (Paris: Cerf, 1951) 234-35.

15. Ibid.

16. Commission Francophone Cistercienne, *Tropaires des dimanches*, Livre d'Heures d'En-Calcat (Dourgne, 1980) 20. (Fiches de chant G LH 106 and P LH 131).

Fourth Sunday, Year A—Pages 119-126

1. The story of David is recorded in the books of Samuel, the First Book of Kings, and the First Book of Chronicles. See "David" in *Vocabulaire de théologie biblique*, cols. 247-50. For the musical instruments, see Amos 6:5.

2. See the genealogies of Matthew (1:1-17) and Luke (3:23-38). See also Matt 1:20; 22:42-45; Mark 12:37; Luke 1:27, 32, 69; 2:4, 11; Acts 2:29, 34; Rom 1:3; 2 Tim 2:8; Rev 22:15. To these we must add the texts in which Jesus is called "Son of David": Matt 9:27; 15:22; 20:31; 21:9, 15; Mark 10:47-48; Luke 18:28.

3. See in what is called the "Book of Signs" (John 2-11) the sign of Cana (2:1-12), the purification of the Temple (2:13-22), the cure of the son of a royal official (4:46-54) and of a crippled man at the Sheep Gate pool (5:1-18), the cure of the man born blind (9:1-41), and the raising of Lazarus (11:1-44).

4. Jesus knows well that evil—disease, pain—and death come from sin, and the evangelist knows this too. But Jesus denies the bond between the handicap of this man born blind and personal sin committed either by himself or his parents. By doing so, he returns our attention to what counts before all else: the meaning of this cure, of this "sign."

5. St. Augustine, *Traités sur la Pâque*, 44:2, Patrologie latine, P.-M. Migne, ed., 35, 1714.

6. See in the Jerusalem Bible, the title of the section in John's Gospel going from 7:1 to 11:21.

7. These are bigger than lemons and are the fruit of the citron tree. To this day, for the feast of Tabernacles (Sukkôth in Hebrew), pious Jews prepare a *lulab* made from the branches of four trees—palm, myrtle, willow, orange—carefully selected. John is the only evangelist who shows us the crowds waving palm branches as a sign of victory to welcome the King and Messiah (12:13, Passion Sunday, Procession).

8. These details are reported by Flavius Josephus, *Antiquités juives*, 4:9; 5:2.

9. The "scrutinies" of former times aimed at verifying the preparation of candidates for baptism; today they are still part of the Rite of Inititation of Adults and the Rite of Baptism for Children of School Age. They are now celebrations preparatory to the administration of the sacrament.

10. The questions the Pharisees fire at the blind man, now cured, are not purely and simply identified with ritual questions asked in the course of pre-baptismal scrutinies. But they remind us that catechumens must give an account of their journeying toward full faith.

11. Text by J. Gelineau (Fiche de chant G LH 108).

Fifth Sunday, Year A—Pages 127-133

1. In particular in the books of Nehemiah and Ezra, in Jeremiah, Ezekiel, and Zechariah.

2. See "Exil" in *Dictionnaire encyclopédique de la Bible*, 453-54.

3. See "Exil" in *Vocabulaire de théologie biblique*, cols. 419-22.

4. The great vision of the dry bones, which immediately precedes the text of this Sunday, is probably better known. Ezek 37:1-14 is read at the Mass of the Vigil of Pentecost. In effect, these are two consecutive oracles (37:1-11 and 12-14). It is therefore not arbitrary to read the second independently from the first.

5. After this, John records the session of the high council (Sanhedrin) at which Jesus' death was decided. Jesus, henceforth, avoids the public eye (11:46-54). Then follow the anointing at Bethany (11:55-12:11), the triumphal entry into Jerusalem (12:12-19), the Last Supper with the disciples (13-17), and finally, the passion and resurrection (18-20).

6. John 2:11; 11:40; 14:10, and so forth.

7. This is the longest narrative in all the Gospels: forty-five verses.

8. John 12:23, 27; 13:1; 16:32; 17:1.

9. This remark in no way invalidates other interpretations of Jesus' being troubled. The proper preface for the Fifth Sunday in Year A says of Christ, "As a man like us, Jesus wept for Lazarus his friend."

10. Thus, the cures of the sick man (5:1-18, 19-47) and the man born blind (9:1-41; 10:1-21), the multiplication of the loaves (6:1-15, 22-71).

11. M. Moret, *Assemblées du Seigneur*, 2nd series, No 18 (Paris: Publications de Saint-André—Cerf, 1971) 22.

12. St. Augustine, *Traités sur saint Jean*, 44:14, Patrologie latine 35, P.-M. Migne, ed., 35, col. 1755.

13. ". . . You did not abandon him to the power of death,
but helped all men to seek and find you.
Again and again you offered a covenant to man,
and through the prophets taught to hope for salvation."
(Eucharistic Prayer IV)

14. Commission Francophone Cistercienne, *Tropaires des dimanches*, 26. (Fiche de chant G LH 110).

Third Sunday, Year B—Pages 136–144

1. There are several ways to divide the precepts of the Decalogue into ten commandments. According to Jewish tradition, the introductory sentence forms the first; then come verses 3-6, 7, 8-11, 12, 13, 14, 15, 16, 17. According to the Greek tradition, also followed by Protestant Churches, we have verses 3, 4-6, 7, 8-11, 12, 13, 14, 15, 16, 17. According to Catholic and Lutheran traditions, we find verses 3-6, 7, 8-11, 12, 13, 14, 15, 16, 17a, 17b. In the text itself, we see a grouping into three parts: God speaks in the first person (vv. 2-6); he is spoken of in the third person (vv. 7-12); last, in the third part, he is not named (vv. 13-17). See, Cl. Wiener, "Le livre de l'exode," *Cahiers Evangile* 54 (1985) 36–38.

2. Thus the Bishops of Belgium, *Belief and Belonging: Living and Celebrating the Faith*, Part 3, "Living the Gospel" (Collegeville, Minn.: The Liturgical Press, 1990) 147–219. See the two facing pages, "The Ten Commandments of the Old Testament" and "The Ten Commandments in Catholic Catechesis," 166–67.

3. See, Cl. Wiener, "Le livre de l'exode," 36–38; A. Cazelles, *A la recherche de Moïse* (Paris: Cerf, 1979) 95, 97.

We recognize here a very old nucleus that could date back to Moses, to his great encounter with God on Sinai, where he received the charter of freedom for the people.

4. Text by J.-F. Frie. (Fiche de chant G 242).

5. Hos 2; Jer 2:1-3; 31:22; 51:5; Isa 49:14-21; 50:1; 54:1-10; 62:4-5; Ezek 16:23. The image is also used in the New Testament: Matt 22:2-3; 25:1-2; John 3:28-29; Eph 5:25-33; Rev 19:7; 21:2.

6. The Name is God himself. See *Vocabulaire de théologie biblique*, cols. 827–29.

7. "The Tools for Good Works" is the title of the fourth chapter of the *Rule of St. Benedict*. This chapter includes all the commandments of the Decalogue.

8. In the Synoptics, this episode is placed after the triumphal entry of Jesus into Jerusalem (Matt 21:1-10; Mark 11:1-11; Luke 19:28-38) and is followed, according to Matthew and Mark, by the decision to put Jesus to death. As for John, he reports this episode at the beginning of Jesus' ministry, after John the Baptist's testimony (1:19-34), the call of the first

disciples (1:35-51), and the sign of Cana (2:1-12) and before the conversation with Nicodemus (3:1-21).

9. Thus at the end of his Gospel, John states his intention when he wrote down a certain number of signs worked by Jesus "in the presence of [his] disciples" (20:30).

10. See "Temple," *Vocabulaire de théologie biblique*, cols. 1266-70.

11. The way Jesus acts emphasizes this. He expels merchants and money changers with their sheep and oxen; he throws the coins down and overturns their tables. But he is careful not to cause the slightest harm to people and property, which was easily recovered. Thus, he simply says to those who sell doves, "Take these out of here." John does not say what happened immediately afterwards and on the following days. Have the merchants come back, perhaps timidly at first, after having made sure that Jesus was nowhere to be seen? One single thing is of interest to John and his readers: Jesus' action and its meaning.

12. "The love of thy house has led me to ruin" according to *Le psautier: Version oecuménique, texte liturgique* (Paris: Cerf, 1977).

13. We may regret that the translation of the Lectionary, in verse 22, has not used the expression "to get up again" or "to get up" (as in the *Traduction oecuménique de la Bible*) "from among the dead."

14. To tell the truth, the theme of the Temple is found in the New Testament: in Paul's writings when speaking of the Church (Eph 2:19-21) and of individual Christians (1 Cor 3:16; 6:19), in the Letter to the Hebrews (9:11-12), and also in Revelation (11:19). See, Y. Congar, *Le mystère du Temple*, Lectio divina 22 (Paris: Cerf, 1963).

15. See Eph 2:21-22.

16. Commission Francophone Cistercienne, *Sur la trace de Dieu* (Paris: Desclée, 1979) 141. (Fiche de chant K 145-1).

Fourth Sunday, Year B—Pages 145-151

1. See the introduction to the books of Chronicles in the *Bible de Jérusalem*, 439-42, and in the *Traduction oecuménique de la Bible*, 1771-77.

2. Eucharistic Prayer IV.

3. This scandal is expressed by such reflections as "How can God let such things happen?"

4. In 1940 in France, how many preachers and writers on current affairs proclaimed, "The military defeat is the punishment for the country's sins"? Was, then, the victory of 1945 the reward for its conversion? We see where such explanations can lead; they are also grist for the mill of opponents, oppressors of all sorts, who never fail to exploit such ways of speaking.

5. Jer 2-3; 31; Ezek 8:11.

6. Jer 11:18-12:6; 15:10-21; Ezek 3:4-9; 33:30-33.

7. The Acts of the Apostles place the ascension forty days after Easter. But we must not understand this way of presenting the mystery as if, during this period, the risen Christ kept wandering, one knows not where, between heaven and earth.

8. "So Jesus said [to them], 'When you lift up the Son of Man, then you will realize that I AM, and that I do nothing on my own, but I say only what the Father taught me' " (John 8:28). " 'And when I am lifted up from the earth, I will draw everyone to myself.' He said this indicating the kind of death he would die" (John 12:32-33).

9. Eucharistic Prayer IV.

10. Ibid.

11. J. Akepsimas and M. Scouarnec, *Des mots et des notes pour célébrer*, 99. (Fiche de chant G 213).

Fifth Sunday, Year B—Pages 152–161

1. Ezek 16:60, 62; 37:26.

2. Isa 50:3; 59:21; 61:8. These texts, integrated into the Book of Isaiah, are the work of anonymous disciples of the great prophet. See the introduction to Isaiah in the *Bible de Jérusalem*, 1078–79, and the *Traduction oecuménique de la Bible*, 732–43; *Cahiers Evangile* 20 (1977).

3. Jer 7:23; 11:4; 30:22; 31:1; 32:38.

4. Ezek 11:20; 14:11; 36:28; Zech 8:8.

The writing down of certain parts of Deuteronomy that treat of the covenant could have been inspired by preexisting models: codes of law and documents of covenants in use at the time in the lands of the Near East. Also, the northern kingdom had kept the tradition of a covenant between the tribes (see Josh 24), a covenant whose religious basis was the recognition of the Lord as God of all the tribes (see Hos 6:7).

5. See, R. de Vaux, *Les institutions de l'Ancien Testament*, vol. 1 (Paris: Cerf, 1958) 18–19, 86–87, 173.

6. What is meant here is Deuteronomy or its legislative part. This "discovery" and what resulted from it are recorded in chapters 22–23 of the Second Book of Kings.

7. This oracle of Hosea is read at Mass on the Saturday of the Third Week of Lent.

8. Matt 26:36-46; Mark 14:32-42; Luke 22:39-46.

9. "Abba, Father, all things are possible to you" (Mark 14:36); "Father, if you are willing. . ." (Luke 22:42).

10. "But not what I will but what you will" (Mark 14:36); "Still, not my will but yours be done" (Luke 22:42).

11. See Eucharistic Prayer IV.

12. Georges Bernanos, *Joy*, trans. Louise Varèse (New York: Pantheon Books, 1946) 45–46.

13. First week: 1:19–2:12. Last week: ch. 12.

14. We cannot ignore that the coming on the scene of Greeks who want to see Jesus is a literary and theological summit of chapters 11 and 12: the raising of Lazarus (11:1-54), the anointing at Bethany (11:55–12:11), the triumphal entry into Jerusalem (12:12-19), this Sunday's Gospel (12:20-33), the words on the glory and the cross (12:33-36), the epilogue on the conditions of true faith (12:37-50). Then comes the narrative of the passion (13–19), which begins with the last meal of Jesus with his disciples and his washing their feet.

15. There were "proselytes" among those who heard Peter's first speech on Pentecost (see Acts 2:11). Nicholas, one of the seven chosen for the service of the Hellenists, was a proselyte. Others followed Paul and Barnabas (see Acts 13:43).

The Roman centurion to whom Peter was sent was "God fearing" (see Acts 10:2). In Antioch, Paul addressed Jews and those who feared God (see Acts 13:16, 26) and converts to Judaism (see Acts 13:43). Lydia from Philippi was "a worshiper of God" before her baptism (see Acts 16:14-15). There were many of them in Thessalonica (see Acts 17:4) and Berea (see Acts 17:17). In Corinth, Paul lodged at the home of one of them, Titus Justus (see Acts 18:7).

16. John 1:14, 18, 51; 3:11, 32; 8:56; 14:9, 19.

17. John 2:4; 7:6, 8, 30; 8:20.

18. John 3:14; 8:28; 12:32.

19. See the marginal notes in the *Bible de Jérusalem*.

20. Matt 13:1-9; Mark 4:1-9; Luke 8:4-8.

21. Matt 13:31-32; Mark 4:30-32; Luke 13:18-19.

22. "Whoever finds his life will lose it, and whoever loses his life for my sake will find it" (Matt 10:39). "For whoever wishes to save his life will lose it, but whoever loses his life for my sake and that of the gospel will save it" (Mark 8:35). "Whoever seeks to preserve his life will lose it, but whoever loses it will save it" (Luke 17:33).

23. See above, the Fifth Sunday of Lent, Year A.

24. In his account of the passion, John does not mention Jesus' agony in Gethsemane.

25. As the crisis caused by Jesus' coming develops, the "world" takes on, for John, a pejorative meaning. We are no longer speaking of the world as God created it—good—but of the world vitiated by sin. On the other hand, the term "to judge" has a twofold signification: "to condemn" and "to separate."

26. See John 3:14, 16; 6:37-44; 10:15-16; 11:52; 16:25, 30; 17:1; 19:37.

27. J. Servel, text, and J. Gelineau, music. (Fiche de chant G 228).

Third Sunday, Year C—Pages 162-170

1. The redaction of the Pentateuch—and therefore of Exodus—was probably completed under Esdras (in the fifth century B.C.); it incorporates several traditions already set down in earlier times. See the introductions in the *Bible de Jérusalem*, 24-27, and in the *Traduction oecuménique de la Bible*, 32-34, and Cl. Wiener, "Le livre de l'exode," 7-10. For what concerns this Sunday's text, see, J.-L. Déclais, "Moïse à la montagne de Dieu," *Assemblées du Seigneur*, 2nd series, No 16 (Paris: Publications de Saint-André—Cerf, 1971) 6-11.

2. The omitted verses (8b-12) concern Moses' mission to Pharaoh.

3. Descendants of Abraham (Gen 25:2, 4), the Midianites were nomads (Gen 37:28, 36; Isa 60:6). The Bible places their territory to the northwest of the Sinai (1 Kgs 11:18).

4. The "mountain of God," designated here under the name of Horeb, is called Sinai in Deuteronomy and in other sources of the Book of Exodus.

5. The "angel of the Lord" designates God himself when he manifests himself.

6. In religious traditions of the Near East, trees, springs, and mountains were the privileged places for theophanies. Abraham had a vision in Shechem—an established place of worship—"by the terebinth of Moreh" (Gen 12:6). Moses encounters the same God in a traditional holy place of the desert. Moreover, there is an assonance between *sineh*—Hebrew for "bush"—and Sinai. The reader can then associate the fire of the bush (*sineh*) and that of Sinai (Exod 19:18).

7. "Adam again had relations with his wife, and she gave birth to a son whom she called Seth. 'God has granted me more offspring in place of Abel,' she said, 'because Cain slew him.' To Seth, in turn, a son was born, and he named him Enoch.

At that time men began to invoke the LORD by name" (Gen 25-26).

8. See the notes in the *Bible de Jérusalem*, 87-88, and in *Dictionnaire de théologie biblique*, cols. 1387-90.

9. See n. 1, above.

10. Must we not see here a reflection on the mystery of God himself? The tradition—called Elohistic—to which our text belongs, "willingly echoes the prophetic movement of the Northern Kingdom; now, in the cycle of Elijah, this prophetic movement comes to the point of truly posing the 'question of God.' It is enough to recall the scene of Elijah on Mount Horeb (1 Kgs 19): casting aside all the religious symbols of the gods of storms, Elijah finds himself before Yahweh, the God of Israel, who radically escapes human perceptions." J.-L. Déclais, "Moïse à la montagne de Dieu," n. 1, which refers to A.-M. Besnard, *Le mystère du Nom*, Lectio Divina 35 (Paris: Cerf, 1962) and J. Courtney Murray, *Le problème de Dieu: de la Bible à l'incroyance contemporaine* (Paris, 1965) 19-40.

11. It is a refusal of this kind that Jacob receives from the unknown being who fought with him for a whole night. Answering his question, Jacob has said, "Jacob." But when he in turn asks, "Do tell me your name, please," the other replies, "Why should you want to know my name?" (Gen 32:28-30). The angel of the Lord also refuses Manoah's request, "Why do you ask my name, which is mysterious?" (Judg 13:18).

12. The *traduction oecuménique de la Bible*, 138, uses this translation. The verb used in Hebrew can be in the future tense or present tense.

13. See, G. Auzou, *De la servitude au service*, Connaissance de la Bible 3 (Paris: Orante, 1961) 111–29.

14. See "Yahvé" in *Vocabulaire de théologie biblique*.

15. After the Exile, people took the habit, through respect, of not pronouncing the name of Yahweh, and saying instead Adonai (the Lord). Normally, Hebrew was written without the vowels being indicated. Around the fifth century, a system of dots and dashes, which were placed under the letters to indicate vowels, was devised. This form of vocalization, called the "Tiberian System," invented between the eighth and tenth centuries, replaced earlier systems from the twelfth century on. In order to remind the readers that one had to say Adonai when they met Yahweh, the word was punctuated with the vowels of Adonai, transliterated into e, o, a. Thus, when the consonants of Yahweh were mistakenly read with the vowels of Adonai, the result was Jehovah. Jehovah in the old translations of the Bible is an artificial name. The Lectionary says "the Lord" where the Hebrew has "Yahweh."

16. The Bible, indeed, says that the people crossed the sea on dry land, the waters forming a wall on the right and on the left (see Exod 14:21-22). Still, the analogy is no less to the point; for it centers solely on the fact of the crossing of the sea.

17. See also Pss 78:25; 105:40.

18. J. Bonsirven, *Textes rabbiniques des deux premiers siècles chrétiens* (Rome, 1935) 252; G. Bienaimé, *Moïse et le don de l'eau dans la tradition juive ancienne: Targum et Midrash* (Rome: Biblical Institute Press, 1984) 178–86.

19. Thus when Paul evokes the relationship Adam—Christ—it is Christ who comes in the first place (see 1 Cor 15:21-22, 45-47).

20. Commission Francophone Cistercienne, *La nuit, le jour*, 32–33.

21. D. Rimaud, *Les arbres dans la mer*, 105. (Fiche de chant H 124).

Fourth Sunday, Year C—Pages 171–178

1. The Book of Joshua is divided into three parts: the entrance into the Promised Land and its conquest (1–12), the division of the land among the tribes (13–21), and the end of Joshua's career (22–24). In the beginning of the first part, we successively find the preparations for the entrance into the Promised Land (1–2), the crossing of the Jordan (3), the erection of memorial stones (4), the stop at Gilgal, with the circumcision of all males (5:1-9), and the celebration of Passover (5:10-12).

Many questions are raised concerning the Book of Joshua: its composition, the events it relates, etc. But the understanding of the liturgical text of this Sunday does not depend on the answers exegetes and historians may give to these questions. See, A. George, "Les récits de Gilgal en Josué 5,2-15," *Mémorial J. Chaigne* (Lyon, 1950) 169–86; "Pâque," "Manne," "Héritage" in *Vocabulaire de théologie biblique*.

2. Gen 12:7; 13:14-18; 15:18; 17:8

3. Gen 26:3; 35:12; Exod 6:4. See "Terre" in *Vocabulaire de théologie biblique*, col. 1289.

4. In Greek, Joshua and Jesus are one single name. On the theme Joshua-Jesus, see J. Daniélou, *Sacramentum futuri* (Paris: Beauchesne, 1950) 203–56.

5. Col 1:15-20; 2 Pet 3:13; Rev 21:1.

6. See also Eph 2:10; Col 3:10.

7. It is the verb *katallaso*, composed of *kata* (toward) and *allos* (other). The noun *katallage* (reconciliation) is derived from it. See, R. Swaeles, "La réconciliation: Thème biblique," *Assemblées du Seigneur*, 1st series, No 76 (Bruges: Publications de Saint-André, 1964) 42–63.

8. See also 1 Pet 2:22; 1 John 3:5.

9. The Jerusalem Bible translates, "God made the sinless one into sin."

10. Some think that "sin" means "sacrifice (or victim) for sin." The same Hebrew word—*hatta't*—can indeed have the two meanings: see Lev 1:4–5:13. But then we must suppose that Paul, writing a Greek word with a precise meaning—*hamartia* (sin)—had in mind a Hebrew word having two meanings.

Others propose that "sin" be understood in a concrete sense. Thus, God would have made Christ "sinner par excellence" for having assumed all human sins. But Paul knew the word *hamartolos*, which means "sinner" (see Rom 3:7; 5:8; Gal 2:15, 17; 1 Tim 1:9, 15; 2 Tim 3:13; Tit 3:11). Why did he not use it here?

11. The parables of the lost sheep (15:4-7), the lost coin (15:9-11), the lost son (15:11-32). Only the first of these three appears in another Gospel, that of Matthew (18:12-14).

12. It underlines the fact that in Luke's Gospel, chapter 15 forms a unit distinctly separate from what precedes and what follows. It is read in its entirety on the Twenty-fourth Sunday in Ordinary Time, Year C. See *Days of the Lord*, 6:210-16, "When God Finds What Was Lost."

13. We follow J. Dupont, "L'enfant prodigue," *Assemblées du Seigneur*, 1st series, No 29 (Bruges: Publications de Saint-André, 1965) 52–68; "Le fils prodigue," *Assemblées du Seigneur*, 2nd series, No 17 (Paris: Publications de Saint-André—Cerf, 1971) 64–72; *Les Béatitudes*, vol. 2, new edition completely rewritten, Etudes bibliques (Paris: Gabalda) 233–42.

14. Gospel of the Twenty-seventh Sunday in Ordinary Time, Year C. See *Days of the Lord*, 6:245-49, "The Service of Faith."

15. Gospel of the Thirtieth Sunday in Ordinary Time, Year C. See ibid., 273–78, "God Vindicates the Humble."

16. In fact, one usually speaks of the parable of the prodigal son, a title so traditional that it is retained even when one notices how inadequate it is.

17. Tertullian (160–220), *Traité de la pénitence*, trans. Ch. Munier, VIII:7-8, Sources chrétiennes 316 (Paris: Cerf, 1984) 179.

18. Commission Francophone Cistercienne, *La nuit, le jour*, 40. (Fiche de chant G 184).

Fifth Sunday, Year C—Pages 179–186

1. "Once more," because throughout the whole Bible, and especially in the prophetic oracles, God, in one way or another, reveals himself as the Creator.

2. See, G. von Rad, *Théologie de l'Ancien Testament*, vol. 1, *Théologies des traditions historiques d'Israël* (Geneva: Labor et fides, 1963) 123–26; vol. 2 (Geneva: Labor et fides, 1967) 207–14.

3. See also Phil 2:16; 1 Cor 9:24-26; Gal 2:2; 5:7; 2 Tim 4:7. And also Heb 12:1.

4. See, J. Dupont, *Gnôsis: La connaissance religieuse dans les épitres de saint Paul* (Bruges-Paris: Desclée de Brouwer, 1949).

5. See also Hos 5:4; 6:3.

6. See also Jer 31:34.

7. Paul uses a very strong word (see also 1 Cor 4:13). However, we should not understand that he calls obedience to Moses' Law and the observances he was taught and formerly followed with faithfulness and zeal (2 Cor 11:22-23; Gal 1:13-14; Rom 11:1; Phil 3:4-6; see also Acts 22:3-4; 26:4-5) "rubbish" to throw to the dogs or into the trash can. He regards all this without value when compared to "the supreme good," the gain that surpasses everything.

8. Commission Francophone Cistercienne. (Fiche de chant N 20).

9. On this question see the notes in the *Bible de Jérusalem*, 1542, n. *e*, and in the *Traduction oecuménique de la Bible*, 311, n. *i*; with more details, see, D. Muños León, "Jésus pardonne

à la femme adultère, *Assemblées du Seigneur*, 2nd series, No 18 (Paris: Publications de Saint-André—Cerf, 1971) 55–60.

10. The historicity of the fact and the canonicity of this Gospel passage cannot be doubted. See D. Muños León, ibid. There are three testimonies, that of Papias, bishop of Hierapolis in Asia Minor, writing around 130, *Expositions of the Oracles of the Lord*; more explicitly, the *Apostolic Constitutions* and the Syrian Didascalias of the third century.

11. Luke 5:16; 6:12; 9:18, 28-29; 10:21; 11:1; 22:32, 40-46; 23:34, 46.

12. On the prayer of Jesus, meeting place with his Father, see Luke 10:21; 22:42; 23:34, 46.

13. Jesus spent his last night before the passion on the Mount of Olives (Luke 22:39-44).

14. Luke's Gospel places the last teachings of Jesus in the Temple, where he stayed daily and where "all the people were hanging on his words" (Luke 19:47-48).

15. "The scribes and the Pharisees," is an expression frequently used in the Synoptic Gospels. John usually speaks of "the chief priests and the Pharisees," especially at the end of Jesus' life (11:47, 57; 18:3) as well as in the passage preceding the episode of the adulterous woman (see 7:45).

16. After World War II, in countries formerly occupied by Germans, there were similar scenes, painful and humiliating, in which women were dragged into the middle of the crowd and had their heads shaved because they were convicted or suspected of having had sexual relations with members of the occupying forces.

17. "If a man commits adultery with his neighbor's wife, both the adulterer and the adulteress shall be put to death" (Lev 20:10). "If a man is discovered having relations with a woman who is married to another, both the man and the woman with whom he has had relations shall die" (Deut 22:22). Curiously enough, only the woman is mentioned in the Gospel narrative, without the slightest reference to her accomplice in sin. Is it because he was able to escape those who came upon them? Or is it because this married woman seduced an unattached male? It does not matter for the understanding of the story. But we must not conclude that in the Bible only the guilty woman was punished (see Deut 22:23-30).

18. To those who wanted to arrest and condemn Jesus, Nicodemus, a Pharisee, said, "Does our law condemn a person before it first hears him and finds out what he is doing?" (John 7:50).

19. Nothing in the story suggests the hypothesis of bad faith on the part of the witnesses or husband, although some exegetes have held this opinion. But is it not a normal reaction to ask questions on the reality of the crime a person is charged with? In any case, Jesus would have shown himself guilty of carelessness and cruelty if he had simply said, "Go ahead. Kill her."

20. We especially recall how he avoided the trap prepared for him on the question of the tax due to Caesar (Matt 22:17-22; Mark 12:14-17; Luke 20:22-25).

21. "The most likely explanation is undoubtedly that which sees in Jesus' gesture a refusal to utter judgment. . . . Jesus' mission is not to apply Moses' Law. Although he has other principles of conduct, he does not oppose them to the precepts of the Law." D. Muños León, "Jésus pardonne à la femme adultère," n. 9, pp. 62–23.

22. St. Augustine, *Traités sur saint Jean*, 33, H. Tissot, ed. and trans, *Les Pères vous parlent de l'Evangile*, vol 1, *Le Temporal* (Bruges: Apostolat liturgique, 1954) 329.

23. Ibid., 330.

24. Commission Francophone Cistercienne, *Tropaires des dimanches*, 28. (Fiche de chant U LH 84).

Jeremiah—Pages 187–209

1. Jacques-Bénigne Bossuet (1627–1704), "Méditations sur l'Evangile au 109e jour," *Oeuvres* (Paris: Firmin-Didot, 1879) 3:667.

2. E. Renan, *Histoire du peuple d'Israël* (Paris, 1891) 3:154.

3. We have only five excerpts in the Eucharistic liturgies of Lent: 31:31-34 (Fifth Sunday, Year B); 18:18-20 (Wednesday of the Second Week); 17:5-10 (Thursday of the Second Week); 7:23-28 (Thursday of the Third Week); 20:10-13 (Friday of the Fifth Week). As for the Office of Readings during Lent, it offers copious excerpts from the Book of Exodus (First, Second, and Third Weeks), a few passages from Leviticus and Numbers (Fourth Week), as well as several important portions of the Letter to the Hebrews (Fifth Week).

4. Among many others, P. M. Bogaert, ed., *Le Livre de Jérémie: Le prophète et son milieu: Les oracles et leur transmission*, BETL LIV (Leuven, 1981); A. Neher, *Jérémie* (Paris: Stock, 1980); H. Cazelles, "La production du Livre de Jérémie dans l'histoire ancienne d'Israël," *Masses ouvrières* 343 (1978) 9–31. And simpler, but well documented, J. Briend, "Le Livre de Jérémie," *Cahiers Evangile* 40 (1982).

5. St. Augustin, "Elévations sur le Ps 85," Patrologie latine, ed. P.-M. Migne, 37: col. 1086.

6. Cazelles, "La production du Livre de Jérémie."

7. See, A. Gelin, "Avant le nouvel Exode," *Cahiers Evangile* 20 (1955) 12, who proposes, as a hypothesis, a chronological order.

8. Ibid.

9. See Jer 11:18–12:6; 15:10-21; 17:12-18; 18:18-23; 20:7-18. On these texts, see, G. Behler, *Les Confessions de Jérémie* (Paris—Tournai: Casterman, 1959).

10. Jer 24:7; 31:33; 32:40 and Ezek 11:19-20; 16:60; 36:26.

11. Jer 31:33 and Isa 51:7; Jer 1:5 and Isa 49:1; Jer 11:19 and Isa 53:7-8.

12. E. Bonnard, *Le Psautier selon Jérémie*, Lectio Divina 26 (Paris: Cerf, 1960).

13. On Jeremiah, legendary figure, see 2 Macc 2:1-18; 15:13-15. On the imitation of his "Confessions," see the Book of Job. See also 2 Chr 36:21; Esdr 1:1; Dan 9:2.

14. See 2 Kgs 22:3–23:2. The origin of Deuteronomy must be sought in Levitical circles of the northern kingdom, who seem to have saved this "second Law" (Deuteronomy), when Samaria was ruined. Hezekiah, king of Judah, would have based his own reform on this text in Isaiah's time. Having become a secret and forbidden book under Manasseh and Amon, it was rediscovered by true believers when repair work on the Temple was in progress. See, F. Garcia-Lopez, "Le Deutéronome: une loi prêchée," *Cahiers Evangile* 63 (1988).

15. See "Confessions of Jeremiah."

16. See also Jer 30:3; 31:27, 31, 38.

17. See Gen 12:7; 13:15; 15:7; 23:1-20; 50:12-13.

18. See his criticism of the Temple (7:1-15; 26:1-9); of worship not matched by faithfulness (7:21-22; 11:1-14); of false circumcision (4:4; 6:10; 9:24-25); of false prophets (14:13-16; 23:9-32).

19. He has, among his ancestors, Abiathar, a priest supplanted by Zadok and exiled by Solomon (see 1 Kgs 2:26-27).

20. See 1 Sam 2:27-36; 3:11-14; Mic 3:12. In the Gospels, see Mark 11:17 and parallel passages.

21. Thus 1 Sam 15:22; Isa 1:11-20; 29:13; Amos 5:21-26; Jer 26:20-28.

22. Heb 10:14 and Mark 15:38. See John 19:34; 1 Cor 3:16-17.

23. J. Danielou, "Penseurs et mystiques d'Israël," *Etudes* (June 1951) 315.

24. See Jer 2:11-12; 3:7, 12; 7:19; 22:13; 35:15.

25. See Jer 4:4; 6:10; 10:16; 9:24-25.

26. See Jer 5:23; 11:3; 13:23; 17:1, 9.
27. See Ezek 16:59; 36:25-28; 14:12.
28. See Jer 23:29; 50:23; 51:20.
29. See Jer 31:34.
30. See Jer 31:31-34.
31. See Jer 16:14; 30:3; 31:1, 27, 29, 31, 38.
32. G. Bernanos, *Le Journal d'un curé de campagne* (Paris: Plon, 1936) 70.
33. A. Neher, *Jérémie*, 163-94 (n. 4).
34. See Hos 11:1; 12:14; Deut 5:1; 6:3.
35. Jer 7:21-23. See Jer 6:20; Amos 5:21; Hos 6:6.
36. Thus Jer 15:7; 18:8; 23:14, 22; 25:5; 35:15; 36:3, 7; 44:5.
37. Jer 3:10, 17; 4:14; 24:7; 29:13; 30:21; 31:21.
38. Jer 7:24; 9:13; 13:10; 16:12; 23:17.
39. The same demand is found in Deut 10:13-16; 30:6, etc. The theme of spiritual circumcision will be taken up often by Paul: Rom 2:25-29; 1 Cor 7:19; Gal 5:6; 6:15; Phil 3:3; Col 2:11; 3:11.
40. In Hebrews, a play on words expresses the intimate connection between conversion and return from exile: it is the theme of the *shub-shebuth*. From the similarity between the two roots, *shub* (to come back) and *shabah* (to capture, to take prisoners), people have interpreted the often recurring locution as the return from captivity. Finally, it took on an eschatological meaning, as E. Jacob notes in *Théologie de l'Ancien Testament* (Neuchâtel—Paris: Delachaux and Niestlé, 1955) 258, 233.
41. See Jer 31:10-14 = *Prière du temps présent*, Cantique de l'Ancien Testament 36.
42. This expression was coined by M.-L. Dumeste, "La religion personnelle de Jérémie," *La vie spirituelle* 66 (1938) 45. A whole modern trend—process theology—makes a formal recognition of this "difference" between the God of biblical revelation and that of Aristotle's "unmoved mover."
43. A. Gelin, *Jérémie*, Témoins de Dieu 13 (Paris: Cerf, 1951) 110.
44. Matt 26:36-39; 27:46 quote Psalm 22. Other psalms seem to be inspired by experiences similar to Jeremiah's: Pss 88:1-9, 15-19; 102:1-12. See also Lam 3:1-18.
45. A. Ridouard, *Jérémie, l'épreuve de la foi*, Lire la Bible (Paris: Cerf, 1983) 73-74, proposes a literary reshuffling of the verses, thus: 7-9, 14-18, 10-13. This most dramatic passage of the "Confessions" would then end with an affirmation of faith and a thanksgiving.
46. Gregory of Nyssa (ca. 335-94), *Contemplation sur la vie de Moïse ou Traité de la perfection en matière de vertu*, Sources chrétiennes 1 (Paris: Cerf, 1941) 149-50.

Passion (Palm) Sunday—Pages 210-231

1. M. L. McClure and C. L. Feltoe, trans., *The Pilgrimage of Etheria*, Translations of Christian Literature, Series 3, Liturgical Texts (Ann Arbor, Mich: University Microfilms International, 1978) 64-67.
The *Martyrium* (testimony) was dedicated to the memory of the Lord's death. *Eleona* (olive trees), on the north slope of the Mount of Olives, was a church that reminded the faithful of the last teaching given by Jesus to his disciples. The *Imbomon* (high church), at the top of the Mount, commemorated the ascension. Finally, the *Anastasis* (resurrection) was the church of the resurrection. The *lucernare* was the evening office during which lamps were lit.
2. The day was divided into twelve hours, from sunrise to sunset, the sixth hour thus corresponding to noon. This liturgy, therefore, began shortly after noon and lasted until dusk.
3. In the fifth century, at the time of St. Leo the Great, the Church of Rome still opened Holy Week with extreme simplicity, by a Eucharist during which the Passion According

to Matthew was read. A few centuries later, under the pressure of pilgrims back from Jerusalem, the West adopted the custom of the procession with palms; in the Middle Ages, other elements from various origins further enlarged this rite. See A. G. Martimort, *The Church at Prayer*, vol. IV: *The Liturgy and Time* pp. 71–75, which describes the simplifications introduced by the New Order for Holy Week (Mar. 25, 1956) as a result of the decree *Maxima Redemptionis Nostrae Mysteria* (Nov. 16, 1955), and the adaptations brought about by the Missal of 1970.

4. See, J. Comblin, "La liturgie de la nouvelle Jérusalem," *Ephemerides theologicae lovanienses* 29 (1953), 5–37. On the liturgical significance of the procession, see, S. Marsili, "La procession des rameaux: reconstitution historique ou mystère?" *Assemblées du Seigneur*, 1st series, No 37 (Bruges: Publications de Saint-André, 1965) 7–20.

5. Or even—more questionable—by the Blessed Sacrament.

6. Text of D. Rimaud (Fiche de chant H 96).

7. Matt 21:1 and Mark 11:1 simply say "When they drew near [Mark adds "to"] Jerusalem." Luke 19:1 begins his narrative by taking up his favorite theme, "He proceeded on his journey up to Jerusalem." As to John 12:12, it is the crowd gathered for the feast that comes to meet Jesus, upon learning of his arrival.

8. On this point, see A. Paul, "L'entrée de Jésus à Jérusalem: Mc 11,1-10; Mt 21,1-11; Lc 19,28-40; Jn 12,12-19," *Assemblées du Seigneur*, 2nd series, No 19 (Paris: Cerf—Publications de Saint-André, 1971) 4–20.

9. See Num 19:2; Deut 21:3; 1 Sam 6:7.

10. See J. Comblin, "La Fête des Tabernacles," *Assemblées du Seigneur*, 1st series, No 72 (Bruges: Publications de Saint-André, 1964) 53–67.

Along with other exegetes, the author thinks that the entrance into Jerusalem could, in reality, have taken place during one feast of Booths, as diverse indications suggest. Be that as it may, the ideological connection between this entrance and the Passover of the crucifixion established by the Synoptics does not necessarily guarantee the actual chronology of the recorded events.

11. See Gen 49:10-11; Zech 9:9; Ps 118:26; Matt 11:3.

12. According to the Greek translation called the Septuagint.

13. See Matt 26:6-13; Mark 14:3-9.

14. See John 11:53; 12:9-10; 18:33-38; 19:19.

15. See A. Paul, "L'entré de Jésus à Jérusalem," 26, n. 8.

16. Twenty-six times in the Gospel and thirty-nine in Acts; whereas, Mark uses it only once. See I. de La Potterie, "Des deux noms de Jérusalem dans l'évangile de Luc," *Parole de grâce: Etudes lucaniennes à la mémoire d'Augustin George*, eds. J. Delorme and J. Duplacy (Paris: Recherches de science religieuse, 1981) 70.

17. Commission Francophone Cistercienne, *Tropaires des dimanches*, 29. (Fiche de chant H 171).

18. The first of these oracles (Isa 42:1-4) emphasizes the Servant's divine election in view of a universal mission. The second (49:1-6) stresses the fact that he will accomplish his mission only through failure and contradiction. Finally, the fourth one (52:13–53:12) will be rightly meditated during the celebration of Good Friday.

These four songs were probably inserted into the fabric of Isa 40–55 after the first redaction of this ensemble, of which they in effect give another version.

19. "He hardened his face" (Luke 9:51, trans. of the *Traduction oecuménique de la Bible*).

20. To be truthful, we must say that no one translation can pretend to render the exact meaning and nuances of the Greek, to the exclusion of all others. See the *Bible de Jérusalem*, 1696-1697, and the *Traduction oecuménique de la Bible*, 590–91, with the notes justifying the respective translations. These notes mention the nuances that should be expressed or the way the chosen translation must be understood. These same difficulties were present when

the liturgical version was established with, besides, the demands of a text destined to be proclaimed in the assembly. The unavoidable choices of any translation entail risks.

21. Phil 2:6 literally means "he did not consider the state of equality with God a prey to be seized" (see Isa 53:11).

22. One should say, "He reduced himself to nothing" (in theological language, the term "kenosis of Jesus" is used).

23. See Acts 2:33-36; Ps 110:1; Mark 12:35-37. The title "Lord" belongs to him who calls himself "I Am." See Exod 3:13-15 (Third Sunday of Lent, Year C).

24. Romano Guardini, The Lord, trans. Elinor Castendyk Briefs (Chicago: Henry Regnery Company, 1954) 212.

25. With the exception of Luke, who omits the anointing in Bethany.

26. See A. Vanhoye, "Les récits de la Passion dans les évangiles synoptiques," Assemblées du Seigneur, 2nd series (Paris: Cerf—Publications de Saint-André, 1971) 38–67 (repeated in A. Vanhoye, I. de La Potterie, Ch. Duquoc, E. Charpentier, La Passion selon les quatre évangiles, Lire la Bible 55 [Paris: Cerf, 1981] 13–63).

See also "Disciples d'un Maître crucifié," Foi et vie: Cahiers bibliques 21 (1982); Cl. Wiener, "Le mystère pascal dans le deuxième évangile. Recherches sur la construction de Marc 14–16," Mélanges F.-X. Durrwell. La Pâque du Christ, mystère du salut, Lectio divina 112 (Paris: Cerf, 1982) 131–45.

27. It is not always easy to distinguish historical facts in the strict sense from scriptural commentary on what happened. Be that as it may, what counts in the last analysis is the meaning of events the historicity of which is undeniable.

28. Nerses Snorhali (12th c.), Jésus Fils unique du Père, Sources chrétiennes 203 (Paris: Cerf, 1973) 178, nos. 713-14.

29. See G. Minette de Tillesse, Le secret messianique dans l'évangile de Marc, Lectio divina 47 (Paris: Cerf, 1968).

30. Nerses Snorhali, Jésus Fils unique de Père, 184–85, nos. 744, 748.

31. Ibid., 192, nos. 735–36.

32. The Masses of Monday, Tuesday, and Wednesday in Holy Week certainly should not be overlooked. These three days must be lived as an extension of Passion Sunday and an expectation of Good Friday. The Gospels relate in turn the anointing in Bethany, "six days before Passover," according to John, with the reaction of Judas, shocked by the expenditure incurred by Mary, Lazarus' sister, and the project of the chief priests to put both Jesus and Lazarus to death (John 12:1-11, Monday); the announcement of Judas' betrayal, made during the meal Jesus took with his disciples at the hour "to pass from this world to his Father" (John 13:21-33, 36-38, Tuesday); and finally, the story of Judas' offering to hand over Jesus, who unmasks him (Matt 26:14-25, Wednesday).

Moreover, the Old Testament readings, drawn from Isaiah, present for our meditation the first (42:1-7, Monday), second (49:1-6, Tuesday), and third (50:4-9a, Wednesday) songs of the Suffering Servant. In effect, these three days are a sort of vigil during which the Church recollects herself and continues to meditate upon the Gospel of the passion.

Lent and Sacramental Reconciliation—Pages 232–241

1. Ch. Péguy, "Le mystère des saints innocents," Oeuvres Poétiques complètes, La Pléiade 60 (Paris: Gallimard, 1957) 686–87.

2. As early as the end of the third century or the beginning of the fourth, the yearly reconciliation of penitents took place in Lent. See, A.-G. Martimort, The Church at Prayer, vol. 4, The Liturgy and Time, 65–70; A. Nocent, Célébrer Jésus Christ, 89–100.

3. "After having attained the age of discretion, each of the faithful is bound by an obli-

gation faithfully to confess serious sins at least once a year" (1983 Code of Canon Law, no. 989). The Code of 1913 said "After having attained the age of discretion, that is to say, the use of reason, each of the faithful of either sex is bound by an obligation to confess all sins at least once a year" (no. 906). Today, the prescription concerns "serious sins" and no longer "all sins" without distinction. This is due to the fact that, on the one hand, a "penitential rite" takes place at the beginning of each Mass and, on the other hand, in accordance with tradition, other means of obtaining forgiveness for daily faults are taken into account. See, for instance, the Rule of St. Benedict, which prescribes that at the end of Lauds and Vespers, the superior should say the Our Father so that the community may be absolved of its daily sins (chapter 13).

    4. *Célébrer la pénitence et la réconciliation: Nouveau rituel* (Chalet—Tardy, 1978).

    Since the promulgation of this rite, numerous theological and pastoral studies have been published. Among those most easily available: "Les signes de la réconciliation," *Notes de pastorale liturgique* 107 (1973); "Renouveau pénitentiel," *Notes de pastorale liturgique* 126 (1977); "Pécheur réconcilié," *Notes de pastorale liturgique* 144 (1980); J. Potel, "La Pénitence, quelques traits du contexte français," *La Maison-Dieu* 167 (1986) 43–62; S. Breton, "Grâce et pardon," *Revue des sciences philosophiques et théologiques* 70 (1986), 185–196; *Communautés et liturgies* 65 (1983). Also, L.-Cl. Sagne, *Tes péchés ont été pardonnés* (Lyon: Chalet, 1987); J. Vanier, *La communauté, lieu du pardon et de la fête* (Paris: Fleurus, 1979); B. Bro, *On demande des pécheurs: Le livre du pardon,* new edition (Paris: Cerf, 1973).

    5. This is what the "obligation" enjoined by canon law means; we must not understand it as a mere disciplinary prescription.

    6. The difficulties arising from the necessity to have recourse to a priest could come from different causes. The most objective among these causes have been—and remain—taken into account. Hence, provisions such as the freedom to choose one's confessor, the anonymity of the penitent, the coming into parishes and communities of outside confessors, etc.

    But these difficulties can cause one to go so far as to reject, more or less consciously and explicitly, any human intermediary between oneself and God. We have here a grave misunderstanding of the place and the nature of the Church and, even more deeply, of the mystery of the incarnation.

    7. This is true especially of the practice of confession: the confession of sins constituting the essential part—often the only one—on the part of the penitent, after a sign of the cross, a formula; afterwards, the imposition of a "penance" (usually the recitation of a prayer) and the recitation of an act of contrition while the priest gives the absolution.

    8. For too long, by dint of concentration on what is essential in a sacrament, people reached a sacramental minimalism that, while guaranteeing the effectiveness of the rite, ended up blurring its signification. Thus, a few drops of water on the forehead of a baptized person, a little oil on a sick person . . . the confession of sins and the absolution. As though the model to follow were the way one proceeds in extraordinary circumstances: the danger of imminent death.

    9. See "Ash Wednesday" text pp. 13–21.

    10. See *Rituel,* nos. 53–65.

    11. This initial abruptness and lack of respect for preambles to the meeting may come from one or the other of the interlocutors.

    12. *Rituel,* no. 55.

    13. Ibid., nos. 55–65.

    14. *Rite of Penance,* The Rites of the Catholic Church (New York: Pueblo Publishing Co.) nos. 17, 6.

    15. Nothing reveals this confusion more clearly than the often-expressed affirmation according to which, today, the psychiatrist has replaced the confessor. This sort of statement shows that there has been an erroneous practice of confession.

16. Fourth Sunday of Lent, Year C.

17. Fourth Sunday of Lent, Year A.

18. In certain cases, it was accompanied by "reparation for the wrong committed against one's neighbor," in particular if property was concerned.

19. During the early Middle Ages, succeeding to earlier modes of penance, what historians have called "tariff" penances (fixed and prescribed amounts) came into usage. The priest imposed a penance proportioned to the fault committed, the "tariff" of which was predetermined. See, P.-M. Gy, "La pénitence du haut Moyen Age," *L'Eglise en prière* (Paris: Desclée, 1984) 3:123-25. The spirit, if not the form of this custom, continued until recent times, when the priest imposed on all without distinction the same "tariff," usually one Our Father and one Hail Mary, or a decade of the rosary.

20. Still, we should not forget that the fulfillment of this penance expressed as well the sincerity of the contrition, "I ask pardon of God and of you, Father, penance and absolution." Moreover, it was recommended that one say before confessing one's sins, "It has been . . . since my last confession."

21. *Rituel*, no. 71.

22. Reread, for instance, Joel 2:12-18; Deut 30:15-20; Isa 58:1-9a; 58:9b-14. See "The Porch of Lent" above.

23. *Rituel*, nos. 72-84.

24. *Rite of Penance*, no. 46. For more developed forms, see nos. 202 and 203.

25. Fourth Sunday of Lent, Year C.

26. Preface of Lent I.

27. If this celebration were to cause sadness or leave a bitter taste, there would be reason to question this serious anomaly and search for its causes.

28. *Rite of Penance*, nos. 48-59, 94-100.

29. P.-M. Gy, *L'Eglise en prière*, 121 (n. 19).

30. This is read during the Paschal Vigil.

31. J.-P. Lécot, *Chants notés*, vol. 2 (Paris: Cerf—Chalet, 1988) 111. (Fiche de chant G 162).

Lent, a Parable of Christian Life—Pages 242-244

1. The Rule of Benedict, ch. 49.

2. What should we think of an especially plentiful meal—or a banquet—consumed on Tuesday before Ash Wednesday (Mardi Gras) under pretense that tomorrow the Lenten fast begins?

3. St. Ireneus (ca. 135-202).

4. Such are the sentiments with which, according to St. Benedict, we must approach and live Lent.

5. P. de La Tour du Pin (Fiche de chant G 103).